DiY Culture

DiY Culture
Party & Protest in Nineties Britain

Edited by George McKay

VERSO

London • New York

First published by Verso 1998
© in the collection George McKay 1998
© in individual contributions the authors 1998
All rights reserved

The moral rights of the authors have been asserted

Verso
UK: 6 Meard Street, London W1V 3HR
USA: 180 Varick Street, New York NY 10014–4606

Verso is the imprint of New Left Books

ISBN 1–85984–878–8
ISBN: 978-1-85984-260-7 (pbk)

British Library Cataloguing in Publication Data
A catalogue record for this book is available from the British Library

Library of Congress Cataloging-in-Publication Data
DIY culture : party & protest in Nineties Britain / edited by George
McKay.
    p.   cm.
    Includes bibliographical references (p.   ) and index.
    ISBN 1–85984–878–8. — ISBN 1–85984–260–7 (pbk.)
    1. Protest movements — Great Britain. 2. Subculture — Great
Britain. 3. Youth — Great Britain — Political activity.   I. McKay,
George. 1960–
HN385.5.D59 1998
306′.0941 — dc21   98–7504
                                                               CIP

Website address for this book
www.verso-nlr.com/diy.html

Typeset by SetSystems Ltd, Saffron Walden, Essex
Printed and bound in Great Britain by
Marston Book Services Limited, Oxfordshire

This book is for Emma McKay, for Ailsa and Dora

Contents

CONTENTS

Acknowledgements

Biggest single shout of thanks to Malcolm Imrie, without whom . . .

For DiY-related things, thanks to Bookcellar in Lancaster, Eric and someone else at Advisory Service for Squatters, Camilla Berens, Keith Mann, Laugh of the Dongas Tribe, Barbara Lisicki of Disabled Action Network, Roger at Nine Ladies Stone Circle for telling us druidic secrets one summer's day in the Peak District, Jez at *SQUALL*, Ally Fogg.

For putting me on to other sources and documents, thanks to Mike Waite, Sylvia Ayling, Alan Rice, Godfrey Featherstone, Tom Cahill, John Moore, Tim Jordan, Anne Beech, Fabiana Forni, Chris Atton, Alan Dearling, Nina Taylor, Jo Norcup.

Thanks to Mum and Jim, for arguments about New Labour, and much else besides, and Ran, too.

Finally, at Verso thanks to Jane Hindle, Sophie Arditti, Amelia la Fuente, Robin Blackburn, Sebastian Budgen.

Any loss of judgement or of contact with reality or fact in the 'notes towards an intro' is down to me; any problems with the individual chapters, hey, give their writers the grief.

1

DiY Culture: notes towards an intro

GEORGE McKAY

In the mid-Fifties the jazz revival had produced an offshoot, a musical phenomenon which became much bigger than itself, the skiffle craze. Skiffle was do-it-yourself music, primitive jazz played on home-made or improvised rhythm instruments as an accompaniment to the singing of folk-blues and jazz songs of the simpler and more repetitive sort.... It is significant that 1958, the year that saw the climactic boom in jazz popularity, also produced the first Aldermaston march. The jazz revival and the rise of CND were more than coincidental; they were almost two sides of the same coin.

Ian Campbell, folk singer and peace activist

The venue was the Roundhouse.... The posters went up, in a scattered fashion, around the autumnal city. 'All Night Rave' they proclaimed.... That Saturday, 15 October, the ravers had come home to roost, this time accompanied by Strip Trip, Soft Machine, a steel band, and Pink Floyd.... It didn't even start until 11 p.m. How the ravers were to find their way out of Chalk Farm and into their bedsits would also be a challenge worthy of the do-it-yourself times into which the metropolitans were moving.

Nigel Fountain, on the launch of underground magazine *International Times* in 1966

In the first week of October, both *Melody Maker* and *Sounds* ran extensive features on the festival which propagandized the new generation. Caroline Coon uttered for the first time the incantation: 'Do it Yourself'.... Mark P. had been one of the first people fully to articulate the 'Do it Yourself' ethic and in *Sniffin' Glue* 5 he had lain down the gauntlet: 'All you kids out there who read "SG" don't be satisfied with what *we* write. Go out and start your own fanzines.'

Jon Savage, on punk rock culture in 1976

In the eighties, a lot of people who were hacked off with the way we were living, or were just plain bored, got off their arses and did something about it. . . . DiY culture was born when people got together and realized that the only way forward was to do things for themselves. . . . Ingenuity and imagination are the key ingredients. . . . Free parties, squat culture, the traveller movement and later Acid House parties pay testament to the energy and vision of people who decided it was now time to take their destinies into their own hands.

Cosmo, DiY activist

that's the real strength of Newbury and all the 90s counter-culture protests – we're not fighting one thing we don't like; we have a whole vision of how good life could and should be, and we're fighting anything that blocks it. This is not just a campaign, or even a movement; it's a whole *culture.*

Merrick, road protester[1]

These five epigraphs offer a pretty neat (too neat) and correspond-ing cartography of DiY Culture in Britain since the Second World War. DiY Culture, a youth-centred and -directed cluster of interests and practices around green radicalism, direct action politics, new musical sounds and experiences, is a kind of 1990s counterculture. DiY Culture likes to think that this is the case and says so often enough. The purpose of this book is to open up some space for a number of key figures and other happeners in it to tell their stories, their histories, their actions and ideas. Like the 1960s version we tend to associate the word 'counterculture' with, DiY Culture's a combination of inspiring action, narcissism, youthful arrogance, principle, ahistoricism, idealism, indulgence, creativity, plagiarism, as well as the rejection and embracing alike of technological innovation. There is now quite a lot of writing about it that says 'We are new, we are different, we are great, cheeky, active'; there's surprisingly little writing, especially from within, that starts 'Are we? Is this new?'

For this book I wanted in-depth pieces of writing by people involved in DiY Culture. For someone like me – a mid- (okay, *late-*) thirties academic, with two kids, urban-born and country-raised, with a past in punk, anarchism, experimental music – the explosion

of positive energy around what I found out was being called DiY
was a keen rejoinder to the cynical narratives maybe activists of my
generation had offered about the depoliticised nature of Thatcher's Children. *Green Anarchist* writer Stephen Booth has observed
with some accuracy that, in the Britain of the 1990s, 'the main area
of political dissent and resistance to the status quo has not been
the struggle in the workplace – indeed there has been virtually no
struggle there at all beyond tokenistic one day stoppages, and many
people do not even have a workplace. The main area of dissent has
been in the anti-roads movement and in animal rights.'[2] This local
view of the situation is widened out by the internationalist perspective offered by *Guardian* writer John Vidal:

> there is increasing evidence that globalism and localism . . . may be
> intimately linked, opposite sides of the same coin. The more that
> corporations globalize and lose touch with the concerns of ordinary
> people, the more that the seeds of grass-roots revolt are sown; equally,
> the more that governments hand responsibility to remote suprana-
> tional powers the more they lose their democratic legitimacy and
> alienate people.[3]

In the space between such local and global readings as *Green
Anarchist*'s and the *Guardian*'s are located these 'notes towards an
intro'. My aim in writing them has been *not* to offer an authoritative
view of 1990s protest and radical culture, but to outline some
historical strands, explain some social context, raise what I think
are some significant problems. The chapters following these 'notes'
deal with the often overlapping achievements of DiY Culture, in
the particular areas of direct action campaigning (Earth First!,
road protests, Reclaim the Streets), the development of its own
media (*SQUALL, Aufheben, Undercurrents, Do or Die*), and its own
spaces of protest, pleasure and living (the Exodus Collective, The
Land is Ours, warehouse and free parties, the E generation). These
chapters have their own authority, and are written by DiY activists
and cultural workers. One further point: I do think that, even if it
doesn't overtly espouse it, DiY Culture practises an intuitive liberal
anarchism. So I have woven through my piece a number of threads
related to anarchism, less to try vainly to claim DiY Culture for an
old -ism than to suggest where there seem to be correspondences,

repeated problems. My hope in doing this is that DiY-ers who reject established politics or even a sense of history for the immediacy of action or subjective pleasure might take time to find out more about earlier groups who may also have acted like that; while grumpy old 'revolutionaries' might make a bit more effort to see that maybe today's youth is *doing* more radical politics than they ever thought of! Maybe.

Do it . . . !

Action! This is one of the real strengths of DiY Culture. DiY and non-violent direct action (NVDA) feed each other: NVDA is the preferred form of politics. Here I want critically to look at the features of NVDA in relation to DiY Culture, discussing first direct action, and then non-violence.

Unlike other more straightforwardly *cultural* moments of resistance, such as, say, 1970s punk and 1980s anarchopunk, there is a tremendous emphasis in DiY Culture laid on actually *doing something* in the social or political realm, and rarely is that something as banal as traditional forms of mobilisation like marching on a demo and shouting in ragged unison 'Maggie Maggie Maggie – OUT OUT OUT!'[4] As we see throughout this book, action takes many forms, from throwing a free party to setting up a long-term protest camp, from swooping *en masse* on a destructive quarry to producing and distributing an alternative press, from trawling round the revived summer festival circuit with your message to organising one-off spectacular mediagenic stunts like climbing Big Ben. Stephen Duncombe (reluctantly) criticises the 'zine' (fanzine) scene, and wider DiY community, in America for mistaking cultural production for political action:

> Within the underground culture, the alienation that marks the rest of society is challenged, denounced, battled, and vanquished. But since all of this happens on a purely cultural plane, it has little real effect on the causes of alienation in the wider society. In fact, one could argue that underground culture sublimates anger that otherwise might have been expressed in political action.[5]

I don't think that such a pessimistic reading is available in British DiY. Activism means action: whereas in earlier decades opposition to, say, a construction project or an industrial pollutant might have meant a group standing at the gates handing out leaflets, today it's more likely to be voiced by invading the offices and disrupting work, trashing the computers and throwing files out of the windows. Writer and peace activist Per Herngren describes a number of 'expressions of resistance', versions of action, showing the diversity of approach: blockades, occupation, camps, conscientious objection, sabotage, monkeywrenching. Herngren's concern is civil disobedience rather than direct action as such; for him action is merely the first stage, and the others, equally important, are dialogue (in court and in the media) and punishment (as often as not, imprisonment).

> In a public action, the participants do not try to avoid the consequences of the action. . . . Only in combination with punishment does the action become a true challenge of obedience. The opponent's reactions are a necessary part of resistance, whether they make concessions or put people in jail. Yet this is not because the opponent shows its true nature through its reactions, as some guerrilla groups claim. . . . By forcing a reaction, the whole society, with its officials and citizens, is drawn into a dialogue.[6]

Clearly the Gandhian notion of self-suffering is fundamental here, but few British direct activists are quite so prepared to be publicly principled in this way.[7] Indeed for some, such as Class War, such a 'fluffy' (non-violent) nobility aligns you as part of the problem, as this characteristically vitriolic piece of rhetoric from *Green Anarchist* shows:

> Neither fluffies nor Gandhian NVDA wank-offs regard self-defence as legitimate – but the latter welcomes violence against protesters as proof of their own moral superiority. The call to 'keep it fluffy' is essentially one of cowardice, but it is also a confession of radical failure.[8]

Other direct activists also veer from Herngren's line, though for different reasons. For Corrine and Bee in the American punk/ feminist *Femzine*, civil disobedience is 'a political act in itself, and its efficacy and the cause that it serves are of less importance. . . . the value of civil disobedience lies not in "the effect" of a long-term strategy to bring about political goals, but in itself as an act of non-compliance, an act of authenticity to one's own beliefs: propaganda of the deed."[9] This punk version is perhaps more in keeping with the self-empowerment aspect of DiY Culture's direct action than with the more heavily principled stand of Herngren and others in the peace movement.

Direct action has important historical roots for DiY Culture, both in campaigning and in lifestyle politics. In terms of campaigning, for example, the anti-poll tax movement set up first in Scotland in the late 1980s is a clear and inspiring successful precedent for further direct action against government policy in the context of road-building from 1992 onwards. Officially called the community charge, the poll tax was designed by Margaret Thatcher's government, and introduced in 1989 in Scotland and 1990 in England and Wales; its renaming by opponents was a deliberate echo of a poll tax from centuries before, opposition to which had contributed to the Peasants" Revolt of 1381. Effectively it was a restructuring of the domestic rate system based on a universal flat rate rather than one related to wealth (that is, it redistributed capital from the poor to the rich), and employed the electoral register to compile lists of payers (that is, had the effect of disenfranchising many poor, mostly non-Tory voters). The divergence of tactics in the anti-poll tax campaign was critical: while the parliamentary Labour Party sought to campaign against the tax by protest and debate, more grassroots organisations sprung up dedicated to *resistance*.

> Their call for resistance differed from the protest calls because its purpose was not solely to express personal morality or to influence opinion but to influence events. The actions taken would have a direct impact on the outcome of the struggle and would not be dependent on the results of elections. Resistance meant confrontation. Advocates of resistance believed that the Anti-Poll Tax campaign needed to be built on a direct challenge to implementation, not the false hope that someone might agree not to implement it. . . . Community Resistance activists rebelled against the bureaucratic models of organisation inherited from the labour movement, these were seen as exclusive and alienating. . . . They took political inspiration from anarchist and autonomist direct action in Spain and Italy,

self-organisation characterised by squatters in London, Berlin and Amsterdam, and the 1968 uprising in France.[10]

Scottish people power has a proud history which was frequently invoked, so that an awareness and retelling of radical history contributed to a contemporary struggle: 'There were also *direct* precedents for resistance of this kind. In Scotland the Glasgow rent strikes of 1915 were an important inspiration.'[11] Significantly the organisation and success of the anti-poll tax campaign was itself invoked only a few years later with the road protest camp on the South Side of Glasgow, and the creation of Pollok Free State.[12] The most important difference between the direct action of the anti-poll tax campaign and that following it in the 1990s is that the community focus was not an alternative one. By this I mean that the community of resistance around the poll tax was an actual community – a council estate, for instance – while the community of resistance celebrated in DiY Culture is more of an alternative community – such as the Temporary Autonomous Zone of a protest camp or street party.

In terms of lifestyle politics, writing of the late 1960s and early 1970s, Steve Platt notes that 'Squatting was a natural extension of direct action into the fight for decent housing.' Platt goes on to unpack some of the interlocking origins of direct action politics and culture, in a passage which illustrates some of the history, but also the range of issues, the development of strategy, and the crossing of activists between the campaigns of different historical moments:

In the late fifties and early sixties, extra-Parliamentary political activity was centred on the Campaign for Nuclear Disarmament and the Committee of 100. The latter openly advocated direct action to further its fight against nuclear arms and this marked the revival of the use of direct action in non-industrial settings. . . . In many respects the direct action of the Committee of 100 against nuclear armaments was purely symbolic, challenging the state at a point where it could least afford to yield. In contrast the activists of the late sixties began to make more realistic demands and moved into areas which affected people's everyday lives. The main impetus for the 1968–69 squatting campaign came from a loosely knit group of radicals, many of whom had been involved with the Committee of 100 and the Vietnam Solidarity Campaign.[13]

CND, Vietnam, squatting: the trajectory of issues is from the global to the local. There are similarities between 1960s squatting and 1990s roads as issues, too: both are issues that affect everyday lives, both have stressed the positive benefit of creating a community – a festive urban street of squats, a string of treehouses in an ancient (not for long) wood – to balance protest with practicality. And, as we see with the No M11 Link Road campaign and Claremont Road in London, housing provision and road-building can be directly connected, too. But 1990s direct action around roads protest is in part a response to the *failings* of earlier groups as well. Institution-alisation and the desire for respectability of established environ-mental pressure groups bred impatience, as Brian Doherty explains:

> The two groups in a more difficult position were Friends of the Earth and Greenpeace. . . . Greenpeace had . . . been subject to the criticism that it was too hierarchical and that as the largest of the campaigning environmental groups its ban on ordinary members taking part in action in the name of Greenpeace had hindered the growth of [the] environmental protest movement. . . . Friends of the Earth was held responsible for its failure to mobilise its local groups to become involved in protests. . . . [T]o road protesters it was the absence of any push at the national level that suggested that FoE was still too concerned about alienating its members and losing respectability in the eyes of political elites if it supported direct action.[14]

Yet elsewhere more credit is given to groups like Greenpeace, which were, after all, at the forefront of direct activism for the environment in the 1970s. Rik Scarce calls Greenpeace the 'bridge to radicalism': 'Greenpeacers were *active* activists. They not only sailed, climbed, and hiked to the sources of environmental prob-lems, but they became daredevils who constantly created new tactics.'[15] Such a description of action as so heroic, so male even, remains resonant. Alex Plows has written of the way in which the 'ego-warrior' rather than the 'eco-warrior' can dominate some protest camps – usually young men who 'are a real danger on site with their macho-aggressive attitudes (it comes from taking the

word warrior too literally)'.[16] The 'womanly culture' that evolved
at Greenham Common peace camp in the 1980s can seem curiously
distant from the 1990s community of resistance. And to move
further again from the image of activist as daredevil – what about
*in*direct activism? One notion of indirect action is the politics of
disappearance or withdrawal. This is well expressed by Laugh, one
of the post-Twyford Dongas Tribe living with horses and carts on
the Freedom Trail in the West Country:

> it is possible for a culture of resistance not to openly 'engage'. NO. We
> don't want to resist – that's negative, we want to create. . . . Similar to
> direct action where 20 people in a rural hamlet can achieve more
> than 50,000 on a march in London can, we believe that lots of people
> doing lots of small gatherings is just as effective in creating social and
> political change. . . . Empowering individuals and re-connecting
> them with the land, whilst largely going un-noticed by the state. We
> try our best to keep them out of our reality, making our reality
> stronger for it.[17]

Sociologist Michel Maffesoli recognises 'the vitality at work within
the *avoidance* lifestyles', and goes on to suggest that 'the essential
quality of group and mass resistance is to be cagey rather than to
go on the offensive.'[18] While not necessarily agreeing with the
second comment, I wouldn't want to ignore the possibility of
'avoidance lifestyles' as a strategy if not of all-out resistance then of
conscious evasion of majority culture/the system/Babylon/UK
PLC/whatever you want to call it. Some dance culture has also
embraced a strategy of disappearance, which may explain the shock
and instant demonisation of acid house a few years back: it seemed
to come from nowhere.

   '[D]irect confrontation and the media . . . are essential qualities
of today's radical environmentalism,' writes Rik Scarce, taking his
cue from the embryonic Greenpeace in Canada in 1969.[19] While
political battles still took place at source, the focus of debate has in
many ways shifted to a different arena, into the reporting of
struggles in the media. The awareness of the significance of the
media, if not actually of television itself, is seen in the very first
Greenpeace ship campaign against nuclear testing at Amchitka in
1971. 'We saw it as a media war. We had studied Marshall

McLuhan,' writes Robert Hunter. The (all-male) crew of twelve included three journalists – one mainstream, one countercultural and one from radio:

> The idea was to hit the establishment press, the underground press, and the airwaves all at once.... So, from the beginning, there was a major departure from the spirit of the earlier Quaker voyages against bomb tests. Whereas the Quakers had been content to try to 'bear witness', *Greenpeace* would try to make *everybody* bear witness – through news dispatches, voice reports, press releases, columns, and, of course, photographs.[20]

Thomas Harding, who writes in this book about video activism, argues that things have moved on since Greenpeace, again to a new level of local, DiY activism: it's the individualisation of protest now, maybe even the privatisation of activism:

> Getting television coverage for a banner-drop or the blocking of a waste pipe for a few hours might alert people to the environmental crisis but does nothing to stop the crisis from continuing the next day. Instead, Earth First! chose to intervene at the point of destruction – lying in front of a bulldozer, getting between a tree and a chainsaw, blockading an entrance to a mine for a matter of months rather than hours.

For video activist Harding, developments in technology are claimed for their radical potential in a more utopian way: 'a camcorder becomes a powerful political instrument that can deter police violence. An edit suite becomes a means for setting a political agenda. A video projector becomes a mechanism for generating mass awareness.'[21] Such embracing of technology for its liberatory or expressive possibilities was found in the 1960s counterculture, too, in spite of its reputation for being anti-technology. The underground press, for instance, took advantage of offset litho printing equipment as well as other, newer developments, as Nigel Fountain explains: 'Offset was exciting. Offset was freedom.... New on the market were IBM electric golfball typewriters. Once typed on to special paper, the copy could be pasted on to the boards and, with no need for hot metal, or skilled printers, was camera-ready.'[22] Nineties technology is generally fully embraced:

DiY activists and cultural workers have employed innovations in information technology from desk-top publishing to the Internet for the purposes of publicity, campaigning and mobilisation, while the computer-generated rave scene produces music, image and, for some, narcotic influence in a kind of luvdup ecstatic utopianism.[23]

Yet, in the context of the media and imagery, Rik Scarce asks the question 'will monkeywrenching monkeywrench the movement?' In North America, 'the radical environmental movement is suffering from an image crisis, one it brought upon itself' – the strategy of ecotage can rebound, both as some direct activists become more extreme in their use of tactics, and through media representations of actions.[24] In Britain, for instance, there has been something of a deliberate retreat from the crustie eco-warrior image recently. As South Downs Earth First! activists explain, of a *successful* action against agricultural development in their area (and, by the way, illustrating a sophisticated awareness of the cultural and historical signifiers likely to appeal to their constituency):

> Our group has long had the policy of not labelling campaigns. Despite numerous TV interviews no-one ever mentioned they were from EF!, describing themselves instead as 'local people'.... As a result, large numbers of Lewes people did come up and get involved, who might have been alienated if the campaign had been labelled as FOE [Friends of the Earth] or EF! [Earth First!] – or worse, a camp of 'eco-warriors'. The fact that no-one on the hill looked much like the media stereotype of 'an eco-warrior' probably helped. In fact most of the interviews were done by two women who put across more of an image of second world war 'land girls' than crusties.[25]

Of course, there are, or can be, problems with a single-minded focus on direct action. These include the fact that media representation of it encourages not involvement but vicariousness, or that we fetishise that special mindset or moment, let alone the other issues that we ignore or other *activities* that we devalue: writing, for instance. A frequently expressed sentiment in the free weekly newssheet of DiY Culture, *SchNEWS*, is that 'A single action is worth a thousand words.' Really? *Any* action? *Any* thousand words? This is said by Brighton-based DiY-ers Justice?, one of whose main achievements is the production and national distribution of a free news-sheet – and it's said in that very newssheet. Even a definition by Justice? of DiY itself is surprisingly anti-discursive: 'DiY Culture is creating homes and entertainment by the people for the people captured in the philosophy of Deeds not Words' (yes – this is quoted from their directory of active groups, a book called *The Book*).[26] Thinking too much can be frowned on too, leading to an anti-intellectualism: academics are a particular target, which I feel slightly sensitive about I suppose.[27] For instance, *Do or Die: Voices from Earth First!* asks for contributions in the form of 'articles, rants, artwork, photos, poems, letters, international news, reviews and turgid pseudo-academic tracts (whoops, I forgot – we take care of them . . .)'. Justice? go to pains to emphasise their preference for the words of activists rather than academics:

> SchNEWS is also written by activists – not academics. . . . And Finally, when History is written, our words – words of people out there actually doing it – will be in black and white and cyberspace for the academics, historians and analysts to pick over the bones with and come up with amazing theories.[28]

In some ways this is obvious: they're activists because they're *active*. Action means movement, spectacle, confrontation; what it doesn't mean is reflection, history, theory. Awkward demands for these kinds of activities are usually dealt with by being rejected in favour of action itself or, worse, uttered platitude – though I do hope that readers will find in this book engagement by contributors with historical and theoretical narratives. Rik Scarce explains that 'Most eco-warriors have no interest in a well-conceived philosophy. . . . Activist after activist, when asked to consider the events, ideas, and inspirations which led them to adapt their uncommon principles, acknowledge that it is intuition which spurs them to act, not some clear, rational, deductive thought process.'[29] This can of course be seen as a further aspect of the culture of immediacy I discuss below – and it's worth emphasising that such a reluctance to engage with theoretical ideas has *not* always been a feature of countercultural activism. From the events in France in 1968, for instance, Daniel and Gabriel Cohn-Bendit sought a history in the form of 'a running commentary on the day-to-day *practical and theoretical activities* of the students and workers' involved.[30]

The other main danger of focusing on direct action is that it contributes to a culture of immediacy, that what can be overlooked or lost in the excitement of the moment is the past – history, tradition – as well as the future – strategies for development. The apocalyptic tone of eco-radicals in particular contributes to this culture of immediacy: Earth First! demand *Do or Die*, and confront with the question/ultimatum, 'If not now, when?' Even road protest camps, an ongoing symbol of 1990s radicalism, are inherently temporary communities. Invariably the one common feature they all share is that they are eventually going to be evicted, bulldozed. John Jordan justifies what he calls this 'obsession with the collective present' as a symptom of the unique awfulness of the current situation:

> Unlike other political issues and historical moments, being a radical environmentalist at the end of the twentieth century gives one a very fixed time frame, one which looks out on an incredibly fragile future. Even the armageddon fears of the peace movement were always based on *if* – *if* there is a Third World War, *if* a nuclear warhead is dropped – out of the ordinary events. But ecological collapse is not based on *if* but *when*: business as usual, growth economics, globalization, etc . . . is all normal everyday activity, all leading to collapse. Time means something completely different to DiY Culture – time is short – and that is why there is an obsession with the collective present. There can be no long term strategy when there is no long term.[31]

The culture of immediacy is a factor in the continuing rhetoric of newness around DiY. To some extent such a rhetoric of newness is a generational feature, claimed in the 1960s (the New Left) and the 1970s (the inverted newness of punk's eschatology, Bob Marley's 'New wave, new braves') alike. But it may be that being new isn't news any more, especially when we're quite old, or rather the tactics and in particular the political ideas and implicit social theories are quite old. And to what extent does claiming newness equate or contribute to ahistoricism? There is some evidence of a lack of historical awareness on the part of youth activists.[32] A clear potential downside of youth can be its rejection of both expertise and history, of radical history which is often hard enough to narrate or recover anyway, without the next generation of activists – the very people that history is of most use to – contributing to its erasure by their focus on youth and the self.

Yet it's in its focus on direct action that one of DiY Culture's connections with anarchism can be traced. In *The Slow Burning Fuse*, his history of British anarchism, John Quail makes the point that 'the Anarchist movement grows in times of popular self-activity.... The Anarchists have preached direct action, spontaneity and self-activity and evidently grow on what they preach. But they have also been consistent utopians.... This combination of utopian aspiration and immediate tactical creativeness seem to be distinctively Anarchist.'[33] Ironically, this immediacy is one of the features of lifestyle anarchists (which he rather caricatures as yuppie radicals) so vehemently criticised by Murray Bookchin. Bookchin seems reluctant to recognise that this may be a feature of anarchism itself, throughout its history, rather than simply of what he sees as the diluted or corrupted version going among today's youth:

> history itself becomes a degrading monolith that swallows up all distinctions, mediations, phases of development, and social specificities. ... What stands out most compellingly in today's lifestyle anarchism is its appetite for *immediacy* rather than reflection....[34]

It's also ironic perhaps that DiY's most consistent historical and theoretical antecedents lie in anarchist thought and practice, ironic because in some ways DiY repeats some of anarchism's (supposed) flaws: partial narrative, inchoate organisation, a naive utopianism, micropolitics, a preference for spectacle and gesture over long-term strategy. (I've often been attracted to these loose features of anarchism myself, not least when the alternative has been hierarchical and centralised avant-gardism. The at best non-hierarchical organisation of direct action campaign groups is intuitively anarchist: 'The system which brings about untold social and environmental ruin relies on people respecting and obeying hierarchy. Don't mimic the system – fight it!' is the advice from Road Alert!)[35] As Michel Maffesoli observes on the social movement of neo-tribalism, its 'sole *raison d'être* is a preoccupation with the collective present'.[36]

I want also to look at some of the issues and debates surrounding the other, related part of NVDA, non-violence. NV is related to DA in a very practical way in the sense that, as protest has become more 'in-yer-face', action ever more direct, so reactions by the authorities in protest situations become more critical and potentially more extreme. Debates around non-violence and violence have raged in DiY Culture, because the reaction of public or private security is an immediate concern for protesters, of course, but also because of the effects violence or non-violence can have on the general public's sympathies, or on media representations of events for the general public. There is a more fundamental reason for debating this, too: an individual activist's vision of a better world is often predicated on his or her position on non-violence and violence. So while few activists may really be *that* interested in discussing, say, the place of anarchist thought in DiY Culture, or the relation of their politics to those of the traditional left, debates about the politics of non-violence have been important. That lines were drawn is seen by advice given at actions or demonstrations: 'Keep it fluffy' meant non-violent, being responsible, setting a positive example by behaviour; 'Keep it spiky' meant confrontational, violent, 'by all means necessary'. *Aufheben* magazine offer a critical view on some of the issues around the fluffy/spiky debate in their chapter here. For others in DiY, though, the fluffy/spiky debate was a diversion, as Miss Pod of underground magazine *POD* explains: 'The whole Fluffy/Spiky debate was seen by most activists as a fuss about nothing. . . . But more than anything, it showed the huge gap in communications between some factions of the far left and those involved in NVDA campaigns.'[37]

Having recalled that neat binary opposition of fluffy/spiky, immediately I have to complicate it, by asking the basic question: what *is* violence? Or rather: what do different activists consider to be violent and non-violent? Pat Arrowsmith recalls that this question vexed the Campaign for Nuclear Disarmament during its early days: 'did [blocking lorries] constitute violence towards the drivers? . . . And what about damaging property? Would using wire-cutters . . . amount to violent sabotage?'[38] When trying to decide what constitutes violence, Road Alert! offer some useful advice to the would-be protester: 'Watch a bulldozer ripping up irreplaceable wildlife habitat so that rich corporations can get a bit richer, and

ponder the meanings of "criminal" and "damage".'[39] Peace activist
and writer on civil disobedience Per Herngren has one of the most
extreme responses, fluff *par excellence*: violence is 'any kind of
action that can cause psychological or physical damage, including
actions that create a panic situation. Police can, for example,
become provoked if people run or yell slogans.'[40] For others the
definition of violence is a fluid one, as Rik Scarce shows in *Eco-
Warriors*:

> others refer to sabotage and vandalism as violent, [but] for the
> purposes of this book *'violence' means inflicting harm on a living being or
> a non-living natural entity*, such as a mountainside. The practical
> implication of this definition is to exclude the destruction of human
> artifacts – machines and the like – from the realm of violence.
> Australian radical environmentalist John Seed goes even farther,
> saying that ruining a bulldozer to preserve the environment is
> 'property *enhancement*', the highest and best use of a place being to
> leave it in its natural state.[41]

So property destruction by ecotage or monkeywrenching is seen by
many as acceptable, though possibly less so if in the form of acid
attacks on the windows of butchers' shops, and less so again if in
the form of, say, firebombing the fur coat departments of major
shopping stores.

> [T]he interpretation of non-violence varies. Most protesters regard
> damage to property as non-violent. Hence, on invasions of the offices
> of road-building firms they have damaged computers, and in site
> invasions they have disabled construction machinery. A sharp distinc-
> tion is drawn between such actions and violence against people and
> living things. ... [S]ome saw nonviolence as primarily tactical,
> arguing that if protesters used violence they would simply be
> repressed. Others viewed nonviolent means as linked to the goal of a
> less violent society.[42]

Some activists believe that both a fluffy and a spiky attitude are
necessary in the wider movement. David Henshaw's pretty sensa-
tionalistic account of the Animal Liberation Front in the 1980s
describes one ALF activist as saying that 'he had nothing to do with
direct action "and never had", but still believed that the movement

needed "a hard, cutting edge" so that the "opposition" would realise that the threat was still there. Where would Martin Luther King have been without the Black Panthers?'[43] The anti-live veal export protests in Britain by a wide range of animal rights activists with a groundswell of sympathy from the animal-loving British general public in the mid-1990s had a fluffy and a spiky side. The fluffy was supplied by news images of old grannies and Second World War veterans out on the protest line, with flasks of tea and sandwiches; the spiky came memorably in the form of a brick through the driver's window of a truck transporting calves to a ferry, and was followed by more serious actions such as the nighttime torching of a lorry depot.[44]

> Listening to the squeals of condemnation from Thatcher, Kinnock and co after the Poll Tax riot [in 1990], you'd think that violence and direct action has never happened before in Britain. In fact, the working class heroes of Trafalgar Square were carrying on a very long and honourable tradition of violent struggle against the state and the bosses.... Neil Kinnock might bleat 'violence is alien to the British working class' but fortunately reality tells a different story. Everything we've ever gained has been through fighting.[45]

Class violence sits uncomfortably in DiY Culture, partly because DiY presents itself as being blind to class (that is, is dominated by middle-class activists), partly because the language of class struggle is identified with a boring politics of yesterday, and partly because it strives to offer something positive, creative. The slightly more spiky side of things is visible in events in the 1980s like the Class War 'Bash the Rich' actions against the rise of the yuppie, or the increasing violence of hunt sabbing as hunts around the country employed heavier and heavier 'stewards'. The use of violence, or the willingness to fall back on it, was a source of unease for some in the development of the ALF in the 1980s, while for others it was a necessary tactical choice. Ronnie Lee, ALF veteran, on non-violence:

> Total pacifism is an immoral philosophy: violence is the only language some of these people (vivisectors, huntsmen and farmers) under-stand. This may be a hard home truth for the pacifist ideologues of the movement to understand, but it is a home truth nevertheless....

> To my mind this preoccupation with 'non-violence' has a lot to do
> with the middle-class origins of most of the people in the movement.
> The middle class traditionally don't like to get personally involved in
> violence.[46]

The line that 'Direct action forces the state to show its allegiances'[47]
was one taken to a greater extreme as a justification for the bomb-
ings across Europe by groups like the Angry Brigade, the Red Army
Faction and Action Directe in the 1970s and 1980s. I think it's fair
to say that most DiY Culture would view such an overt embracing of
violence with horror, and, depending on its historical awareness, as
a failed tactic of the old revolutionary left.[48] Yet the development of
the Animal Rights Militia, for instance, in the 1980s showed a drift
towards premeditated violence aimed first at property then at
people: acid attacks and firebombings of department stores that
sold fur were followed by letter bombs and car bombs directed at
what were seen as leading figures in or apologists for animal
research. More recently, *Green Anarchist* has also taken a lurch to
embracing violence, at least in its rhetoric. In a passage illustrating
its sometimes extremely dubious politics, the magazine reads like a
millenarian embracing of misguided and/or deranged killers echoing the *fin de siècle* gestures of those stereotypical anarchists from
one hundred years ago, the propagandists of the deed.

> The unabomber, the ALF Justice Department and ARM, the Okla-
> homa bombers and the Japanese Aum cult all show the direction it is
> going in. Outside of Middle-Eastern terrorism, events like the Okla-
> homa bomb would have been unthinkable 15 years ago. *Such develop-
> ments are inspirational* and open up wide ranges of new possibilities.[49]

DiY Culture has so much ingenuity and creativity it's extremely rare
that it has to go to such lengths to find such a chimera of inspiration
as this.

. . . Yourself!

NVDA contributes to the construction of self; protest is about
conditions and events *out there*, but it's also about *inner* values and
responsibilities, as road protesters repeatedly make plain.

> [D]ircct action implies acting *yourself* ... having the initiative to
> decide for *yourself* what is right ... fighting for control of *your own*
> life ... taking responsibility for *your own* actions on *your own*
> terms.

> The feeling of institutional disenfranchisement may well be comp-
> lemented by a feeling of radical empowerment. When asked, 'What
> message do you want people to take from your action?' it was exactly
> this that Free-Staters were aiming for: 'Do it yourself', said Anna,
> 'You can make a difference', said Lindsay. There was little faith at the
> Pollok Free State in 'representative' channels. The empowerment
> message that Free-Staters sought to convey was that people can have
> a collective influence if only they are prepared to engage in radical,
> and following the CJA [Criminal Justice Act], usually illegal, direct
> action outside the institutional political system.[50]

Subjective freedom and empowerment, the emphasis on self self
self (even when located within a collective practice, even when it
might lead to the self temporarily cracking or being beaten up),
may not always be so praiseworthy. The use of the term 'privatisation' in relation to subjects like politics and religion in the 1990s
is one I don't like, because of its Thatcherite resonance.[51] Yet it
may bear consideration: the turn to a politics of Do it Your*self*,
of self-empowerment, can be seen as a corollary of the Thatcherite
notion of the privileging of the individual ('there is no such
thing as society'). In religion, the shift from established Christianity to embracing a more personal belief system, such as that
of neo-paganism, for instance, can again be seen as part of
an inward turn.[52] The fact that DiY has taken (at least until
recently) little interest in established left and class politics – I'm
thinking in particular of the trades union movement here –
offers an uncomfortable parallel with a central tenet of the
Thatcherite, uh, revolution of the 1980s. Peter Gartside, from the
traditional left of CND and anti-racism marches in the late 1970s
and early 1980s, writes about his fascinated difficulty with DiY
activism:

> it is difficult to 'make sense' of this style of politics partly because the
> languages used by these protesters are not altogether commensurate
> with those of what I understand as 'left', or 'radical' politics. This is

so for at least two reasons. Firstly NVDA protests represent, among
other things, a critique of the rational, positivist languages of existing
political culture, of which the marxist and socialist traditions are
clearly a part; and, secondly, in a sense this is the politics of the
Thatcher generation which has grown up during a period when the
'languages' of collectivism, unionism, even the idea of 'society', came
under radical ideological attack.[53]

An American DiY fanzine writer also connects right-wing government with DiY: 'I think the Reagan Years, paradoxically, were good
to zines. [They] encouraged people to think about being self-
sufficient.'[54] Is DiY Culture, then, some kind of Thatcherism of the
underground? After all, their rise and enterprise is roughly contemporaneous, through the 1980s. Like everything else, countercultural moments are always implicated in capital, even where they try
to escape or subvert it,[55] as eco-anarchist Murray Bookchin observes
with a veteran's critical eye.

> The Ecstasy Industry, for its part, is doing only too well under
> contemporary capitalism and could easily absorb the techniques of
> lifestyle anarchists to enhance a marketably naughty image. The
> counterculture that once shocked the bourgeoisie with its long hair,
> beards, dress, sexual freedom, and art has long since been upstaged
> by bourgeois entrepreneurs.[56]

But of course, we must look at the entire question from the other
way round, too, from where any correspondence between DiY and
Thatcherism is a symptom of the right's appropriation of radical
terminology. As Colin Ward writes, 'bureaucratic managerialism
took over socialist politics so that, in the climate of disillusion,
slogans like self-help and mutual aid were left around to be
exploited by the party of the privileged'.[57] The right has no
monopoly on the rhetoric and practice of self-help (even if it felt
like it did in the 1980s) – is it not the case that Thatcherism *caused*
the negative conditions that gave rise to DiY Culture, which was a
reaction to unemployment, boredom, a grasping materialism, the
denial of alternative pleasures, general social deprivation and
alienation, a growing sense of an establishment looking after its
own?
    It's worth making the point, though, that the notion of subjec-

tive revolution has a lengthy tradition in the context of anarchism, the self being both that most problematic and celebrated of anarchist constructions. John Quail writes of nineteenth-century anarchist practice and problems, and more generally the wider utopian cooperative movement, that 'no matter how subjectively revolutionary these enterprises were, objectively they represented a withdrawal from the fray in the absence of a general revolutionary movement'.[58] And the me generation of the sixties was in some ways little different from the alt.culture of the E generation today: is it fair to say that both extol a solipsism which is radical in terminology but conservative in its self-interest? I think not: 'the green children of Thatcher' (a phrase which seems to recognise, even embrace, the contradiction),[59] like the best elements of the counterculture, *can* be truly radical and subversive. One road activist from a campaign in Yorkshire in 1993 does give the right-wing government some credit, sardonically: 'Maybe it is Mrs Thatcher who should be thanked most because many of our activists were unemployed, early retirees or redundant and were able to give all of their time to fighting the campaign.' To offer another slight caricature, if in the sixties it was student activism that was all the rage, in the nineties it's activism by unemployed graduates, the products of Thatcher's mass higher education programme.

Still, in spite of suggesting that there may be some uncomfortable connections between right-wing and DiY self-promotion (an issue I'll return to later when discussing the politics of DiY), it needs to be remembered that, fundamentally, (right-wing) government is implacably opposed to radical political self and collective non-hierarchical mobilisation. Government distrusts politics like these, which don't involve it, probably because such extra-parliamentary forms exist in the main to challenge its authority. As Prime Minister, Margaret Thatcher said as much in 1984, when she sought to ridicule direct action:

> A fashionable heresy is that if you feel sufficiently strongly about some particular issue, be it nuclear weapons, racial discrimination, or animal liberation, you are entitled to claim superiority to the law, and are therefore absolved. This is arrogant nonsense and deserves to be treated as such.[60]

There is an impressive Conservative tradition of 'treating it as such'. It involves using the full range of the law against alternative cultures, from police brutality to crazy (or what would be crazy if it wasn't so serious) repressive legislation. In 1974, following the Miners' Strike, police trashed the People's Free Festival at Windsor; in 1985, following the Miners' Strike, police trashed the Peace Convoy on its way to Stonehenge during the Battle of the Beanfield; in 1994, following intense animal rights activism, the resurgence of festival and traveller culture at Castlemorton, and the development of road protest at Twyford Down, the government passed the Criminal Justice and Public Order Act (CJA).[61] Maybe Thatcher's Children *did* learn something from Thatcher, though: there was no U-turn for activists and others targeted in the CJA, as Newbury protester Merrick notes in his terrifically energetic account of the camps and the campaign, *Battle for the Trees*:

> Through the Criminal Justice Bill I met some of the most inspiring, beautiful, life-lovers ever. . . . Blank Generation? Slacker Generation? Thatcher's Children? It's all bollocks, just another weapon to bleed your strength and drain your hope. There's hundreds here, seeing clearly, and acting with dedication, humanity, love and *style*.[62]

Activism is about the self as well as the cause, but sometimes the self needs protecting. For inexperienced eco-activists at the Newbury bypass camps of 1996–97 a booklet manual called *My First Little Book of Peaceful Direct Action* was produced which includes this advice on preparation:

> Get an early night, if you can. Work could start at any time from first light, and could go on well into the night, if contractors bring in lighting.
> Respect yourself – hangovers can reduce your body's reaction time, which could prove dangerous to your health, if you have to duck or dive.
> Try to do some muscle warm up exercises before you go to the action. At least one person was out of action for a week, due to a 'cold start'. . . .
> If this is your first action, try and join with some more experienced people, who are prepared to look out for you.[63]

Further self-protection for activists comes in trying to avoid activist stress, a kind of battle fatigue caused by the life on protest camps, those ad hoc communities of resistance that thrive under daily pressure of confrontation and destruction – 'burnout'. Symptoms of this kind of politicised stress on the pressured self include 'chronic fatigue, minor illnesses, frequent headaches, stomach pains, backache, disrupted sleep patterns, depression, anxiety, a sense of being overwhelmed and hair-trigger emotions which quickly produce tears or flare-ups'.

Self and pleasure are entwined in DiY: 'Party & Protest' is the slogan, after all. But is DiY Culture a movement or a scene? One feature of an underground magazine like *Frontline* has been what's basically a fashion or lifestyle photoshoot: among stories about protest and arrest are photo-features of, for instance, 'real women': 'Not media and fashion manipulations of what women should look like and be. Women with a positive sense of self and unique style' are the lines accompanying a number of portraits. In an earlier issue of the magazine is another fashion feature with portraits of alternative types: 'PIERCED UP: Welcome to the wonderful world of body adornment'.[64] Maybe the baggage of rave, ecstatic experience and fashion that Mary Anna Wright explores in her chapter signals it as one in a long line of youth subcultures, the kinds of social phenomena invested with importance and vitality by those in them, but viewed as narcissistic by cynics, with bewilderment or bemusement by other outsiders. The links between subculture, pleasure and politics are worth exploring a little in the context of popular music here. Ever since rock and roll (and before, but it's a convenient starting point) there has been an impulse in popular music towards self-production, part of the cultural politics of autonomy. Music technology is frequently cited as a democratising aspect of dance music in DiY Culture: because of the easy availability of computers and MIDI technology, the production of recorded music is more accessible both in terms of the tools themselves and in the fact that one need not learn the specialised skills of playing an instrument to create music. Earlier DiY moments surely have a stronger case here, though. Consider the skiffle craze of the austerity-tinged 1950s, for instance, when necessity did indeed breed ingenuity. Skiffle bands produced music on home-made instruments, both made in the home and made of domestic

commonplaces: a tea chest and a broom-handle for a bass, a
washboard struck with a thimble for percussion, a jug blown across
like a flute for percussive and melodic notes. In 1956 it's estimated
that there were almost a thousand skiffle groups in London alone,
inspired by Lonnie Donegan's hit 'Rock Island Line'. Skiffle was a
new form, popular, democratic and cheap. Interestingly, the skiffle
and trad jazz boom was associated with the rise of the Campaign
for Nuclear Disarmament – DiY music accompanying extra-parliamentary politics – as folk singer Ian Campbell has noted in one of
the introduction's epigraphs, but the independent space of
pleasure is important, too, as Campbell explains:

> Having no access to any process by which we could influence popular
> music, many of us turned our backs on it and looked elsewhere for
> musical pleasure. We found an underground movement. . . . At any
> jazz event a liberal sprinkling of CND badges, and perhaps even
> leaflets and posters, would be in evidence; conversely, at every CND
> demonstration live jazz music set the tempo for the march.[65]

Pirate radio in the 1960s is in some ways a significant early DiY
moment, too, when the British airwaves were taken over by stations
broadcasting from boats moored outside British territorial waters.
The issue in pirate radio was not just legality but also one of taste:
while BBC radio was stuck in the mentality of offering people what
was good for them, on the Light Programme, in the wider western
world 'youth was busting out all over', in the words of Radio
Caroline's founder Ronan O'Rahilly.[66] Pirate radio has been taken
up on a more local scale by black and Asian urban youth in the
1980s and 1990s; both periods of activity indicate the centrality of
music, and taste in music, in countercultural or oppositional
discourse and identity.[67] It's worth noting, though, that pirate radio
in the 1960s touched on other areas of relevance to DiY Culture: it
connected with the production of independent records, for
example, trying to break the broadcast monopoly of the four main
record companies at the time, EMI, Decca, Pye and Philips. There
was also recognition in pirate radio of the need to promote a
culture of the provinces, a decentralised approach which very
largely predated the development of (legal) local radio. For
instance, in 1966 'Radio Caroline's ship in the North . . . found a

ready market for her wares in the North, the home of beat-groups and the currently popular "Liverpool sound"', while the first Radio Scotland in 1966 was a pirate station.[68] A Conservative MP in Parliament showed he had the usual Tory finger on the pulse when he railed against them: 'The pirates are providing what the people want. To some Members of this House that is sound democracy. It is not. It is pandering to populism.'

In the late 1970s, punk rock, media and style revolved around a DiY ethic, and this is when the term gains a greater currency in alternative culture. Home-produced fanzines championed xerox culture at the same time as they exemplified it. On the anarcho-punk scene, Crass created an independent label and gig network, playing almost exclusively benefit concerts for many years, while Poison Girls exhorted their audience to 'Sing your own songs'. Independent record labels mushroomed, and single record covers by groups from The Desperate Bicycles to Scritti Politti included advice and a breakdown of production costs so buyers could then go and make their own records. To quote from the cover of one 1977 single:

> The Desperate Bicycles were formed in March 1977 specifically for the purpose of recording and releasing a single on their own label. They booked a studio in Dalston for three hours and with a lot of courage and a little rehearsal they recorded 'Smokescreen'.... Three months later and The Desperate Bicycles were back in a studio to record their second single and this is the result. 'No more time for spectating' they sing and who knows? they may be right. They'd really like to know why you haven't made your single yet. 'It was easy, it was cheap, go and do it' (the complete cost of 'Smokescreen' was £153).[69]

More jokily, one of Ian Dury's albums on the Stiff independent record label was called *DIY*; the record came with a cover available, I seem to remember, in a choice of wallpaper patterns. (Look under Do It Yourself in a Brighton telephone directory in the 1990s and you will find an entry for the DiY group Justice?) In terms of style, punks ransacked the domestic sphere, turning bin liners into dresses (while Rotten sang 'We're the flowers in the dustbin'), safety pins into jewellery or body adornment.

Murray Bookchin's recent scathing attack on lifestyle politics is

only slightly marred by an uncomfortable sense of an old man
railing against youth for being young, for having fun: 'The black
flag . . . now becomes a fashionable sarong.' Such 'socially innocu-
ous' 'narcissistic anarchism', according to Bookchin, is characterised by 'its aversion for institutions, mass-based organisations, its
largely subcultural orientation, its moral decadence, its celebration
of transience, and its rejection of programs'.[70] Not only are many
of these easily identifiable as features of DiY Culture, but there are
echoes of such criticism from within DiY itself. Following events at
the Newbury bypass protest camps, one Earth First! activist
reflected:

> I became increasingly worried that the cultural vanguardism of the
> campaign was alienating people from getting involved. If we are to
> break free from the media stereotype of us as hippy dropouts, then
> we should not live up to it. We must not pander to their puerile
> attempts to shift the agenda from why the planet is being trashed to
> lifestyle bollocks. . . . Although the DIY culture has grown in the last
> few years it has become more and more of a clique because there
> seems to be a certain style which one must conform to.[71]

In practice as well as in discussion, then, many of the problematic
areas in DiY Culture *are* being addressed from within. In particular
here, the potentially narcissistic hedonism of youth party and
protest is balanced by a serious effort at collectivity, massive-style.
The construction or reclamation of space for a group or a group
event is a continual project, and indicates the extent to which DiY
Culture *is* active, *does* want to move by practical example rather
than rhetoric. The almost lost history of the 1980s warehouse party
scene around Blackburn in Lancashire which is uncovered and
told here by Drew Hemment, the tribulations and celebrations
of the Exodus Collective in Luton in Bedfordshire written about
by Tim Malyon – both are versions of a practical collective
experience around pleasure. Consider, too, the wider variety: self-
organised workers'/unemployed centres, activist spaces, zones of
squatted pleasure in urban areas, protest camps in trees and
tunnels, wasteland occupations, street parties and free festivals.
Anything from a drop-in advice centre to a living space is evidence of DiY's aim to combine party and protest, to blur the

distinction between action and living. In a discussion of a DiY European punk festival in that city, Edinburgh-based activist Angela explains that 'for me, these gatherings of people are something really important, that I need. *An essential part of resistance is the coming together of people.*'[72] As John Jordan shows in his chapter here, one of the main forms of protest developed by the anti-car culture group Reclaim the Streets of course is the street party, when an urban road (even motorway) is suddenly blocked off and thousands of revellers turn up in full party mode to make their pleasure-filled political point. Social criticism is combined with cultural creativity in what's both a utopian gesture and a practical display of resistance. The annual direct action conference organised by Justice? in Brighton combines political discourse and dancing (even if three times as many people turn up for the dance as for the politics . . .):

> last weekend saw the doors of the old [squatted] Top Rank Bingo Hall flung open for a Justice? organised National Direct Action Conference. Nearly 600 people (CCTV provided police estimates!) schemed, swapped ideas and watched Conscious Cinema. . . . Following on from the day and continuing in the great tradition of party and protest the former theatre saw 2,000 people partying until 10 o'clock on Sunday morning.[73]

I should point out that collectivity can be a forced as well as voluntary choice: state legislation against DiY Culture has made it look more to itself, at its strengths and weaknesses. In particular here there's an inspiring irony that the CJA galvanised rather than dispersed activists.[74] Yet I hope it's clear that the potential pitfalls in DiY Culture of the focus on self, on narcissism and hedonism, on being tainted with some residue of Thatcherism, are balanced from within by a practical insistence on collectivity. Possibly the term that's come into favour is misleading (or is just very accurate?): as some of the contributors do in this book, maybe we should be talking less of Do it Yourself than of Do it Ourselves.

Space

Land is what it's all about.
Ideal Home[75]

The anarchist-produced manual *Ideal Home*, published in the wake of the extraordinary New Traveller movement (literally) of the mid-eighties, offers alternative housing and living options from squatting houses and land to moving around in a bus or truck to building a tipi or a bender. The construction or reclamation of space, with its attendant problems, is a central area of action and concern in DiY Culture, too. In such spaces, both rural and urban, the social and the cultural come together. As a number of the chapters in this book show, the space constructed or reclaimed by DiY can be as grand as land, as ambitious as the earth, or can be as microcosmal as the blank space of a post-industrial warehouse or a disused quarry. Short or long term, space is a prerequisite for community.

> The JCB digger then tried to drive ... on to the site. So we started again; taking turns in ones and twos we jumped in front of the digger, lay down and were dragged away by the police. It is an unnerving feeling to be lying in front of a machine when you can't see the face of the driver who keeps edging nearer and nearer to you, the great metal shovel spikes on it inches from your body – and he keeps coming, an inch at a time, forward, forward. I don't know how we manage to stay calm at times like this.[76]

These are the words not of a road protester at a camp in the 1990s but of a peace protester at a camp in the 1980s, as part of the campaign against American cruise nuclear missiles being kept on British land ready for deployment. Jane Lockwood kept a diary of her time at Greenham Common Women's Peace Camp, and this is her description of activists blocking work on the airbase in 1982. By 1983 'there are peace camps outside military bases all over the country now: Lakenheath, Faslane, Molesworth, Fairford, Caerwent, Burtonwood, Burghfield, Waddington, Upper Heyford', while on 9 November 1983, 102 peace camps were set up in Britain, in the form of 24-hour vigils outside every American airbase.[77] This countrywide spread of living spaces of resistance anticipates and informs the protest camps of the 1990s, especially perhaps at camps such as Greenham Common, where one sometimes overlooked aspect of the protest was an effort to *reclaim* what had once been common ground, land owned communally. The expression of resistance through the construction of community, the vision of 'our alternative reality' – as well as the more profound experience of nature – creates an important precedent for newer protest communities.

> Living at Greenham ... makes few compromises with mainstream society, it is an alternative, an outdoor community of women. ... We experience autumn, winter, spring and summer as we've never experienced them before. ... We gained gypsy knowledge and learnt to build warm, spacious, comfortable homes for ourselves – benders – that two women can build in an afternoon. ... From our alternative reality, the world from which we come looks pale and comfortless. We have to transform it.[78]

DiY communities affirm 'the force of example in facilitating cultural change ... opposition is converted by the power of ideas and example'.[79] Well, maybe not converted too often, but certainly confronted, challenged, and even shamed sometimes: while government maunders on about communitarianism, youth, budgetary priorities, and so on, young and youthful people are out there *doing it*, with no money, little support, sometimes only harassment.[80] Of course for others the fact that such space *is* outside the mainstream is part of the point. Not all DiY living communities are overtly resistant, though; an initial distinction is between one whose primary purpose is to contribute to a protest campaign, which is almost invariably in the form of a temporary camp, and an alternative community, whose aim is to offer a sustainable living example of alternative, low-impact lifestyle.[81] I want to consider both in the context of a return to the rural, and look at some of the issues around the experiences of metropolitan space, and briefly at the relation of the local to the global.

A major impetus in the founding of Earth First! in North America was around the rural, the protection of the wilderness, a key signifier in the American psyche that taps into grand narratives of the West, freedom, individualism. Meanwhile in Britain the reinvention of romanticism, via allotments and countryside actions (even a weekend's hunt sabbing's a chance to get out in the fields, experience an authentic landscape), insists on a socio-critical edge:

> At the '96 EF! gathering there was much discussion about getting together a 'farmageddon' campaign. While campaigns against infrastructure growth like Manchester & Newbury are essential, they give the illusion that ecological destruction mainly happens in the realm of 'mega-developments'. In fact the way we grow our food is the main cause of devastation in this country.[82]

The countryside living spaces of protest camps are themselves significant by their flaunted difference: up in the air, under the ground. Tree-living from Darwen in 1994 and Newbury in 1995–96, to Vietnam War-style tunnelling at Fairmile in Devon in 1996 and the Manchester Airport camps in 1997 – these captured the imagination of the public, were intended and seen as practical instances of striving idealism. Living in trees, with aerial walkways connecting them, symbolises both a sense of utopian striving and a practical, hands-on defence strategy. Tunnelling moves literally into the earth, to delay both by obstructing the passage of heavy machinery (cherrypickers, bulldozers) over the top of it and by protesters having to be safely dug out. It's a potentially extremely dangerous otherworldly experience made possible by eminent practicality:

> Each occupant should create a comfortable space for their bed, and somewhere to store food and water. Keep this clean with food stored in metal boxes, otherwise rats will move in. Have lots of empty bottles for peeing in, and plastic bags for crapping in. Don't forget toilet roll, and ash to cover smelly business. Prepare ways of dealing with boredom and isolation. The best lighting system seems to be a car battery powering a few small bulbs – for instance white fairy lights.[83]

When eviction comes, rural DiY ingenuity comes into its own against technocratic culture: 'To map out the tunnel system and find where you are, they may use heat-seeking equipment and radar. To confuse them, consider burying human-sized bags of

silage (which rots without using oxygen, producing heat).' Newbury protester Merrick stresses the community aspect of the protest
camp, that it is a space for living as well as protesting:

> A camp needs to be an *uplifting* place to come to.... A camp that
> looks good feels good. If your camp isn't a bleak, squalid place but a
> friendly, comforting home, then your energy isn't drained just for
> being there, and it can be directed to the places where it's really
> needed.[84]

If a camp *isn't* an uplifting place to be, this is often blamed on a
'lunchout' element within. Yet the lunchout problem looked at by
Aufheben in their chapter here, where alternative space such as
protest camps becomes a repository for wasters, Brew Crew, acid-
heads, whatever offensive term you care to come up with, is in itself
nothing new. An unsympathetic visitor to the late-nineteenth-
century anarchist community of Whiteways in Gloucestershire
describes the problems: 'While some worked hard, the majority
sponged idly.... No idea can be given of the indolence and sheer
animalism of this Whiteway Anarchia with its lawless licence and its
cadging.'[85]

As well as protest communities, DiY alternative ones also seek to
reclaim the countryside. Simon Fairlie notes that 'Britain's rural
economy has been moulded by a singular set of historical circumstances: enclosure and industrialisation'.[86] He's involved with the
campaign group The Land is Ours, whose arguments George
Monbiot looks at in a chapter in this book. Fairlie advocates a
direct action approach (living on the land as part of a bender
community at Tinker's Bubble, Somerset), but one combined with
effort to achieve within the current legislative framework, a non-
revolutionary approach:

> Without radical changes to the planning system, apparently insoluble
> social and environmental problems can be combined to provide a
> democratic solution: ... the people presently excluded from the rural
> scene can participate in its revival. If permission to build or live in the
> countryside were to be allocated, not just to those who can afford
> artificially inflated land prices, but to anyone who could demonstrate
> a willingness and an ability to contribute to a thriving local environ-
> ment and economy, then a very different kind of rural society would

emerge. Low impact development is a social contract, whereby people are given the opportunity to live in the country in return for providing environmental gains.

There's an awkwardness here, though, in trying to reconcile apparent opposites: direct action with the propertied classes,[87] state legislation with producing a participatory and sustainable environmentally responsible society. Fairlie's book aims for a reasoned respectability, signified by its preface by a leading Liberal Democrat MP, Paddy Ashdown, who can write unironically in it of 'progress'; it is produced in cooperation with The Land is Ours, which campaigns for 'greater access to the land for *all* social classes' (my emphasis). Is this not a bit too liberally inclusive? Especially when one social class already – still! – owns most of the land? Hidden in Fairlie's text is the more radical project, seen in such calm statements as 'a sustainable lifestyle will require something close to the abolition of the private car'.[88] Fairlie's is a gradual revolution:

> Changes tend to begin at the margins of society: the organic farmers who thirty years ago were regarded as cranks are now given grants by MAFF; the 'alternative technology' pursued by hippies in the early seventies has now become 'renewable energy', the subject of a Planning Policy Guidance.

A key point of approval for DiY-ers is that the campaigning power of a group like The Land is Ours comes from its practical example: Fairlie has authority because *he lives it*, not (simply) because he is an expert on the subject. DiY Culture is predicated on such authenticity, such commitment, such rooted realness of action.

It's surely significant that, when DiY Culture wants to transform the dread urban space, it chooses to transplant into the city motifs from nature. The vibrant urban street parties thrown by Reclaim the Streets illustrate the desire to question the urban/rural binary opposition, in order to challenge the restrictions placed on citizens by car culture. City limits are interrogated by rural signifiers of freedom and pleasure, whose incongruous import and subsequent report function as a flash of possibility. A central London road is blocked off and covered with sand, deckchairs laid out and cocktails served to a tropical beat; an urban motorway is pedestrianised and a party thrown for thousands, while the tarmac is dug up and trees planted anew. Small images of small wilderness are smuggled into the patrolled urban zone – subversive, funny, daring. An urban squat on wasteland by The Land is Ours throws up a countryside community of benders and open fires in the midst of concrete London. A key project by Exodus Collective in Luton is the community farm. Such efforts as these are all far distant from the dystopian vision of activists for whom 'the city is implicitly totalitarian',[89] or even for the nomadic Dongas Tribe, wandering with horse and cart along the lost green lanes of southern England. As Laugh, one of the Dongas, put it to me:

> We have spent so long in the countryside now that going into towns let alone cities seems alien and oppressive to us. We see these feelings as healthy. Humanity is rooted in nature not concrete. You say that large free festivals bring the city to the countryside. This is true. The tribe collectively once went to the Glastonbury Festival, many of us felt as if we were in inner city London and vowed never to go again.[90]

Isn't a problem with championing the countryside as radical space that it's too white, too straight, though? That race is totally overlooked in a valorisation of rural over urban is shown by Rupa Huq, showing the invisibility of Asian popular music and style in much British popular culture and writings about it:

> Britpop bleaches away all traces of black influences in music in a mythical imagined past of olde England as it never was, whereas Beyond Bhangra and Jungle are rooted in the urban reality of today's Britain. *It's village green versus concrete jungle and we know where we'd rather be.*[91]

Huq pinpoints the evident danger in valorising *the land*, the rural landscape, which is that we tap into a Little Englander narrative, that old distrusting position of insularity that harks back to days of Empire, that parallels a right-wing, white and superior construction of Englishness. One of the problems with, say, attacking progress is that one of the alternatives on offer is nostalgia, and nostalgia in the British countryside is a black-free zone. According to Peter Gartside,

It is also possible to think of this strange youthful invocation of nation
(young Britain meets Old England) – contemporaneous, incidentally,
with the monocultural idea of Britpop and Blair's 'New Britain' vision
of a 'young country' – as a complex and confused response to
unsettling forces of globalisation and cultural fragmentation: a longing for belonging, for a comforting sense of rootedness and
authenticity.[92]

A dominant form of reclamation of space by alternative culture
has been squatting. Anarchist writer Colin Ward identifies 'ideological squats' intermittently in history, efforts at living in spaces
that themselves challenge property law and convention, or seek to
make political or social points about poverty. Most famously of
course there are the Diggers of 1649, protesting against enclosure
and for communal living, but there are stronger echoes of the city
wasteland squats of The Land is Ours in the 1990s in urban actions
of nearly a century ago:

> 'land-grabbers' occupied empty sites in several towns including Man-
> chester, Leeds, Plaistow and Bradford. The basic idea of the move-
> ment according to one writer 'was to grab land (or in some cases
> borrow it) that was not being used and to cultivate it whereby the
> hungry could grow their own foods and obtain a living from their
> own methods.' It was a response to massive unemployment, poverty
> and hunger, and the organisers saw the 'back-to-the-land' approach
> as a way of breaking workers' dependence on the capitalist system.[93]

The squatting movement as alternative lifestyle peaked in the late
1960s and 1970s, though it continues to an extent today in spite of
the recent extra restrictions of the CJA. Steve Platt recalls that in
the heady days of the seventies 'people had a sense of living
somewhere special, symbolised by the street carnivals and parties
which became a regular feature ... squatting began to be more
than simply finding a roof, it became fun, it offered new freedoms,
a sense of community ... almost a way of life in its own right.'[94]
Squatters claimed not only living spaces, but also action spaces:
community meeting rooms, women's refuges, gay centres, city
farms, workshops, small business premises, and so on. In antici-
pation of the DiY road communities and independent free states of
the 1990s,[95] Platt continues:

The notion of the squatting community was taken to its ultimate conclusion in 1977 when 120 squatters in Freston Road, West London, occupying GLC [Greater London Council] property, carried out an imaginative stunt. They made a unilateral declaration of independence from Great Britain and declared a 'Free Independent Republic of Frestonia'. Full membership of the United Nations was applied for, and a telegram sent to the Queen.... The GLC only recognised families as a unit for rehousing, so all the inhabitants adopted the surname Bramley, and Frestonia's motto was 'We are all one family'.[96]

After this highpoint of the seventies, London squatting hasn't always been so filled with such creativity since, as Rob of Hackney Squatters' centre notes: 'People say "I'm going to London, getting a squat and getting seriously fucked up." There's too many bad drugs.' One solution Rob offers to this negative city attitude is to take advantage of London's international situation, the global pull only a metropolitan locale has:

> The community is just so important. One thing that's been nice about this place is there's a lot of people here who come from different countries where there's more of a history of this kind of living, having social centres. They're used to the politics and working without hierarchies. . . . I like that organisation.[97]

More and more direct action protest as well as living seeks to connect the local with the global, in a conscious example of the green mantra 'act local think global'. This is one of the main and often overlooked reasons I think why we've seen direct action campaigns focus on export and overseas trade. During only two or three years in the mid-1990s there was an extraordinary upsurge in using the space of a local protest to project outwards to raising a global issue. I am thinking here of animal rights activists at Coventry Airport, Shoreham and Brightlingsea and other seaports, protesting against the live export of animals in 1995. I am thinking of the Reclaim the Streets activists who organised a party and protest action in collaboration with Liverpool dockers to show solidarity with striking trade unionists in 1996. I am thinking of the eco-tunnellers and other activists at the camps protesting against the development of the second runway for Manchester Airport and for the preservation of greenbelt and other landscape in 1997. It's surely significant that what all of these campaigns have in common is that they embrace import/export issues. This means of course that transport is always an underlying concern, but more important perhaps is the tactical point of overcoming the limitations of single-issue politics by connecting the local to the global. Such a magnification of action space offers a degree of unity and an ambition of scale for otherwise apparently disparate actions. Such micro-based internationalism also seeks to bypass any danger of Little England-erism, and signals solidarity with campaigns and struggles overseas. DiY activists are aware of the possibilities, of course, as made clear by a 1997 flyer in the form of a political essay put out by Earth First! and Shoreham Wilderness Defence for an anniversary day of action at Shoreham:

> The second anniversary of the Battle of Shoreham harbour is upon us. Now an even greater battle faces us – against the ecologically destructive practices of the global corporations. By going on to the streets and taking Direct Action aginst live exports in 1995 we stopped the trade at Shoreham. With our combined strength we can do the same again. . . .
>
> The three main industries at Shoreham are Oil, Timber and Aggregates. Communities just like ours are fighting these corporations all around the earth. Wild Nature is being destroyed everywhere and turned into frivolous items to feed the demands of western consumer culture. . . .
>
> By ignoring single issues and attacking the whole thing we can begin to highlight the consumption end of the process.

We can see here how DiY Culture wants (has?) the capacity to shift from micro to macro – or from the rural to the urban, from the urban to the international. Its construction and reclamation of a variety of protest and living space alike underline both its potential and its ambition for radical change, even as the project has problems and dangers within it.

DiY politics

That the political positions of DiY activists and cultural workers can be vaguely expressed, or can be simply reactive or problematic or even unsophisticated in themselves, is touched on throughout the intro and in the book itself, so here I want to look at two specific areas of political concern. These are the cluster of questions and problems around single-issue campaigning, with reference to animal rights, and the dangers of right-/left-wing blurring in the rhetoric and practice of eco-activism.

The main single issues of DiY Culture, the focus of its NVDA, apart from its self-interested concerns around the right to protest and the right to dance of the anti-CJA coalition in 1994, are the environmental ones of road protest and, to a lesser extent, animal rights. Why these seemingly marginal political subjects? Partly, and this has been understated by observers, because of the relative *novelty* of roads and animal rights for mass and ongoing direct action. Partly these are the areas of DiY Culture's overt political protest because they're *not*, say, the Bomb (1950s and 1980s), or Miners' Strikes (1972 and 1974, and 1984–85), or racism (late 1970s), or the poll tax (1988–90). To an extent DiY has chosen its own battlefields for struggle and self-definition, ones comparatively untouched by earlier generations of activists.

While suggesting that animal rights mass direct action is a relatively new phenomenon, it's important to qualify this by noting the history of the Animal Liberation Front in the 1980s, or the fact that a group like the Hunt Saboteurs Association was founded as long ago as 1962 – and this in turn needs extending back to the actions of, for instance, early feminists (even then there were no single issues) who spoke out against vivisection in Victorian times. But in the light of the increasing industrialisation of animal husbandry, animal rights campaigns have refocused their targets in the past decade. In *The Price of Meat*, Danny Penman notes that 'the sheer scale of cruelty inflicted by the meat industry merits special attention. About 720 million creatures are killed each year for meat in Britain. About 2 million are used in experiments and many thousands are killed for so-called "sports" like hare-coursing and fox-hunting.'[98] So in the nocturnal acid attacks on butchers' shop windows in the 1980s, the etching on plate glass of MEAT IS MURDER was a favoured tactic. But Penman identifies 'the weakest link' of the meat and dairy industries as the period 'when the waste calves of the milk industry [are] shipped to continental veal crates' – so for him it's no surprise that sea- and airports such as Shoreham,

Brightlingsea and Coventry were blockaded *en masse* by direct activists in 1994–95. Writing of the live export campaign, gaoled animal rights activist Keith Mann illustrates the politicisation of individuals through a single issue:

> a so-called single issue has galvanised the support of a whole variety of people, many of whom have never campaigned for anything before and who have soon been alerted to other related issues, like the link to drinking cows' milk and the export of calves, the indifference of the authorities and farmers to the suffering of animals (not just veal calves), the fact that the typical animals rights activist no matter what the appearance and opinion of the media is a dedicated and caring member of society with clear ideas of right and wrong, that the police aren't always the honest protectors of law and order it's claimed, etc.[99]

It may be that, as Mann describes taking place, single-issue campaigns need to make conscious efforts to signal their wider awareness and relevance in order to avoid effective criticism – even dismissal – of their campaigns as NIMBYistic (NIMBY: Not In My Back Yard) or ghettoising. But I do have problems with the easy sneer of criticising single-issue protest myself anyway. Consider roads: the 'single issue' of No More Roads includes topics like rural landscape, urban housing, the challenge to government and to big business, the environment, public health, personal political strategy, and social reformation – not bad for a single issue. Protesters have even laid claim to being the protectors of the establishment's defining jewel, the heritage industry itself, as when direct activists squatted a recently vacated monastery in Manchester to publicise its swift and scandalous decline, or with the emphasis placed by activists on the damage to archaeological sites by the bypass at Newbury. The fact that actions embrace a range of single issues is shown by a flyer for an anniversary protest at one of the south coast ports at the centre of the anti-live animal exports campaigns:

OPENCAST MINING,
SUPERQUARRIES,
ANIMAL RIGHTS,
OVERFISHING,
ANTI-ROADS,

WILDERNESS,
TIMBER,
OIL,
WHY WE HATE IT ALL.
SHOREHAM II![100]

The connection, the stress on interrelatedness, of single issues is matched by an alliance of activists themselves. Robert Hunter notes one of the characteristic features of the very first Canadian Greenpeace campaign of 1971:

> we also represented one of the strangest alliances to have ever emerged on the West Coast. The unions were behind us. The churches were behind us. Students were behind us. And housewives, mothers, and politicians on every wavelength of the spectrum from Trotskyite to the prime minister. Normally these factions fought like cats and dogs.... [T]he alliance we represented was a hint of a tremendous future power base, if any environmentalist could find some way to harness it.[101]

As Greenpeace went global in its attempts to build this power base, a rather more mundane and local British version of such a campaigners' alliance has developed, which seems to cut across class and social boundaries, while maintaining the signifiers of such boundaries (whether dreads or strings of pearls). Beneath its name on each front cover, the underground magazine *Frontline* outlines the inclusive breadth of its concerns, its readership constituency: 'travellers parties protests animals reviews contacts', or 'travellers parties politics culture reviews contacts'. Those attending a meeting of animal rights activists in Brighton are described by David Henshaw in *Animal Warfare*:

> Meeting in the upstairs room of a pub just off the sea front, you would find rainbow-haired punks sitting next to pensioners who were happy to march with the local branch of the National Front against ritual slaughter in Jewish and Moslem abattoirs; next to them would be hunt saboteurs, and then activists who had taken part in a raid to free animals from a big south coast laboratory complex; in the corner sat the elderly founder of the local evangelical Christian animal rights group, a heroine of the local press and a woman of selfless good

works. In between, there would be a large number of ordinary local
people, teachers, local government officers and plenty of students.[102]

Merrick captures some of the complexities of the alliance of
protesters against road-building: 'There's hunters and hunt saboteurs on the same side! If we don't save this land, there won't *be*
any countryside here to argue about.' He continues:

> The road protests and the campaign against the CJB [Criminal Justice
> Bill] are different from others in recent history because they're not
> about a single issue, NIMBYism, or students being a bit radical before
> settling down to make money and babies. They are coming out of a
> whole new culture that is emerging. It is a culture derived from a
> common discontent with the self-interest and blandness that is
> endemic in western society, and a rejection of the pyramidic power
> structure that only ever disempowers those at the bottom, and
> corrupts and compromises those at the top. The alternative power
> structure is a networking of self-responsibility and co-operation.[103]

For sure, to previous generations of activists there may be something a bit offensive in the idea that all this is new or that they were
all single-issue campaigners (let alone in the inference that radicalism ends when parenthood begins: at least a quarter of the people
writing in this book have children) – were, say, the alternative
networks constructed by women's peace camps in the 1980s single-
issue? What may be more breathtaking was the extent of the 1980s
DiY culture of resistance's sheer scale of ambition: from a DiY
community of protest such as Greenham Common came a massive
international challenge to the global war machine, to American
militaristic imperialism, the project of the British state, let alone
little things like, well, patriarchy, let alone land rights, travellers'
rights, and so on. (Anyone over the age of, maybe, thirty reading
the chapters in this book may find their reading process inter-
rupted by occasional moments of such enthusiastic youthful arrogance. How to deal with it? Well, not [just] by saying, 'Oh *we* did
that in the fifties/sixties, more and better', please.)

In some ways there may well be a lack of ambition in the scale of
DiY Culture today, compared with earlier more straightforwardly
global countercultural campaigns, like the anti-Vietnam War protests or Greenpeace's global direct action, or the anti-cruise missile

Peace Camps of the 1980s. All of those sought to engage grandly with global concerns, while if we compare that aim with, say, the anti-live exports campaigns of 1994–95, we're left with a sense of parochialism, aren't we? The very fact that *export* is at the centre of things suggests a distrust or even fear of the foreign: continental Europe for animal rights activists blockading ports is characterised by its cruel and distasteful treatment of animals, and worse: don't they eat horses and bait bears over there? A danger of a local politics is that it is another way of mapping on to a Little Englander mentality, even a xenophobia.[104] In the context of DiY Culture, an early example of such a Little Englander attitude is seen in 1976 when Richard Hunt, planting the roots of magazine/organisation *Green Anarchist*, 'argued that in order to maintain the cultural integrity of the small communities he advocated – necessary to keep order in the community on an informal, face-to-face basis – they would have to practise "xenophobia"'.[105] We begin to touch on the dangers of a irrational/authoritarian crossover in eco-politics, particularly as Hunt later resigned from *Green Anarchist* and espoused a much more worryingly nationalistic politics.[106] Celebrating the land and self has its uncomfortable antecedents, as we'll see in discussing both Nazi Germany and more contemporary modes of ecofascism in Germany and elsewhere, but opposing road-building projects and identifying a threat to indigenous cultures can be awkward as well.

[T]he hundreds of thousands of particular cultures that have existed for centuries are disappearing from the landscape at an alarming rate. There currently exist two intertwined and mutually reinforcing trends in European policy-making that have and will continue to contribute [*sic*] to an identifiable change in how people live. The first is the radical transformation of agriculture, largely thanks to Euro-pean policies including the Common Agricultural Policy (CAP). The second is the aggressive promotion of new infrastructure, most notably roads, in the EU's controversial proposals for Trans-European Networks (TENs).[107]

How far is campaigning against CAP and TENs taking one into the territory of suspicion of Johnny Foreigner? One has dreads and ill-fitting combat boots, one offers the argument of the retired colonel. It may be that such awkwardness is reality intruding in the form of contradiction (in the way that the activist's guide against European Union transport policy just quoted from is part-funded by the European Union, for instance), but it's not enough to identify irony or express discomfort. Looking at land, self and environment in the earlier twentieth century reveals some troubling antecedents, ones which should give pause for thought to those in DiY Culture who are engaged in efforts to construct more coherent political perspectives.

Some aspects of the New Age are markedly old, whether it's solstice celebration around stones, bohemian travellers' groups getting back to the land, or a deep interest in vegetarianism and organic farming. All of these, for instance, became or were features of Nazi social practice or policy in Germany between the two world wars. Even the word 'ecology' itself is tainted, and, 'From its very beginnings ... was bound up in an intensely reactionary political framework' in which ideas of natural law and order, the place of the organism in the environment, and authoritarian notions of purity and control contributed to what would become Nazi ideology.[108] The word 'ecology' was coined in 1867 by the German zoologist Ernst Haeckel, who himself 'contributed to that special variety of German thought which served as the seed bed for National Socialism. He became one of Germany's major ideologists for racism, nationalism and imperialism.'[109] More worryingly perhaps, as Janet Biehl and Peter Staudenmaier observe, 'Tenets of "New Age" eco-ideology that seem benign to most people in England and the United States – specifically, its mystical and antirational strains – are being intertwined with ecofascism in Germany today.'[110] The country which has produced perhaps the most dynamic green movement of the late twentieth century is raising fundamental problems which need addressing, or at the very least acknowledgement, by all eco-activists, not just German ones. Peter Staudenmaier notes also 'the neo-pagan elements in the Nazi leadership', which combined the Blood and Soil movement of the German people/history and land with at times 'a level of government support for ecologically sound farming methods and land use planning unmatched by any state before or since'.[111] The relation between authoritarianism and irrationalism is one explored brilliantly by Theodor Adorno, the German Marxist critic exiled to America to escape the Nazis. 'Occultism is the metaphysic of dunces', booms Adorno, authoritatively, and his work from the 1940s and 1950s signals a distrust of the burgeoning West Coast New Age movement in America as much as it is a critique of irrational strands in Nazi ideology or mythology. For Adorno, engaged politics is dissipated in New Age-style discourse. As he puts it, 'Spirit is dissociated into spirits': political energy and reason is dispersed, transformed, displaced by magic, mystery, the intangible of the occult.[112]

At the cusp of the millennium there is in some quarters a 'continuing attraction of the sort of millenarian, apocalyptic and mystical thinking that helped spawn the Nazis'.[113] Matthew Kalman and John Murray have written exposés of the connections between extreme right-wing and eco-issues, in order to 'make the green and New Age movement aware of the racist and neo-Nazi thinking that is trying to masquerade under its banner'. The well-established British paper *Green Anarchist* has itself flirted with right-wing ideas, not only in the past but also in its writings on population reduction, jokily(?) admitting a perspective it has described as 'well eco-fascist'.[114] David Henshaw writes that 'far right groupings saw considerable mileage in both the ecological and animal rights movements as a potential source for the recruitment of the idealistic young. And animal rights as an issue had the useful ingredient of ritual slaughter as a means of promoting anti-semitic and anti-Muslim propaganda.'[115] Meanwhile, in America DiY Culture is adopted by the radical right, as this material from a fascist fanzine called *Third Way* shows:

> The goal of the Third Way is 1) to create an *independent media* for White nationalists; 2) to *educate* young Whites through a *counterculture* which is *opposed to* the sick society of *the present system*; and 3) to allow young nationalists a chance to let off steam. . . . *What sets us apart,* as Revolutionary Nationalists . . . is that we are *a cultural as well as a political movement.*[116]

There's little doubt in my mind that the italicised words here would sound absolutely acceptable to British DiY-ers, which is a forceful argument for the need to put more effort into moving beyond DiY Culture's initial strengths – its capacity for action and its vibrant

culture – to greater consideration and reflection of difficult questions such as organisation, coherence of ideology, relation to
established radical and mainstream politics, future development,
history and theory. Peter Staudenmaier's conclusion on the well-
known preferred political declaration of some environmentalists (a
different kind of third way, maybe) is pertinent to DiY Culture
more generally:

> the slogan advanced by many contemporary Greens, 'We are neither
> right nor left but up front', is historically naive and politically fatal.
> The necessary project of creating an emancipatory ecological politics
> demands an acute awareness and understanding of the legacy of
> classical ecofascism and its conceptual continuities with present-day
> environmental discourse. An 'ecological' orientation alone, outside
> of a critical social framework, is dangerously unstable.[117]

Not just an emancipatory *ecological* politics, either, but for DiY
Culture an emancipatory politics of pleasure or autonomy needs
an awareness and understanding of history and theory, too. In the
context of interrogating the politics of dance culture, for example,
Tim Jordan has observed that 'What a "raver's revolution" might
mean is a barred question, as is the meaning of unending autonomy,
whose very asking would constitute an attempt to stifle the creativity
of raving.'[118] How frequently does DiY Culture deal with difficult
questions simply by not asking them?

Lacunae

The 'unofficial slogan' of the DiY organisation at the forefront of
coordinating opposition to the Criminal Justice Bill in 1993 and
1994, the Freedom Network, was 'unity through diversity'.[119] So,
are there significant gaps in the inclusive, embracing, empowering
and supportive movement that is DiY Culture? Well – what about
sexuality, class, race, gender and disability, for a start? When they
are introduced it's tokenistic, much as it is you might say in
mainstream society and culture generally. I'm not saying that
lesbians and gays, working-class people, blacks or Asians, women,
people with disabilities, aren't involved in DiY Culture as activists

or as cultural workers – DiY has a real strength in its capacity to empower. Rather, there are matters around identity, social and physical access, the politics of invisibility, the production of culture, as well as other single issues and direct action campaigns which seem to be comparatively ignored, that are either excluded from or marginalised within DiY Culture.[120] And, since its buzzwords are things like 'reclaiming', 'self-empowerment', 'action', and its preferred space the pleasure/politics zone of party and protest, when there are other groups in society also occupying that space, it's at the very least surprising that DiY's utopian rhetoric falters in practice. It may be that some of the lacunae I am uncovering are symptoms of DiY Culture's project of newness, whereby these issues are too tainted with having been focuses of activism over previous decades, are somehow too mundane. Also some are issues that have been embraced by parliamentary politics, the subject of manifesto pledges and televised debates over the years, and again that may taint with tedium. DiY is suspicious and sometimes disdainful of -isms, viewing them variously as outdated, as the kinds of things non-activists do instead of direct action, or as simply boring.

It's true that DiY isn't alone in perhaps thinking of certain political issues as belonging to the past, even if others have voiced it more clearly. Gay writer Mark Simpson, for example, has recently said that 'Gay is a grand narrative – come out of the darkness into the light. Like class struggle and feminism, it doesn't work the voodoo any more.'[121] In the context of sexuality, what's surprising is the paucity of occasions when DiY's preference for NVDA leads it to working alongside current gay direct action groups such as Outrage. Turning to consider dance music, again there are potential overlaps between DiY and gay culture, though, as touched on by Hillegonda Rietveld in this volume, the gay pleasure-zone disco origins of dance music seem to be overlooked in the more hardcore, masculine aesthetic of free party sounds. *The danger is that DiY Culture quietens marginalised voices and erases difference, and that, paradoxically, it achieves both of these by a loud rhetoric of inclusivity.* Time for some sweeping generalisations and critical comments, as I discuss DiY Culture and its lacunae.

One of the problems of the project to rewrite activism and social organisation in a green framework rather than a more traditional left/right one is that it may close down as much space as it opens

up. When researchers can write of 'the *green* emphasis on participatory rather than representative democracy',[122] I'm wondering
why participatory democracy is specified as a green feature, when
to me it's much more clearly and much more historically rooted in
the theory and practice of anarchism. Such a shift, to a woolly
contemporary terminology from a historically located political
tradition, is not always useful. A rhetoric of class awareness and
politics has been pretty largely absent from DiY Culture. A consciously expressed reason for this by some activists is that class
politics is an outdated way of approaching issues. This is related to
a vague historical sense of a failed division between right-wing and
left-wing, which valorises the kinds of direct action single-issue
alliances we've seen between the NIMBY (Not In My Back Yard)
twin-set-and-pearl brigade and the NOPE (Not On Planet Earth)
'crustie' eco-warrior, the hunter and the hunt sab defending rural
England side by side, even the neo-fascist and the anarchist doing
animal liberation work together. Publications like *Aufheben* or
Counter Information have offered a class perspective from broadly
within it, but long-established organisations like street-centred, 'in-
yer-face' Class War or the anarcho-syndicalist Direct Action Movement, along with the higher-profile and more centrally organised
Socialist Workers' Party, seem to be missing out on the activist
energy of DiY. Writing in this book, *Aufheben* explore the politics of
road protest in terms of a class framework particularly at the No
M11 Link Road campaign in east London. The most working-class-
located road protests are the urban ones, less concerned with the
preservation of landscape than with issues of health, poverty and
social housing. This is perhaps most true of the 1994 protest camps
against the M77 motorway through a woodland park historically
bequeathed to the city in the Pollok region of Glasgow. The left
Labour group Militant Tendency was central in mobilising the
campaign, and Earth First! acknowledges the class impetus of that
eco-campaign.

> Pollok and Corkerhill lie next to the proposed M77 scheme, and their
> communities have opposed the road for decades. Corkerhill has the
> lowest percentage of car owners in Europe and 1 in 5 children there
> already has asthma. ... Many environmentalists began to see the

campaign beyond wholly moral terms and saw the class and social implications of this fight.[123]

It seems clear to me that some of the chapters in this book are more centred on the experience of one social class than another – a fairly obvious comment, you might think, except that few of the writers or the people who were involved address their situation in such terms. Warehouse parties in post-industrial Lancashire or free community events for local black and white youth in Luton may quite probably be premised on a different social expectation and experience than those of land rights activists talking about the continuation of enclosure – it's a generalisation of course, but maybe not an invalid one. Is another reason for the comparative silence around class that class awareness threatens the 'feel-good factor' of DiY? Efforts in 1996 by Reclaim the Streets to link their transport and environment issues with the trade union-based struggles of London Underground workers and Liverpool dockers indicate that some activists in DiY Culture are addressing its limitations, however.

The African-American cultural critic Michele Wallace argues that 'white people consistently conceptualise resistance in ways that minimize the importance of race, or the vital contribution black artists and intellectuals have made to the discussion of that issue'.[124] Writing against what she terms 'the great American whitewash' of 1968, the way in which African-Americans have been written out of histories of the 1960s counterculture, Wallace offers a revision of the term 'counterculture':

> Afro-American culture was instrumental in forming the aspirations of the New Left, as well as minority revolutions – not so much by its considerable political activity, but precisely by its counterculture. While this 'minor' culture may sometimes be difficult to link directly to political protest, it was always clearly formed in the spirit of subverting a majority culture that tried to choke it at the root. Precisely in its sex, drugs, dance, music, and style, it kept the record of its discontents accurately and well. Perhaps this counterculture is the site where mainstream culture is still most forcefully challenged, even as 'revolutions' come and go.

Black invisibility exists in 1990s protest, in DiY Culture, too. (Green is white, isn't it?) *The White Book* was a project by Justice? in Brighton to publish a directory of activist groups in Britain. When it was completed and published in 1995 it was renamed *The Book*: 'We asked some black groups why they hadn't responded and were answered by looks of incredulity – we're stupid.'[125] The book *Dis-Orienting Rhythms* is part of a recent effort to uncover 'lost' or erased narratives of the new Asian dance music in Britain, and using 1980s Bhangra music as an example it's clear to see the limitations of DiY Culture's professed or assumed liberal or radical inclusivity. The production of cheap tapes of original popular dance music for a youth audience, independent and widespread distribution networks, recognisable subcultural styles, alternative spaces for the collective consumption and pleasure of performance, the updating of an indigenous music form through embracing new technology: all of these aspects of Bhangra contribute to what might – maybe, to what *should* – be identified as a lengthy and thriving DiY Culture, but it's one which has been *completely* absent from the DiY media. 'Play that funky music white boy? We don't think so,' conclude the editors of *Dis-Orienting Rhythms*.[126] I should point out, however, that the invisibility of other cultures in predom-inantly white sub- or countercultural moments isn't confined to DiY Culture in the 1990s. Writing of the Rock Against Racism carnivals in the late 1970s – events whose main purpose was to challenge racism and celebrate racial and cultural diversity through the medium of pop music – Virinder S. Kalra, John Hutnyk and Sanjay Sharma observe that 'the early British Bhangra scene was running parallel to these developments, but there was no involve-ment of Asian bands in RAR'.[127] Racism can be inscribed even within what is frequently presented as the utopian, racially mixed space of dance culture:

> Jungle is what killed Smiley. Remembering 'Smiley's' ecstatic promi-nence as the symbol of a drug-related, happy (white) rave scene from 1989 onwards is useful. It allows us to think about the overtly racialised symbolism of utopia. Even digitally engineered utopias are apparently ruined by the natives. Their science is seen as bad science. It is jungle that disrupts the ordered progress of British culture. Or so the story goes.[128]

While white Britons in the mainstream and the alternative culture alike continue to espouse a cosy multiracial image, others, like the Asian writers of *Dis-Orienting Rhythms*, replace multiracial with *multiracist.*

Rachel of Slampt Underground Organisation, part of the 1990s punk/fanzine scene, does link gender and NVDA, explaining that 'Being a girl in a male-only environment. Wearing exactly what I want. Speaking my mind. I guess all of these are direct actions.'[129] In general, though, the awareness of gender declines in 1990s alternative culture. This can be either implicitly waved away by mutterings of post-feminism – women need struggle no more against patriarchy, because we have the equality of the sexes, that unconvincing kind of line – or, more uncomfortably still, the silence might correspond to the feminist backlash in majority culture. Obviously, and as we've seen, the women's peace move- ment of the 1980s is an important inspiration for DiY protest, yet the separatist space of Greenham Common (declared a women- only space shortly after the Peace Camp was founded) is not repeated, nor is there even that much discussion of the ways in which gender can frame issues or protest. For example, protest against car culture engages with national culture and multinational finance – consider not only the importation of the mass consump- tion of motor cars into Western Europe from the United States, but the fact that related American forms of living and dying are imported too, from drive-thru burger bars (gross out) to drive-by shootings. But car culture is also a *gendered* issue. Winfried Wolf observes that three-quarters of registered car ownership in Germany in 1988 was to men – that is, car culture reinforces a patriarchal domination of property rights. He elaborates on the point, to illustrate the wider implications of gender and car culture:

> The patriarchal nature of the car society expresses itself also in the nature of property ... urban planning and residential structures are unfriendly to women. ... 'Many women see multi-storey car parks as unfriendly and threatening and they avoid them when they can'. ... Car advertisements, especially those for car accessories, are clearly based on the assumption that the car society is male domi- nated. In no other industrial branch is the woman so openly and aggressively used as a sex object. ... 'A woman at the wheel' – that is

a cry of horror and abuse in the male-dominated car society. And this is in spite of the fact that, as the statistics show, women cause fewer accidents and women constitute only 7.9 per cent of drivers who lose their driving licence.[130]

In different ways and contexts Alex Plows, Mary Anna Wright and Hillegonda Rietveld all seek to redress the balance a little in their chapters here, away from a DiY Culture which has a tendency to elide the experience and significance of gender. Perhaps Reclaim the Streets in the 1990s could learn more about the gendered perspectives and fears of public spaces from the Reclaim the Nights marches of the 1970s, too.

DAN is the Disabled People's Direct Action Network, which exists to campaign for disabled people to have the right 'to boldly go where all others have gone before', as one slogan puts it. Lorna Reith explains that 'disabled people were completely excluded from the political process – from inaccessible party meetings, polling stations, an unrepresentational government'. The disability direct action of the 1980s and early 1990s, Reith continues,

> was an interesting campaign because it was saying – we want more law – this isn't against the establishment – it isn't against the state. We're saying the state should intervene. It was therefore turning the stereotype regarding what direct action is about on its head.[131]

The American disability empowerment movement ADAPT inspired British activists, and in 1986 a march under the banner of 'Rights Not Charity' effectively became a direct action event as it turned into a physical blockade by disabled activists. Other direct action followed, and DAN was set up in 1993 as a result of the increasing activism. It organises two national non-violent actions a year, with the fundamental point that, as Barbara Lisicki of DAN told me, 'the campaign is in *our* control: it's about empowerment, strength, determination'. Asked about DiY Culture and disability activism, Lisicki notes that the timing of direct action is connected – late 1980s and 1990s – but also makes the point that 'DiY has a problem around disabled people'.[132] There have been efforts to open up access between direct action campaigners from within and outwith DiY Culture, of course, not only because of the shared common tactic of 'in yer face' NVDA. For example, car culture has its own exclusionary strategies for disabled people, too: Italy has 'a restrictive law which does not permit physically handicapped people to drive any car above a certain rpm',[133] while the systematic denial of access to public transport for people in wheelchairs has been a major focus of DAN actions in Britain. Organisers of a major Reclaim the Streets action in London contacted DAN because they thought it important to signal that public access and safety in the streets was an issue for all city people, and to illustrate RTS's effort at widening the context from single issues to a broader coalition of activist groups (as they have done more sucessfully with striking transport workers, as we've seen). Lisicki remembers that 'RTS was so insistent that they wanted a DAN presence, but they didn't put two and two together: to get to the secret location of the street party people were told to get on the tube, which isn't the most accessible form of public transport for disabled people, now, is it?'

Outro

Possibly the lacunae discussed above illustrate the way in which DiY Culture is implicitly seeking to position itself as powerful and radical but as outside the traditional left, with a mentality quite far removed from that of the Liberation Movements idea that flourished in the seventies. On the other hand, veteran anarchist writer Colin Ward wrote the following in 1972. I think it speaks to DiY Culture in the 1990s, and may signal a route worth pursuing for both historical and theoretical awareness of young or newer activists today.

> The very growth of the state and its bureaucracy, the giant corporation and its privileged hierarchy, are exposing their vulnerability to non-co-operation, to sabotage, and to the exploitation of *their* weaknesses by the weak. They are also giving rise to parallel organisations, counter organisations, alternative organisations, which exemplify the anarchist method. . . . None of these movements is yet a threat to the power structure, and this is scarcely surprising since hardly any of them existed before the late 1960s. None of them fits into the framework of conventional politics. In fact, they don't speak the same language as the political parties. They talk the language of anarchism

and they insist on anarchist principles of organisation, which they
have learned not from political theory but from their own experience.
They organise in loosely associated groups which are *voluntary,
functional, temporary* and *small.* They depend, not on membership
cards, votes, a special leadership and a herd of inactive followers but
on small, functional groups which ebb and flow, group and regroup,
according to the task in hand. They are networks, not pyramids.[134]

Reading the chapters that follow you'll encounter a wide variation
in approach, style, language, analytical concern. You may well
notice a kind of entrepreneurial spirit, an acceptance of the current
situation (which means old battles are ignored or current activists
are ignorant of them), a desire to celebrate/think positive. There's
a microperspectival utopianism, a limited challenge in some ways –
even where combined with a revolutionary rhetoric, which may
well be the least interesting or convincing feature. There is material
in individual chapters, for instance, that I disagree with, or find
problematic or simplistic, and even worrying, but I consciously
withhold comment here, unwilling to use my editorial position to
set the agenda too much: your careful reading will uncover gaps
and contradictions, I'm sure, while hopefully admiring and enjoying much of the energy and subversive imagination DiY Culture
possesses in abundance. For other old(er) readers and (ex-)activists
I've this point to make: if paragraphs or chapters in this book take
your breath away because of their displayed ignorance of or
arrogance about previous radical movements and moments – the
ones you were involved in in the sixties or seventies, for instance –
that's only partly DiY Culture's fault. Remember your breath's
taken away because you're a bit unfit. You need to get out and
about more. Adopt a tree, aggravate some trespass, make the
acquaintance of a D-lock. What about some dance to a pedal-
powered sound system in a blocked-off street? There's some serious
fun to be had out there. There's people out there who want to
hear your history, too. DiY writer Camilla Berens tells me of young
DiY-ers on national anti-Criminal Justice Bill protests in London
through 1994 asking each other, 'Where are the old hippies, and
the punks of the seventies? Where are they when we need them?'
Ahistoricism isn't really a preserve of youth – it's combated as much
by the elders keeping their own ideas and actions fresh, in the

memory. And, if you suspect that DiY has a thick patina of radical chic, well, whose fault is that? Who acquiesced, kept their head down under Thatcher in the 1980s, settled for New Labour in the 1990s? John Vidal pinpoints the altered context of radical expectation within which DiY Culture is located.

> Dismissed as 'one issue' groups by the party politicians, together they may be seen as a realistic new political force, even as the seeds of a new society. *If that seems radical it is just a measure of how unfashionable popular idealism has been made to seem by the free market. It can seem radical these days to get on a bus or walk.*[135]

But also, I ask, how far is it possible to find ways ahead which avoid the pitfalls of over-establishment and centralisation, as well as of the 'tyranny of structurelessness',[136] but which allow the energy, creativity and sheer cheek of activists and cultural workers from the last decade and more to thrive and develop? According to an even more veteran anarchist than Ward, Murray Bookchin, 'If a left-libertarian vision of a future society is not to disappear in a bohemian and lumpen demimonde, it must offer a resolution to social problems, not flit arrogantly from slogan to slogan, shielding itself from rationality with bad poetry and vulgar graphics.'[137] Sometimes the slogans, poetry and graphics aren't that bad, really, but my main concern here is Bookchin's implication that resolution to social problems is not being offered by contemporary counter-culture. One of the aims of this book is that the chapters in it, written by people involved in DiY, demonstrate that the existence *and* the vibrancy of DiY Culture do address and, yes, resolve social problems. Housing and homelessness, the environment, unemployment, the social value of people, the construction of community, poverty, cultural entropy and silence – all of these, and more, are directly addressed by people at grassroots level, outside the mainstream. Solutions include, for instance, squatting and low impact living spaces, camps and campaigns throwing up fresh ideas and energy on eco-issues, an emphasis on self-empowerment through social acts like protest, free parties and newpapers, new music experiences and independent alternative media. But the writing in the following pages tells you all this in more detail and with a closer sense of involvement than I possess, so . . .

Cartoons

KATE EVANS

This and the following page show illustrations from Kate Evans's *Copse: The Cartoon Book of Tree Protesting*. Further details at p. 302 of this book

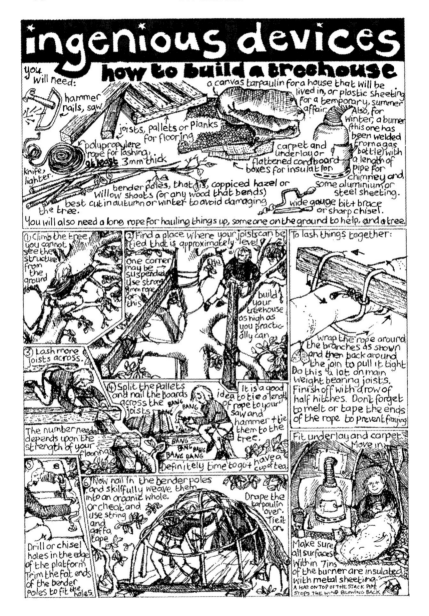

2

Fresh flavour in the media soup: the story of *SQUALL* magazine

JIM CAREY

'So what does it actually mean? ... Squatters' Action for Lively Livers?'

Well no, it's a word, rather than an acronym.

The dictionary offers its definition as a sudden strong wind or commotion (CoMotion).

Attention all shipping. Sea area Dogger Bite, squally showers. Gale force 8.

The office lexicon also proffers the Scandinavian root word '*skvala*' meaning 'to shout'.

There is a need to be heard.

'So what does *SQUALL* mean?'

We risk an incomplete picture and apply the minimum of spray paint. It lies written on the wall thus: *SQUALL* is a storm, the course of which disturbs the choking waters, unsettling the sediment, preventing stagnancy, and providing breath to a gasping truth.

Bit grand yer think? Well lying behind the poetry is a diagnosis of malaise and a prescription of medicine:

Global media are now increasingly owned by a small number of media barons who, despite assurances to the contrary, directly influence the news agenda on the basis of their market intent. And from the barons to their editors to the staff to the career freelancers, this economic sub-agenda looms large in the reportage.

Neither is the voice of national media comment in Britain remotely representative of a diverse nation – rather it is the distilled opinion of a select clique of mostly Oxbridge journos who feel dutybound to protect their monopoly on social comment.

SQUALL is a serious attempt to provide a more socially relevant representation, unfettered by the usual sycophancy to advertisers and spin doctors; an attempt to rejuvenate the independence, accuracy and liveliness of British journalism.

Phew!

The six-year history of *SQUALL* magazine has been fuelled by such outrageous and grandiose aspirations. Each new generation contributes to the achievement of what was previously thought impossible – simply because they did not consider it so. We have not reached our destination but the journey has already borne significant fruit.

A journey of a thousand miles begins with . . .

Kenneth Baker doesn't deserve much of a mention in this story. But as Home Secretary in 1992, he stood up at the Conservative Party Conference to utter words significant to the history of farce: 'We will get tough on armed robbers, tough on rapists and tough on squatters.' It was a laughable juxtaposition of course, and, coming from the mouth of a British Home Secretary, one deserving of scornful media criticism. There was none. Instead it was left to the likes of the *Daily Mail* and *Daily Telegraph* to dredge up nightmare after manufactured nightmare in order to lend weight to the demonisation.

Armed robbers, rapists and . . .

For one group of North London squatters leaning on their brooms, Baker's words breached an already stretched threshold of tolerance. If casual demonisations like this passed as acceptable political currency, then the gap between reality and rhetoric yawned in emergency. Operating under the name lowLIFE?!, this collective of squatters had been the prolific organisers of large cultural events in London squats since 1989. Their regular Arts Feasts brought together diverse performance from all round the world, their Cooking Club presented live music, their galleries were packed with photography, painting and sculpture, their all-night parties offered both live music and DJs, whilst their free lowLIFE?! magazine provided a forum for community art and writings. The entire operation was run by volunteers, with the aspirational rollercoaster kept on the rails with passion, commitment and the money collected in a donation bucket at their free events. They were nutters for a cause, and the cause was financially accessible communal culture.

So it was with brooms in hand that the lowLIFE?! team read the *Daily Telegraph*'s editorial (7 June 1993) describing squatters and travellers as a 'swarming tribe of human locusts' and then observed the political dribble build into a hysterical flood. Our space to live and celebrate in ways outside the official market formula were being legislated away along with basic necessities like the only affordable roof over our heads. And there to facilitate this cultural attack was and is the likes of the *Daily Telegraph* with its sales figures of over a million a day, the *Daily Mail* with over two million a day, and the poorly written *Spectator* magazine shoring up the prejudices of its 50,000 readers with fortnightly dollops of right-wing pseudo-intelligentsia.

After operating for over two years, the members of the lowLIFE?! collective felt a long way from 'armed robbers' and 'rapists', and a far cry from John Major's reference to squatters as 'creators of municipal rubbish dumps'. By 1992, however, the lowLIFE?! project had run its course. Having started with very little money and few possessions, the project was left with even less after Labour MP Frank Dobson and thirty-five coppers forced their way into a Camden warehouse, confiscating speakers and injuncting the venue two days before a lowLIFE?! event. What little money the project had was lost, leaving the group with nothing but a sleep debt, two years' valuable experience and a small computer.

Published in 1992, the first edition of *SQUALL* magazine was constructed on this computer. Its front-cover cartoon depicted a snail leaving its shell.

Lockjaw: media silence on the CJA

Issue 1 – now lodged in the British Library – was with hindsight a modest affair: a photocopied A5 eight-pager, lovingly (nay, deter-minedly) assembled by pressing over binding staples with redden-ing thumbs. It has to be said that this collector's item was not greeted with the expected uprising of the oppressed, the eradication of injustice and a revolution in British journalism's willingness to investigate the truth behind the spin. Instead the conspicuous chirrup of uninterrupted cicadas was only punctuated with a few head-pats and a trickle of feedback suggesting it wouldn't mean a thing unless there was an issue 2, 3, 4 . . .

In word and indeed, there was plenty to publish, as the political demonisation of squatters proved to be merely the tip of a large, dirty iceberg. Within a few months of launching *SQUALL*, it became apparent that the government's intention to stamp out squatting was just a part of a much larger assault on British culture. Contained within the 1994 Criminal Justice and Public Order Bill's large number of disconnected clauses were new police stop and search powers, the removal of the traditional right to silence, as well as criminal sanctions against travellers, ravers, festival-goers, public assemblies and political protests.

Issue 1 of *SQUALL* magazine described itself as 'a magazine for squatter/homeless', a strap line which evolved into 'a magazine for squatters, travellers and other itinerants' by issue 5, and then to 'a magazine for sorted itinerants' by issue 10. By issue 14, the magazine's brief had galloped full pelt into a vast unpopulated savannah of British journalism we referred to as 'the missing agenda in culture and politics'. The list of the unrepresented quickly grew wider than those targeted by the CJB, or CJA (Criminal Justice *Act*), as it became when passed by parliament in late 1994.

Social ills resulting from a compassionless politics were rhetorically reapportioned as blame on single mothers, itinerants, homeless people, dole scroungers and disrespectful youth. The Old Testament origin of the word 'scapegoat' proved more than apt as a commentary on current circumstance: a goat used in the ritual of Yom Kippur was symbolically laden with sins by the authorities and cast into the wilderness to die. The people were led to believe that the ritual of sending an innocent goat to its death relieved the populace of responsibility for their own sins.

Single mothers were a classic example. According to both John Major and the then Social Security Secretary, Peter Lilley, women were having babies out of wedlock to ensure that they got a higher priority status on the housing waiting list as single mothers. Those involved in the growing *SQUALL* team observed such farcical rhetoric appearing in national newspapers with barely a sniff of journalistic dissent. And yet it was laughable that a woman would gestate a child for nine months, go through the trauma of childbirth and accept the responsibility of looking after a child simply to put a few extra points on her housing priority status. Even if she did, what did this say about the availability of affordable housing! Nevertheless, this 'burden on the welfare state' was deemed unacceptable and legislation to remove the welfare premium paid to single mothers was drafted by the Tories and carried forward by the incoming Labour government.

As Tory MP for Luton North until the 1997 general election, John Carlisle was candid about his selected scapegoats when he offered his opinion that 'All gypsies should be banished into the wilderness.' Once again it was difficult to believe that such racially inflammatory comments could pass from the lips of a British MP during the passage of the Criminal Justice Bill and not become the subject of media outrage. It is more than ironic that the Bill itself included a clause which created a criminal offence out of racially inflammatory comment!

Nevertheless gypsies, like most of the social groups targeted by the Act, had little by way of access to a media reply. No champions in the media, no press releases, no media spokespeople, no lobbying power in parliament, no significant economic clout. And, being the object of a historical prejudice easy to re-inflame in the pages of the *Daily Mail*, they were perfect scapegoat material. When the home affairs' correspondent of the left-leaning *Guardian* newspaper approached me after a press conference, I asked him why none of the media seemed interested in the plight of gypsies – given the kind of bigoted comments emanating from parliament. 'I don't know,' he said before changing the subject, though in reality nothing was changing except for the worse.

As a result of *SQUALL*'s coverage, one of its journalists was invited over to the Czech Republic by some prominent British-based gypsies, in order to attend a large family christening. During the course of her visit, she was warmly welcomed by the entire community, hearing countless tales of gypsy mythology, whilst ably aiding the families with their customary demolition of countless bottles of vodka. Squatters Action for Lively Livers after all! She also took part in the ceremony of pouring some of the precious spirit on the graves of dead gypsies. One more for the road. Her subsequently written 'international special' was published in the pages of *SQUALL* 12, and left readers in no doubt that 'banishing gypsies into the wilderness' was tantamount to a crime against humanity.

In every direction *SQUALL* cast its investigative eye, it found such scapegoats being fattened up with manufactured sins ready for the wilderness and certain slaughter. The goat needed kick.

Despite experiencing a series of disruptive evictions from several squats, possibly exacerbated by the climate change engineered to precede the CJA, *SQUALL*'s co-editors attended night classes in journalism in early 1993 and pressed on with issue 5, 6, 7 . . . Several members of the team cut their political teeth on activities surrounding the CJB. Whilst some of the co-editors were heavily involved with meeting MPs, drafting potential amendments and attending interminable committee stage meetings, others were familiarising themselves with publishing techniques and building liaisons within the so-called 'underground' movement. This move-ment was emerging from its subterranean status as a prominent voice of political dissent. Groups representing the different minor-ities targeted by the CJB began organising themselves and dissemi-nating more representative information. The term 'DiY' movement sprang up and found resonance as an encapsulation of the notion of not sitting around just waiting for things to improve. In reality, though, 'DiO' (Do it Ourselves) captures more accurately the communal rather than individual response.

The two anti-CJB marches held in London in 1994 attracted unusually large numbers of people, including many not normally seen at such protests. Though often ignoring the underlying issues of concern, the national media began passing comment on this new political phenomenon. Even parliamentarians slumbering through the passage of the Bill in the House began taking notice. Something unusual was happening in the state of Britain: the goats weren't accepting the load. Meanwhile, now blind to their own indis-cretions, politicians were revelling like Caligula in their own warped sense of decadent social injustice and widespread political corruption. The only rule now was not to get caught and, except for a few rare incidences, the national media were failing miserably

The cover of *SQUALL* 6, published during a period of particularly active resistance to the passage of the Criminal Justice Bill

in providing the investigative background information essential for such exposure.

It was both educational and alarming to meet MPs during the passage of the Criminal Justice Bill. Those principled enough to stray from the regurgitation proffered by the usual party line admitted there were reasons behind the legislation which had little to do with the farcical rhetoric used to present it to the public. None of them, however – much as they might realise what was happening behind the scenes – would risk their political necks by standing up for travellers, squatters, ravers and the rights of public protest. Labour MP John Battle – then shadow Housing Minister – had a history of representing travellers and homeless people. We were actually thankful for at least his honesty when he told us that he was unable to risk his neck and create too much of a fuss. The climate for principled speakers in the Labour Party, we were told by several of its MPs, was becoming more rarefied by the minute. We were advised and duly wrote to the shadow Home Secretary, asking for a meeting to discuss his response to the Bill.

'I'm afraid I don't have time to meet you at the moment,' wrote back Tony Blair. 'But I can assure you I will oppose anything that is wrong.' Rest assured? We thought not. The Labour Party refused to oppose the Bill, allowing the new law through with a casual ease, pin-pricked only by the forty-three principled MPs prepared to risk the rungs of their career ladder and vote against it. No-one was impressed by Tony Blair's honesty even then.

It was more than ironic when several of the MPs whom we met during the passage of the CJB arrived to our appointment carrying books on media and politics. We did not remark upon it and neither did they, but it left a notable impression. Ever since the power-dressed Margaret Thatcher refined her provincial accent to beat the duffle-coated Michael Foot in the 1983 general election, the sacrifice of substance for salesmanship has become ever more prevalent as political currency. We've all seen them, driving up and down the M1, salesmen with their selling suits on coat hangers in the back, ready to be donned at the crucial moment in the cause of unconscious consumer persuasion. False and phoney by any definition of the words. And so to politics with its increasingly formulaic oratorical techniques, profuse verbal obfuscation and an increased political power base afforded to spin doctors and

image makers. Presentation oozed from every photo-opportunity
to plaster the face of politics with cheap foundation.

And the medicine for this malaise . . .

The majority of us enjoy good presentation; it is an art form in
its own right. But when used as a duping technique its art is
harnessed to the cause of falsity, its techniques used to sugar-coat a
poison. Hearing persuasive words, gestures and pictures only to
find them lacking in reality serves only to rob us all of language.
Our aural and visual sensitivity readjusts to cope with the onslaught
of hidden agendas and, whether we realise it or not, we begin to
switch off. To steal back the significance of language simply add at
least as much substance to the recipe as garnish.

In the subsequent pursuit of this aspiration, the designers and
production staff at *SQUALL* began adapting and absorbing the best
creative techniques around whilst inventing a few of their own.
Were the magazine to lie on the shelves next to any other, the
casual browser should not immediately be able to tell that one was
produced by a fully paid commercial staff and one by a bunch of
committed volunteers. Despite very little formal training, *SQUALL*'s
designers learned on the job and, with the introduction of high-
quality photography to the magazine in issue 8, began producing a
magazine second to none. The resultant presentation served the
message well, although problems have arisen when some of the
magazine's diverse readership consequently assume *SQUALL* must
be running with a full staff on wages. To this day few people realise
the core staff at *SQUALL* numbers about six, all of whom are
voluntary and all of whom work for a publication which survives on
donations, subscriptions and magazine sales, having eschewed the
usual deluge of advertising.

Attending the standing committee stage of the CJA was also a
swift education in the processes of parliament. Almost every new
law goes through such a stage, the aim of which is to consider
and vote on every clause and potential amendment. The process involves thirty MPs supposedly chosen according to their
'interest' in the subject and apportioned according to party political divisions in the House of Commons. The sessions are held in a
committee room within the Palace of Westminster, which, with its
swinging gates and two small wooden grandstands, bears resem-
blance to a Wild-West courthouse. In contrast, the public gallery

consisted of two tight rows of plastic chairs only a matter of feet away from the government MPs on one side and the opposition (although they provided little of such) on the other. Being so close to the (in)action provided a close-up view of what we are taught to respect as democracy. It was possible to see MPs pondering over the crossword in the *Daily Telegraph*, doing their constituency work, reading the sports results and falling asleep during the passage of the debate. Triple-chinned Tory MPs would suddenly blurt 'hear, hear' whenever their minister spoke, even though it was patently obvious they had not been listening. I wanted to stand up, stop the proceedings, and ask these MPs what it was that they had just given their vocal consent to. I also wanted to speak up when MPs confidently littered the debate with factual inaccuracies and I twitched with the desire to berate the acquiescent 'opposition' benches; this was my life and the lives of many others they were legislating over.

But the public were only allowed to observe; they were not allowed to take part. And so in the cause of observation, I sat on my tongue, knowing that if it dared articulate the truth of what was occurring before me I would be evicted forthwith. Better to observe now and reveal later.

A live debate on Granada Television in 1993 did provide *SQUALL* with a rare opportunity to call an MP to account. Granada had originally promised us a face-to-face with Home Office minister David McLean – Michael Howard's field marshal on the government benches during the committee stage of the CJB. Having reined in my tongue whilst observing him at work during committee, I relished the prospect of having it out in front of a live studio audience. However, much to my disappointment, he refused to appear at the last minute. Instead the TV station hired in local Tory MP Geoffrey Dickens, a red mass of a man, who, I was told, had appeared on the programme several times previously to talk about whatever they wanted him to talk about for an appearance fee. Dial-a-comment!

A first-class train ticket awaited me at King's Cross station – costing more money (£150) than I usually lived off for three weeks. I was put up in a Manchester hotel at a further cost of £100. In front of a live studio audience I listed the organisations who had strongly expressed their reservations about the government's extreme measures against squatters. They included the Institute of Housing, the Metropolitan Police and the Law Society. I then asked Dickens to point out who, beside the right-wing compliant press, was actually in favour of such draconian measures. On live TV he pulled an envelope out of his back pocket and proclaimed it to be a 'long list of organisations which supported the measures'.

However, I knew, because I also had such an envelope in my back pocket, that the document he was waving was in fact the appearance fee cheque we'd been given for coming on the programme. Bang to rights – or so I thought as I informed the Granada audience that this was the case. Immediately, however, the boom arms swung away from me and the presenter of the programme – ex-head of leading indie company Factory Records, now media careerist Tony Wilson – asked the studio audience if they had any further questions. I could hardly believe the speed with which they'd made a decision not to put the MP on the spot. Dickens, meanwhile, looked over at me out of camera, and smiled.

In the hospitality room afterwards I sat sipping a glass of rough red wine and watched as one of the blonde cropped female presenters – who had hosted a debate about Barbie dolls in the second half of the same programme – flashed her eyelids and doted on the reptilian MP. Media and politics inseparable, in league, insufferable and insulated.

Sharp words: accuracy and (Mc)Libel

One of the prescriptions offered by *SQUALL* as a contribution to journalism is its insistence on accuracy. This was considered an absolutely essential prerequisite for two very important reasons. Firstly, given the deluge of information and messages now available in the media and on the World Wide Web, a reputation for accurate source material will become ever more important if organs like *SQUALL* aren't simply to drown in the media soup.

It is sometimes said that journalism is the first draft of history. And yet from the word off, it became clear to *SQUALL* that the national media's commitment to factual accuracy is temperamental. Only by developing a reputation for researching published material thoroughly can any sense of faith be worthily reinvested in a media source. Information is your weapon, but what use is a blunt sword? However, a reputation for sharp observation and accuracy is not something achievable overnight. It is necessary, quite rightly, to do it again and again before such a reputation is earned and it has to be said that such an aspiration produces a huge workload of research and double checks.

Secondly, the last thing anyone in *SQUALL* wanted to get tied up in was a lengthy legal battle over a careless libel. British libel laws are a lengthy and costly business even before they get to trial, rendering them a tool largely at the disposal of the wealthy. As a consequence they are commonly adopted as a political strategy designed to intimidate truth-tellers into silence. Rather than compromise ourselves however, *SQUALL* decided to print without fear but to always go armed with a sharpened lance of factual accuracy. To accompany the lance, a shield . . . If you print what you know, when in fact you firmly believe there to be more, individuals and organisations are less likely to sue you if it will inevitably result in the exposure of more than what has already been printed. Running the gamut of this fine line takes considerable care.

Not only does *SQUALL* aspire to be more accurate than most of the national media, but we have so far managed to do so without the much needed services of a trained libel proof-reader. We simply studied hard and learned on the job. To this day, and much to many media professionals' amazement, no attempt has been made to counter-attack *SQUALL* with a libel suit. We are, however, in no doubt that certain quarters would rather the magazine wasn't around to stir the sediment.

At least some of the credit for this clean libel sheet must be extended to a small group of people who set a powerful precedent with their stance on behalf of free speech. Driven by Helen Steel's and Dave Morris's tenacious refusal to apologise to the McDonald's corporation, and more than ably aided by a support group coordinated by Dan Mills, the McLibel team provided *SQUALL* with both extensive investigative material and a crash course in British libel laws.

When *SQUALL* visited Helen and Dave at each of their homes, it was difficult not to view them as modern-day heroes – a tag they themselves would strongly disapprove of. Files bulged from the shelves of their small living spaces, sometimes spewing across their bedrooms to invade the sanctuary of their sleep. As a single parent, Dave was forced to digest mountains of relentless documentation whilst also looking after his eight-year-old son, Charlie. Meanwhile, whilst co-defending her way through the longest court case in English legal history, Helen worked nights in a West End bar to earn her living. Dan Mills, on the other hand, had left his job with a top UK legal firm in order to support Dave and Helen's stand. Throughout the four years he coordinated the McLibel Support Campaign, he slept on the floor of the tiny McLibel office, his dreams punctuated with bulging faxes and late-night international telephone calls.

Their legal struggle began with the service of a libel writ by McDonald's in 1990 and went on to engulf Helen and Dave's lives until a decision was finally delivered in mid-1997. As they emerged from the High Court following a mixed verdict, the media pack surrounded them like scrabbling paparazzi. Despite this flurry of attention, however, the serious issues raised in the case were largely ignored by media analysts. True, the McLibel team had generated copious amounts of attention; McDonald's had twice offered to give money to charity if Dave and Helen would agree to apologise and put an end to the corporation's increasingly troublesome PR disaster. However, the media often treated the story simply as an oddity in the British justice system, playing heavily on the David versus Goliath connotations whilst largely steering clear of the gritty issues raised in court.

Yet from the very start the national media had every reason to view Helen and Dave as champions of their cause. Previous to the McLibel trial, Channel Four and the *Guardian* were among a long list of organisations and individuals forced to apologise to McDonald's under threat of libel. With the massive financial outlay involved in defending libel cases, no-one could afford to fight the formidable McDonald's legal department, even if published allegations were true. Up until Helen and Dave's stance, this policy of persistent legal intimidation had created a climate of paralytic fear. Even those parts of the national media prepared to publish mildly dissenting material steered well clear of criticising the way in which McDonald's conducted its business, despite the international significance of the information.

Helen and Dave, on the other hand, not only remained standing where all others had backed down, they also seized the opportunity to force court disclosure of huge amounts of primary source material about the workings of the world's largest fast-food corporation. In essence, Helen and Dave had turned a libel suit directed against them into a unique opportunity to force a long-required degree of corporate accountability. They had also halted the domino effect of retractions and public apologies which had stifled public debate for so long.

The significance of this tenacious extraction was made even more apparent by McDonald's powerful connections in politics. When the corporation withdrew from purchasing British beef during the BSE crisis, they took £350 million out of the British economy. By the end of this century McDonald's will also be one of the biggest employers in the UK, after doubling its expansion plans in 1996. McJobs for all! By way of courting this economic clout, Margaret Thatcher opened McDonald's new UK headquarters building in 1982, whilst both Michael Portillo and Tony Blair have since posed before the press serving McDonald's burgers to children. *SQUALL* published photographs of each of these episodes. Meanwhile, ministers at the Department of Health, in line with the World Health Organisation, continue to urgently recommend a less fat, less salt, higher fibre diet; in direct contradiction to the political endorsements freely given to McDonald's high fat, high salt, low fibre food.

With transnational corporations like McDonald's assuming a global influence greater than that of many nation-states, such disparities are of large-scale significance. As James Cantalupo, president of McDonald's International, said recently: 'I don't think there is a country out there we haven't gotten enquiries from. I have a *parade of ambassadors and trade representatives* in here regularly to tell us about their country and *why McDonald's would be good for them.*' Whilst *The Economist* magazine now uses international variations in the price of a Big Mac as an economic indicator, the McDonald's Corporation 1995 Annual Report actually has a chapter entitled 'Strategies for World Dominance'. The willingness thus shown by politicians actively to promote McDonald's products stands as a neon signal to one and all that economic clout prevails over health as their currency of political respect. The rhetoric of social well-being thus lies fallow in their field.

As *SQUALL* sat with Helen and Dave watching the television coverage on the day of the McLibel verdict, I could only sigh with exasperation when the election of William Hague as Conservative Party leader, and Tony Blair's decision to go ahead with the Millennium Dome folly, pushed the McLibel verdict story into third place on the BBC's main news. Contrary to so many other national issues, media analysis of the wide-scale implications of the mixed verdict did not appear and the issue was almost completely forgotten about within a couple of days. And yet McDonald's were deemed by the judge to offer poor-quality employment; they had also been deemed 'culpably responsible' for cruelty to animals, for the deceptive promotion of the quality of their food and for 'exploiting' children with their advertising. These big issues were kept at bay in the subsequently sparse media coverage.

Helen and Dave, on the other hand, seemed less bothered and were almost immediately planning their appeals and helping to facilitate the continual dissemination of information released by the trial. A *SQUALL* journalist once asked Dave Morris whether, given the significance of the information uncovered by his and Helen's stance, he was ever disillusioned by the small number of people willing to help. He replied: 'If you call a public meeting about an important issue and only ten people show up, don't worry about the hundreds who didn't or you'll completely waste the presence of the ten.'

The copious quantity of investigative articles written about the McLibel trial in *SQUALL* was partly an attempt to redress the national media's selective deployment of its blind eye. We are lingering much on the McLibel trial with good reason ... Many of the issues raised by the trial were ones which concern us all both culturally and politically (as if these two criteria could be separated) and illustrate much about the nature of media. Given that McDonald's had successfully applied to remove a jury from the trial, it was – we felt – partly our responsibility (*respond to your ability!*) to present the issues to a wider jury. (Respect is also due to the team who put together the incredible McSpotlight website: http://www.mcspotlight.org.) Indeed, it was always *SQUALL*'s intention never to get stuck as a ghetto magazine. From the outset, the project's intentions in this direction were articulated as 'a presentation to the unexclusive bridge', the bridge between diverse backgrounds and social sensibilities. Good-quality writing, photography and production, mixed with factual accuracy, helps attract people of all backgrounds.

Out from the ghettos: a widening readership

Reaching to the bridge is a guiding aspiration rather than a claim of arrival, although *SQUALL*'s successes in this area were most graphically illustrated to the team after 400 replies were returned from a postal survey of *SQUALL*'s subscriber base in 1997. The analysis of responses surprised us. Not only did the majority of subscribers own their own homes (none of the *SQUALL* team do!) but their backgrounds were even more multifarious than the team had supposed. Doctors, teachers, legal professionals, social workers, nurses, librarians, academics and politicians were amongst an eclectic list of readers. (Being annual subscribers of course, the survey sample was largely confined to readers with stable addresses, about one seventh of the magazine's readership.) The survey also revealed that an average of 5.5 people read each single copy of *SQUALL*, with the majority of respondents tending to pass the publication around; an inspiring communal network. Multiplied by the 7000 copies printed of each issue, the survey thus suggested an extrapolated overall readership of around 35,000. *SQUALL* was going places, even without the usual marketing campaigns associated with media source development. What's more, the survey also revealed that readers tended to keep their copies of *SQUALL* rather than, say, lining their cat's litter tray, wiping their bums in lieu of toilet paper, or feeding the council recycling bins, and so on. With bookshops, newsagents and grapevine networks all steadily increasing their orders, the last three issues of the magazine have sold out bar the few we keep for specific requests.

Amongst this swelling readership is a fair quotient of national media journalists interested in the 'unusual angles on a plate' offered in the magazine. When some of these began picking up on *SQUALL*'s stories, it introduced a dilemma. For whilst dissemination of accurate information is a yoke behind which *SQUALL* willingly volunteers its shoulder, national journos were ringing up the office for background material on stories and then using our work to make themselves money. Precious few ever remunerated the project for either the story or the often extensive help with research, and, although respect is due to the few who do support the source, the majority have simply ridden on the project's back acting as if they were doing us a favour. Many never even paid for copies of the magazine sent to them, whilst some directly plagiarised *SQUALL* word for word without either accreditation or remuneration. After a couple of years of battling with this rankling situation, the sheer quantity of insistent parasites reached a point where the *SQUALL* team now has to firmly insist on a better quality of respectful interaction. On the inside front cover of every issue of the magazine are the words: 'Open copyright for non-profit-making use only.' We mean it.

There was little point in fighting for respect on a societal level if we then put up with disrespect in our own backyard, and the scurrility associated with professional journalism is largely a well-deserved reputation. Nevertheless, as long as respect is afforded, *SQUALL* does interact with national media in a profuse way. Indeed, some of the team earn a partial living from freelancing in the nationals. Spokespeople from *SQUALL* have also appeared on almost every terrestrial TV and national radio station in the UK, in nearly every national newspaper, as well as on many cable and local media outlets, talking about subjects ranging from homelessness to youth crime, dance culture to current legislation.

The glare of the lights and the intimidating environment of a live studio were never easy to overcome in the delivery of a calm yet cutting message. However, members of the team threw themselves into the task and once again learned on the job. One of the most laughable requests amongst many came from a staff feature writer at the *Daily Telegraph*. She was keen to write an article on squatting and wanted to know whether we knew any 'middle-class squatters' she could interview. Asked what she meant by the phrase, she replied: 'People who earn a high wage and squat for fun.' She was told that *SQUALL* had never heard of a high wage earner who squatted for fun but that we might be able to put her in contact with some real squatters. She replied: 'Well, er, unfortunately, you know how it is, this isn't what the *Telegraph* readers want to read about. Do you know any that earn a wage, are articulate and preferably good-looking?' We laughed and told her we'd do what we could, and then promptly did nothing in the hope that her phoney agenda would choke on its own lack of reality.

Although the *Telegraph* never ran its feature, the *Daily Mail* picked up on the farce with a two-page spread published a couple of months later. Written by 'undercover investigative journalist Helen Carrol', the article was headlined: 'CAMCORDERS, CANNABIS AND EARL GREY TEA. WELCOME TO THE WORLD OF MIDDLE-CLASS SQUATTERS – THE PHENOMENON OF THE WELL-EDUCATED YOUNG-STERS WHO PREFER TO LIVE IN FILTHY SQUATS.' It seemed unlikely to us that the *Daily Mail* bug the *Daily Telegraph*'s Canary Wharf telephone lines, and more likely that their similar pre-agendas arise from a mutual penchant for news manipulation.

Now, all this shit – when it's so in yer face – can sometimes get you down . . . On the back cover of *SQUALL* 13, we printed a quote from gay South African satirist Peter-Dirk Uys, encapsulating what the team had always thought: 'Politics on its own is deadly dull. Entertainment on its own is deadly irrelevant.' Indeed, much of the politics *SQUALL* was required to understand in the development of a socially relevant magazine was and still is incredibly boring. So boring in fact that it seems almost designed to keep the subject an exclusive preserve for those who derive perverse pleasure or foster perverse financial ambition from learning its terminally turgid intricacies. And yet much of the serious behind-the-scenes manipu-lation in politics is achieved through convoluted means, most of which are a nightmare to articulate to a reader in an attractively accessible way. And yet it simply has to be done . . . politics matters that badly.

Most of us, of course, would rather live life than argue about it, but whilst ignorance might be blissful in the short term, it's downright dangerous in the long term. For, unfortunately, whilst a few million people are still recovering from their 'cultural' week-ends on a Monday morning, corporate and political strategy departments are already having their first meeting of the week. Paying no attention to the hidden intention is perilous . . . but then again so is excessive yawning. 'Act up', 'Lively up yourself', 'Stoke it up' and 'All fired up' have all been phrases used on the front cover of *SQUALL*. And whilst the magazine is undoubtedly political, there is no desire from any of the *SQUALL* team to cease our cultural celebrations.

SQUALL 15's cover, illustrated with an image from the April 1997 Rally for Social Justice in Trafalgar Square

One of the many facets which singled out the CJA as a particularly draconian piece of legislation was the legal definition it placed on the terms 'rave' and 'rave music', the now legendary 'series of repetitive beats'. The Criminal Justice and Public Order Act 1994 had already been preceded by the Entertainments (Increased Penalties) Act 1990, and then succeeded by the Noise Act 1996 and the Public Entertainment (Drug Misuse) Act 1997. This avalanche of legislation targeted against festival and dance culture revealed just how out of touch politicians actually were with modern youth culture, and just how far they were prepared to go in legislating against something they had no understanding of. And yet when asked to make speeches at raves during the passage of the Criminal Justice Bill, *SQUALL* was often heckled: 'Fuck politics, put the music back on.' With necessity breeding ingenuity, *SQUALL* speakers began asking for the music to be left on at a low level and for reverb and phaser effects to be put on the voice. As a result the speeches became that bit more enjoyable both to deliver and receive. Just as politicians seemed hell-bent on squeezing the joy out of people's lives, so *SQUALL* was increasingly interested in the ways and means of reincorporating it as a necessary partner to social awareness.

Despite the initial prevalence of a dismissive dancefloor attitude to imminent dangers, a new consciousness began emerging from the rave and festival scene. Those who realised that culturally destructive forces were plotting strategically behind the scenes began to speak and act up in defence of diversity and cultural space; and there is none so powerful as the combination of consciousness and culture. The most striking example of this new spirit has emanated from the Luton-based rave organisation the Exodus Collective. Ever since *SQUALL* paid a visit to Exodus's housing projects following a brief meeting with some of its members at a Welsh festival in 1993, the two teams have liaised extensively. For just some of the reasons why this interaction has induced such considerable inspiration, Tim Malyon's chapter on Exodus elsewhere in this book is a well-recommended read. Such dances with a new dimension offer entertainment that isn't deadly irrelevant and socially relevant politics that isn't deadly boring.

The inspirational Reclaim the Streets and a host of spirited road protest campaigns like those also written about in the book provide further examples. Both these persistent and well-populated enviro-political stances mix music, theatre, sculpture, craft and ingenuity with serious and urgent political consciousness. As a result, much of the dour laboriousness associated with politics dissolves in a potent concoction of imagination, celebration and dissent. You need a laugh to live, you need a life to laugh; with celebration as an essential prerequisite for personal health, especially when involvement in urgent political campaigns can often leave a person run-down, cynical, angry and unhopeful. Health, after all, is the confluence point for the huge diversity of urgent single issues represented in the magazine's pages. Common ground.

Throughout its journey *SQUALL* has sought to spotlight those who overcome the debilitations, desperations and restrictions of a disrespectful world in order to deliver fresh fire, spirit and solution; those who weave blessings from curses and help twist the mangled environments around us into something emanating more health. It is not possible to say, and even seems rather unlikely, that in fifty years' time a copy of *SQUALL* magazine issue 300 will lie on the newsagents' shelves with 'est. 1992' under its title. However, there is little doubt that the actively deployed ideas presented in its pages will have already offered a contribution to the achievement of what was previously thought impossible: a better quality of media, a better quality of mutual respect . . .

3

Viva camcordistas! Video activism and the protest movement

THOMAS HARDING

All at once twenty people dashed to the back of the building, up the fire stairs, through a top-floor emergency exit and down the carpeted corridor towards the English offices of McMallinan Blowdell – the company responsible for the clearcutting of Vancouver Island in Canada – screaming 'No more logging!' and 'Earth first! Profits last!' I ran with them trying to capture everything on the camcorder I'd borrowed from my sister. The security guards blocked their entry at the doors to the offices, the police arrived and started dragging the protesters downstairs. Meanwhile outside, other activists were dropping a banner from a balcony reading 'Canadian chainsaw massacre'. I called the local TV station on a mobile phone and told them about the story. 'How many arrests were there?' they asked. 'Oh, already ten, but I guess by the end of the morning more than forty.' I knew that if the numbers were too low they wouldn't be interested in the story.

I was the only person with a video camera. The protesters hadn't wanted to tell TV news in case they would have blown the story and passed the information on to the police. Even if they had known, they probably wouldn't have sent a crew to cover it. 'Too risky,' they would have chirped to each other at the early-morning editorial meeting, 'let's do the story about the local conservative politician book launch instead, pictures are guaranteed there!'

The news sent a motorbike courier around to pick up the tape and later that night it made the local news as a short item in the 'roundup' section. Even more exciting, I'd managed to sell the footage also to national TV in Canada. Straight from the streets of London into the homes of those who actually could make a difference in Canada, and all because of a cheap domestic 'let's get it out to video the baby' video camera! If I hadn't been there with my camcorder it would never have made it on to TV. This was the first time I'd videoed a direct action with a camcorder and tried to sell the footage to TV. I had no idea what I was doing but it seemed to be working.

The beginnings of the DiY movement

In the summer of 1991 the 'Direct Action Movement', or 'DiY movement' as it was later called, was just getting going. Of course direct action can be traced back through the Miners' Strike of the 1980s, the peace movement of the 1970s, the Suffragettes of the 1920s, the Diggers of the seventeenth century, and back and back all the way through time. But the most recent wave of direct action to sweep through the UK can be traced to two teenagers – Jason Torrance and Jake Burbridge – who dropped out of their Hastings secondary school in 1990 and went about setting up Britain's first Earth First! group. Brought up on a diet of environmental crisis from televisions and newspapers, inspired by tales of the 'no compromise' attitude of the Earth First! groups in the USA, and mentored by people steeped in the non-violent direct action experience of the anti-nukes campaigns like Angie Zelter, they quickly built up a network of people committed to using direct action to bring about change.

Both Jason and Jake had applied to be volunteers with some of the mainstream environmental groups like Greenpeace and Friends of the Earth, but both groups said they were overwhelmed with similar requests and had no room. This experience was replicated again and again over the next few years and lay the seedbed for the growth of the new radical party 'n' protest movement. Young people shocked and inspired to act by the message of planetary crisis in the 1980s found there was either no opportunity to participate with the major groups or that these groups were too bureaucratic and too conservative to take part in anything 'too radical' or 'extreme'. There was therefore a great need for a group committed to action, open to all comers, that was anti-bureaucratic, anti-hierarchical and fun to be involved with. At first Earth First!, and then later the DiY movement, was a historical inevitability given the massive swing in the popular value system and the inability of the larger groups to adapt quickly enough.

The first major environmental direct action took place at Tilbury Docks in 1991. Making use of bicycle D-locks for the first time, Jason, Jake and other Earth First! activists locked themselves by the neck to the docking area, thus preventing ships carrying rainforest timber from unloading their cargo. After the success of this action a number of peace- and rainforest-orientated direct actions were organised (perhaps most notably the SOS Sarawak action where two English and two Australian activists chained themselves to logging equipment in Malaysia and were thrown in jail for three months). But it wasn't until the anti-road protest at Twyford Down outside of Winchester – which combined the emotions that are wrapped up in a local beauty spot being destroyed with the excitement and colour of people putting their bodies in front of large yellow land-eating bulldozers – that the DiY movement really caught the imagination of a whole generation of activists.

The year-long anti-M3 motorway protest at Twyford Down (1991–92) saw the first use of an action camp at a road construction site. It saw the convergence of the rural 'New Age traveller' subculture (which transformed itself into the 'Dongas Tribe' at Twyford Down) with the direct action environmentalism from the cities. It saw the birth of a new culture of protest where having fun, dancing to drums and telling stories around a fire were as important as press statements and strategy meetings. Perhaps most importantly of all, Twyford Down became a melting pot of people committed to doing something about the problems in the world with those experimenting with different forms of community living.

Twyford Down was treated as a strange one-off by both mainstream environmental groups and the mass media. Friends of the Earth wrote a letter to all their supporters asking them not to become involved with the Earth First! activists. Newspapers like the *Times, Telegraph* and even the *Guardian* wrote articles focusing on the 'likely' extreme tactics that the protesters would use such as spiking trees and use of explosives. TV coverage of the protests at Twyford Down tended to be at best non-existent; at worst a wholesale attack on the values and actions of a generation of people engaged in legitimate civil disobedience. They were denigrated as 'New Agers', 'crusties', 'hairies', 'dole-scroungers', 'layabouts' and that old catch-all 'hippies'. Any coverage of actions or activists that did take place was always 'balanced' by some convincingly sane, middle-class, eminently likeable person who dismissed the whole campaign with ease and who stereotyped the activists as some 'extreme fringe'.

It would take another five years for the public to be able to identify individual personalities within the party 'n' protest movement whom they could talk about in the pub and expect their neighbour to know who they were talking about. The terms 'eco-warriors', 'Dongas', 'pixie', 'fluffy', 'tree-sitter', 'digger diver' were only just beginning to be heard at the action camps, let alone included in articles in the mainstream press.

An example of the early bias against the protesters can be seen in the 'NIMBY'/'outside extremist' paradox. When local residents took up the struggle against a road scheme like that at Twyford Down, TV journalists would describe them as 'NIMBY', or, in other words, Not In My Back Yard. For this they mean us to think, 'selfish, greedy, unpatriotic spoil-sports'. However, if people from the outside come in to try to stop an injustice they are described as 'outsider trouble-makers' or 'professional agitators'. With such pre-set attitudes campaigners couldn't win either way. Such attitudes took many years to change, and the use of camcorders as a campaign tool played a large part in this value shift within the media.

Birth of video activism

This is the arena that we stepped into. When I say 'we' I mean a small group of anti-road activists, former TV documentary makers and film school graduates who at this stage did not know each other, but who all started using video camcorders to support the new campaign movement. This new type of campaign work became known as 'video activism'. The phrase captured the dual, and sometimes contradictory, nature of the role. We learned that at all times the video activist must think like an activist – campaign goals, maximising impact, limited resources, and so on – while at the same time thinking like a video-maker – taking good pictures, maximising distribution, intruding into private space.

Of course the use of video to bring about change is as old as celluloid itself. Right at the start of cinema film-makers like Vertog were using moving images to affect attitudes and to bring about changes in action. The use of film, and later video, as a tactical tool took off during the civil rights and anti-Vietnam protests of the sixties and seventies. At this time small, lightweight cameras became available, first in the 16 mm format, then in the more flexible Portapak system. In Britain during the 1980s community television blossomed under the Channel Four-inspired Film and Video Workshops. The major shift came in the late 1980s with the introduction of the small format 8 mm and VHS camcorders. These were very easy to use, high quality, relatively low in cost and widely available. By 1997 one in seven households owned a video camcorder in the UK. This is why we saw the explosion in the use of video as an activist tool in the 1990s. Three factors converged at the same time: an emergence of a vibrant form of activism; the availability of the new camcorders; and the failure of the mainstream TV to adequately cover the boom in grassroots politics.

The first major DiY video activist site was the No M11 Link Road campaign which started in September 1993. This centred on the building of an unnecessary three-mile link road in Wanstead, East London, which would end up knocking down 350 houses and costing £240 million. The direct action campaign lasted over a year and during the course of it over five hundred people were arrested because they put their bodies in front of the oncoming bulldozers. It was the next 'big' anti-roads action site after the anti-M3 protest at Twyford Down, and the first to take place in a major city.

The campaign proved to be a magnet to socially aware video-makers. Many of us had no idea what we were trying to achieve by being at the protest site, but we came anyway. During the campaign we learned to coordinate our work, and more importantly we developed ways in which we could concretely support the day-to-day efforts of the activists. For example, a video activist might collect footage of an arrest being made, submit the footage to court during the trial and prove that the activist had been falsely arrested. We managed to get the campaign covered again and again on local TV, thereby attracting more people to the site, ranging from more activists to local supermarket managers who gave out food and clothing, as well as lawyers and other journalists. We also learned that video could have a direct impact on the protest itself. For example, having camcorders around actually reduced the violence that was being handed out by the security guards hired by the road-builders to safeguard their project. Someone would shout 'camera!' if they were being assaulted and as soon as a video activist arrived on the scene the assault would usually stop.

Paul O'Connor was one of the key video activists involved in the M11 campaign. Originally a sports photographer in Ireland, Paul moved to England in 1992 and moved around the UK as a roving reporter. In 1993 he travelled to London and soon moved into and squatted one of the houses that were due for demolition to make way for the new road. He joined other activists in the early days of the direct action campaign, blocking bulldozers, getting in the way of the surveyors, and sitting in trees to avoid their destruction. Paul soon realised that there was a great need for video support, especially as the private security firms hired by the road construction companies had started to become violent towards the activists. He traded in his photographic equipment and bought a cheap second-hand Sony all-weather yellow camcorder. Paul became the first, and then later, one of many, video activists at the campaign, providing video support, chronicling its progress and selling footage to local TV.

Undercurrents is set up

Towards the end of the M11 campaign, a few of us decided to join forces. We set up a non-profit organisation, based in London, at first known as Small World Media and later known as Undercurrents. We agreed that our aim was to 'provide media support to grassroots groups working on environmental and social justice issues'. In practice this meant that we sometimes didn't make video programmes for campaign groups if this wasn't useful for their efforts. We might instead help them win mainstream media coverage or show them how they could use video evidence in court. Our golden rule was that we would only work with groups who could identify real needs and where we had the ability to help them meet those needs. This was a radical departure from the traditional TV company whose primary goal was to win broadcast commissions no matter what and to make as much money in the process as they could.

At first we worked by responding to a call for video support from a group, videoing their action and then trying to sell it to TV or hand it over to the campaigners for use in court. We had many successes doing this kind of work. But after a while it grew frustrating. We couldn't get any stories on to TV besides arrest stories, and we didn't feel we were building any long-term strategies with campaign groups.

Box 1: Video activist approach[1]

1. Work with a specific identifiable group.
2. Find out their needs.
3. Devise a media strategy.
4. Make it happen.
5. Evaluate and adapt project.

For these reasons we decided to launch the video magazine called *Undercurrents – the alternative news service*: ninety minutes of in-yer-face footage, shot on camcorder by campaigners themselves, distributed on video cassette, distributed by mail-order and sub-scription. We were fed up with watching documentaries and news items where the journalist gave one side of the story and then the other, leaving the audience totally confused, even though he or she would actually know that one of the sides was true and the other not. So the best bit about having our own distribution mechanism was that we got to control the editorial line. We didn't have to worry about 'balance', 'impartiality', 'objectivity' or any other bogus journalistic concept used to keep the mass audience ill informed and inactive.

At first we had trouble trying to track down the footage we needed to make up a ninety-minute tape. We couldn't rely entirely on our own footage as we wanted to include diverse campaigns from different parts of the country. Mainstream TV was always being criticised for being too London-focused. We didn't want to make the same mistake, especially as we were billing ourselves as the 'alternative' news. We knew there were people out there doing this kind of thing, but where were they? We found someone in Glasgow who had been videoing anti-Trident actions at the Faslane Peace Camp. Another person had captured the action outside the Campsfield Asylum Centre outside of Oxford where refugees were kept for over two years without trial or sentence. Someone else had some great images of an occupation of a super-quarry conference in Edinburgh. This turned out to be people's favourite, probably because of the realism conveyed by the wobbly cam. Finally, and at the last minute, we compiled four short features about the outrageous and then little known Criminal Justice Bill which would reduce people's ability to protest, remove the right to silence and severely limit people's ability to squat, attend and organise raves, and travel freely around the country.

One of the reasons we were able to even contemplate producing a watchable video magazine was that we had acquired our own edit suite. This was one of the latest computer-controlled suites, which enabled us to not only speed up the process, but also to add text captions and digital effects like slides and tumbles; and, most important of all, to maintain a high quality as the edit suite included a professional-standard machine which was able to play camcorder tapes to their maximum capacity. Without this edit suite we would have never been able to afford the hour upon hour of edit time spent viewing and selecting from the hundreds of hours of material we now had at our disposal.

The 'big' feature on the video was a 35-minute epic entitled 'You've got to be choking' (see Box 2) charting the course of the No M11 Link campaign. Including over fifteen different video activists' footage, edited over four months, this video feature ended up being the definitive anti-road movie made at this time. In one classic scene bailiffs are seen drilling into a concrete barricaded bunker where two protesters and the video activist Zoë Broughton are waiting. The images are violent and scary. Scary because the drilling is coming towards you the viewer. For the first time, we were witnessing the campaign from the activists' perspective, and never more effectively than this. This video went on to win the prestigious Okomedia Festival in Freiburg, the first ever film to win that hadn't already been shown on TV.

Box 2: Script for 'You've got to be choking' video[2]

Sequence 1: Sound bites from key campaigners about why they were involved over images of Wanstead and general shots of sitting on bulldozers.

Sequence 2: Images of early days of direct action and discussion by key campaigners about why they use it.

Sequence 3: Activists squat houses in the path of the road to delay building, bailiffs arrive to evict them, discussion about the responsiveness of the police.

Sequence 4: The threatened felling of the chestnut tree on the green, the community responds by setting up camp around the tree, police evict tree dwellers and knock down the tree.

Sequence 5: Campaign moves to three houses due for demolition. Press conference where evicted tenant tells media she is now squatting her own house. Setting up of defences in houses, close-ups of people 'locking-on', sealing themselves in concrete bunker, waiting during the night. Interviews with people about how they feel.

Sequence 6: Eviction from houses, police arrive, bailiffs smash windows, people dragged out. Intercut of general shots with women in concrete bunker, on phone telling people how they feel. Sequence ends with bailiffs breaking into bunker, threatening protesters with violence to get them out and dragging camera-woman away.

Sequence 7: Song sung by women about being strong, final interviews with key campaigners about how campaign will go on, caption saying campaign is continuing, with final shot of people invading construction site as an example.

In April 1994 we sent the tape off to the duplicator, made 250 copies, dropped 20,000 leaflets in friendly magazines and hoped for the best. Nothing happened! What were we going to do? Then orders began to trickle in. We picked up a few favourable reviews: 'The Pathé news of the 90s,' said *Time Out*; 'Compelling viewing,' said the *Independent*; 'The news you don't see on the news,' said the *Guardian*. We made another 250 copies and suddenly we had a viable alternative video news service on our hands. We had become a media phenomenon. National programmes like the BBC's *Late Show* and ITV's *Little Picture Show* as well as international slots like Canadian TV and MTV Europe were making features about us. We estimated that over 50,000 people watched this issue. Copies were being sent across Europe, North America and Australia.

The videos acted as an inspiration to new people to get active and a promoter of new campaigns and campaign methods to those who had not heard of them before. Hundreds of people later told us that they watched the videos and became involved in campaign work for the first time because it demystified what was involved in actions.

For those already involved in campaigns, moreover, the videos acted as a reaffirmation. As Merrick wrote in his autobiographical account of his time sitting up a tree at the anti-road protest at Newbury:

> There are many security guards now, a lot of them on their first day being barked at by hysterical red hats. They're only there to do what they're told. . . . They ask me to leave so I sit down deadweight, and two of them drag me out. I've watched so many Undercurrents and Conscious Cinema videos of stuff like this, I don't fear these people. I've seen so much footage of them being stupid and of people being arrested for stupid and petty things that I've lost my Fear of Authority, that self-policing that is the most powerful force holding us back. . . . Fuck it, I'm here coz I'm right. I'm not scared of that, so I'm not scared of them. Let them deal with me.[3]

Growing pains

Funding was always a problem for us. Radical video groups had come and gone over the years and financial sustainability was one

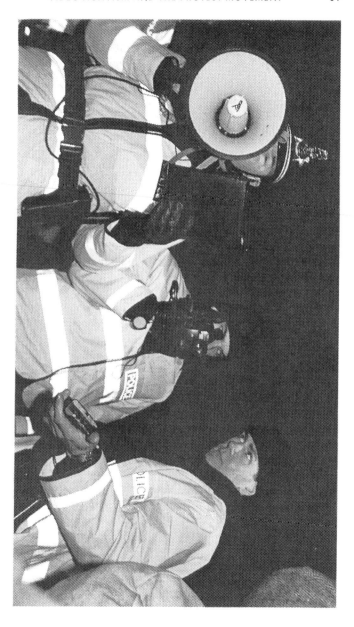

Police counter-surveillance at the Newbury bypass protest site. Photograph by Paul O'Connor

of the key reasons why very few had ever lasted. During the 1970s
and 1980s local arts and council money was available to support
video initiatives. This source of funding had all but dried up by the
early 1990s. We knew we had to find ways to fund our work, and
were realistic enough to know that selling videotapes was never
going to be able to cover all our costs. We tried making semi-
commercial videos for large non-profit groups like the WWF and
Action Aid to help finance the work. But we quickly found that this
work not only took us away from our main goal (of helping
grassroots campaigns) but actually ran counter to some of our
strongly held beliefs (some of the WWF's work we found to be
extremely dodgy). We had some success in raising funds from small
trusts and foundations, but our real saviour came in the form of
the European Commission.

With this perhaps unlikely ally we were extremely fortunate to
raise over £50,000 to support a couple of issues of *Undercurrents*.
Without these funds we would never had been able to survive to
the point where today we can actually financially support ourselves
through training work and sale of footage to television companies.
But this grant was not without its problems. In 1995 the right-wing
Daily Mail heard about the grant and ran a full-page story headed
'Green Militants get £50,000 from Europe' along with a propagand-
ist article which tried to smear us by saying that we fomented
violent campaigns. This would have been okay if it hadn't been for
the European Embassy in London faxing copies of the article to
other parts of the Commission where we had ongoing fund
applications. A few months later the *Sunday Times* picked up on the
story again as part of a larger piece about misspent European
money. Luckily this time they were a bit more sympathetic to our
work. For a while it seemed like we might not get the second half
of the grant we were owed, putting the whole organisation in peril.
In the end we received the full amount of the grant, but it proved
a hairy and exhausting experience.

Meanwhile, we tried to keep our feet on the ground. Another
major anti-roads campaign had sprung up on the outskirts of Bath.
In their great wisdom the Department of Transport had decided to
build a new high-speed road through the ancient Celtic hill-fort on
top of Solsbury Hill. We were there on the first day when eight
people locked themselves to a bulldozer. We continued our video

support throughout the year-long campaign, videoing arrests, sup-
plying footage to TV news, training people how to use video to
reduce incidents of violence, making campaign videos. And we
were there at the end when two hundred people were evicted over
three days from a village of tree houses sixty feet up in the air by
over eight hundred bailiffs, police, and the London-based Reliance
Security guards.

Then other direct action campaigns sprang up. More road
protest sites: Pollok/M77, Blackburn/M66, Honiton bypass, Salisbury, Exeter. Other campaigns were covered too: the live animal
export campaigns that exploded in Brightlingsea, Shoreham, Coventry, Dover; a whole series of 'ethical shoplifting' actions which
took place around the country when mahogany stolen from Brazilian Indian land was seized by activists from stores and taken to the
police for investigation; the anti-Criminal Justice Bill marches and
actions; anti-open-cast campaign sites; and the occupations of
corporate offices which were the focus of campaigns – such as
Tropical Timber Federation, Costains, Tarmac and Celtic Energy.
At each of these, video activists kept pace step by step with the
campaigners to make sure that they were safe and got as much
exposure as possible. Video cameras became seen as an integral
part of almost every campaign around the country. We were
constantly approached to cover actions.

One problem was that there was simply too much to cover! We
decided to concentrate our efforts on training as many people as
possible on how to use video in campaign work. We ran formal and
informal courses around the country. We quickly learned not to
hand out free cameras as they were rarely used and sometimes got
trashed. Instead we encouraged people to find their own equipment, so that they would have more of an investment in both using
and taking care of it, and then would train them how to make best
use of it. We had reasonable success with this. By 1997 we had
trained over five hundred activists how to make use of video
tactically as part of their campaign work, another fifty video activists
to make their campaign videos to be distributed on *Undercurrents*,
and published the *Video Activist Handbook* with Pluto, the first
comprehensive guide to video activism.

But there was another bigger problem. With the ever-increasing
presence of camcorders at actions and demonstrations, the benefits

of video activism became increasingly controversial. During the Brixton riots of 1995 Paul O'Connor was beaten up three times in an evening by *protesters* for carrying a camcorder. A few months later another video activist, Roddy Mansfield, was beaten up by police when he videoed them encouraging (*sic*) protesters

---

Box 3: Pros and cons of video activism[4]

For:	*Against:*
Footage taken at the demo can be used to get people off charges like false arrest.	Footage could be taken by the police and used to incriminate others at the action.
Selling footage to TV can get the issue to a wider audience.	There are now too many people with camcorders and not enough activists.
Video can be edited into empowerment campaign films.	If you sell the footage to TV they can sensationalise and distort the action.
Video can calm things down if police or security are getting violent.	The police have security camcorders; we don't know who's who any more.
Footage sold can pay for tape costs and camera repair costs.	People are using videos to advance themselves not campaigns.

– this time in Luton – to throw stones and rocks! Incidents like these made some people sceptical of camcorders. They argued that camcorder footage could be used by the police to prosecute activists. They were also worried that there were more video activists than activists – at times this did happen, much to the annoyance of the campaigners involved! Pamphlets were circulated telling people not to trust anyone with a video camera, that groups like Undercurrents had passed footage to the police which was then used to prosecute protesters, and that video activists were making a lot of money out of selling footage to TV.

A summary of the anti-video point of view is laid out in Stephen Booth's book *Into the 1990s with Green Anarchist*. Booth heavily criticises groups for trying to use the mainstream media in their campaign work. Quoting a poster from the poll tax riot booklet, 'All photographers, TV crews, journalists are legitimate targets', he goes on to say that 'no cameras on demonstrations should be considered friendly'. He admits that videoing protests could be used to 'inform and inspire people. . . . [but] the danger is that videos of road protests, live exports protests etc. could all too easily become a substitute for radical action'.[5]

But for the most part video activists were able to persuade campaigners that they could play a useful part in terms of legal support, TV coverage and educational video productions. Some protesters continued to be anti-video over the years, but as most video activists arranged to cover an action or demonstration *before* it actually took place on the request of the activists themselves, the problem remained a small one.

Emergence of other groups

By 1994, there were so many video activists that new distribution outlets needed to be formed. In Brighton a group of camcordistas set up the Conscious Cinema video collective in association with the Justice? group. By giving activists access to a just-about-good-enough-quality edit suite and a bit of training, they produced a number of exciting one-hour compilation videotapes of activists' features. These they sent out to as many as sixty local organisers who set up video screenings at community centres, cinemas and festivals. Tens of thousands of people got to learn about cutting-edge grassroots issues and actions they would never had access to otherwise.

Some of these screening groups were running their own regular alternative video nights. Exploding Cinema in London were organising extravaganza evenings in bizarre locations such as disused swimming pools, disused dole offices like Cooltan Arts, and huge squats such as Artillery Mansion in central London. At these events anyone was allowed to come along and show their own home-made video features. The only catch was that they had to face the audience afterwards to take the reaction whichever way it came. In Coventry the Headcleaner Collective pegged up a large white sheet and ran screenings at a local community centre mixed in with poetry readings, sets from bands and a gong which anyone could hit if whatever was going on at that moment was just too bad for them to take any more.

The point being made was that if you want to get people to watch the programmes they had to be entertaining. Of course this should never be at the expense of the informational content of the programming. But many in the DiY video culture realised the mistakes of political video-makers of the past who had made very serious and important films that were almost unwatchable. At Undercurrents, we knew that we had to compete with commercial TV for people's time and attention. They would compare our programmes to broadcast programmes; even if consciously they knew they were made on a shoestring budget, they would subconsciously note bad quality and automatically zone out. If you wanted to show people more than ten minutes' worth of video you had to keep their attention up. The only way to do this is entertainment. Whether that's music, shocking images, stylish cuts, humorous statements, it doesn't matter. A thirty-minute 'the world is fucked' documentary wasn't going to work any more.

Becoming inventive

Meanwhile, the direct action movement moved their campaigns closer and closer to the source of the problem. Shareholder meeting actions, office occupations, invasions of events like the annual Motor Show and excursions into forbidden zones like the Houses of Parliament became increasingly common. So video activists had to become more adept in the use of secret camerawork and sneaking into difficult places with cameras. This was very much in line with the new DiY ethic; it combines brazen in-yer-face action with the latest in technology.

My favourite example of this is the 1995 Lloyds annual general meeting of shareholders. We had been working with a student group who were targeting Lloyds because they were the largest holder of privately owned Third World debt in the UK. We knew that no-one had managed to get a video camcorder into an AGM before. The corporations had started hiring private security guards to frisk the suited shareholders as they went in. They even had metal detectors, we were told!

We had seen plans of the place because the over-zealous PR company hired to promote the event had sent us detailed architectural drawings of the building the week before. The day before the AGM was due to start two of us paid a visit to the conference centre. Jamie and Zoë walked through the main doors, past the metal detectors we would fail at the next day if we had a camera with us and into the main room. After a few moments they were stopped.

'Hi,' Zoë chirped, 'we were just looking for a toilet.'

'Well you can't go in here. Sorry, security reasons,' a tall officer barked back.

'Well we are kind of desperate.' At this point legs were crossed and generally anxious looks were offered. 'Is there anywhere else we could go maybe?'

Zoë went upstairs looking for a toilet. She found one, knowing it was accessible from the main conference room the next day. She quickly prised open the tampon box, suspended a plastic bag inside hovering just above the toxic chemicals at the bottom, placed a camcorder inside and replaced the lid. She was downstairs soon enough. The next day we got inside with no problems. Halfway through the performance Zoë snuck into the toilet and retrieved the camera. Ten minutes later, to the security guards' surprise, protesters started standing up and shouting 'Shame' and 'Why do you give money to oppressive regimes?' I was also standing up capturing the entire scene on a camcorder. As far as I know this is the first secret videoing of an AGM in the UK. We distributed the footage on *Undercurrents* and it later appeared on national TV when we sold the footage to a documentary about shareholder actions.

Undercurrents today

By 1996 we had become eager to branch out to support new grassroots community groups, aware that the DiY culture was

The video cover slip from a recent edition of *Undercurrents*

becoming increasingly self-sufficient and successful in its own media strategies. Some of the most exciting networks we have linked up with have been the broad-based organisations supported by the Community Organising Foundation.

We worked with a group of residents who lived on a housing estate outside of Wrexham in Wales. They were suffering from noise and sound pollution emitting from an aluminium recycling factory. They had spent years trying to improve the situation, talking to council members and the factory itself, to no avail. They decided the last hope was to go directly to the ultimate owner of the factory, Leonard Blavatnik, who lived in New York. We produced a video letter, 'Dear Lenny', with testimonies from the residents and video evidence of the pollution that they had shot on camcorder. Two of the residents flew to New York to hand the video letter to Mr Blavatnik. They were thrown out of the offices by one of the other directors of the factory, but they did manage to give him the video. Back in Wrexham, residents made copies of the video and sent them to the factory workers, all the members of the local council as well as the media. They won huge coverage on local and national radio and TV because their 'story' was so good. The residents gained the support of the local MP and the media, and a few months later the Managing Director of the factory was replaced, and significant changes made to the production routine.

At the same time Undercurrents had accumulated so much unique and important campaign footage that we decided to make sure that it would get maximum exposure. We set up the country's first ever Alternative Video Archive, made up of hundreds of hours of counterculture and campaign footage from the UK and around the world. We raised grants to support the project and won the backing of the National Film and Television Archive, who agreed to house a part of the archive in the main national archive. This means that not only will the footage be used by campaigners, lawyers, teachers and broadcasters, but from now on the video activist coverage of the 1990s will be maintained as one of the country's official cultural records.

Throughout the course of our work we have always been committed to enabling campaigners to shoot their own footage and to edit it themselves. This strategy paid off not only in terms of empowerment and useful support for the campaign, but in terms of excellent video features as well. Over the years Undercurrents features have won major international festivals, including the French Environment Film Festival, the Tokyo Video Festival, the Brazil Video Olympiad and the London International Environment Film Festival, as well as the BT/WWF community award. Not bad for a grassroots non-profit video organisation with a bunch of second-hand domestic camcorders!

By November 1997 Undercurrents had produced the eighth edition of its video magazine. It has grown from a group of three or four individuals loosely collected around a common project, working in someone's spare bedroom on a bunch of 'just about okay' equipment, to having a full-time staff of eight, a computerised database mail-order system, a non-linear broadcast quality edit suite as well as far more experienced staff. We have even been able to get two half-hour compilation shows taken from *Undercurrents* on to national television with Channel Four in a slot called *Major Resistance: The Underground Tapes.* Interestingly, it was watched by only 100,000 people, compared to the approximately 50,000 who watch each *Undercurrents* issue! However, we are resisting the urge to 'move on' and become a 'professional' broadcast production company. We know that the quickest way to destroy all our hard work is to start chasing after broadcast programmes. We won't do this. Our strength remains as a non-profit video organisation capable of independent distribution, the production of radical programmes and the training of video campaigners. We remain committed to supporting grassroots activism now and into the future. Three years after the launch of the video magazine the DiY movement continues to be a key focus of our alternative video work. Long may it last. *Viva camcordistas! Viva!*

4

The politics of anti-road struggle and the struggles of anti-road politics: the case of the No M11 Link Road campaign

AUFHEBEN

> Through the passionate creation of conditions favourable to the growth of our passions, we wish to destroy that which is destroying us.
>
> Ratgeb (1974)[1]

> What we're dealing with here is a small unrepresentative group. They set aside the entire democratic process and try to get what they want by physical means. ... I hope there will be no more resistance, because the road has the full authority of democracy, and any attempt to disrupt it is therefore an attack on democracy
>
> Stephen Norris, Minister for Transport in London (1994)[2]

This chapter was originally written in the summer of 1994, when we were involved in the campaign against the M11 link road in northeast London.[3] The campaign had moved into its final and, in our view, most radical phase: the occupation of Claremont Road. The chapter was written to be presented at a discussion meeting at the Justice? courthouse squat in Brighton. It also appeared in the zine *Claremont Road: The End of the Beginning*, produced after the eviction of Claremont Road. The purpose of the piece was to analyse the political possibilities of the anti-roads movement, and some of its internal tensions, as exemplified in the No M11 campaign.

Aufheben is the name of a magazine, not a group. *Aufheben* has appeared approximately annually since 1992. Issues covered include the 1992 Los Angeles uprising; the anti-roads struggle at Twyford Down; the project of European Monetary Union; an

The cover of *Aufheben*'s summer 1994 edition

analysis of the UN invasion of Somalia; the class struggles in France in 1995; a critique of current anti-civilisation theories; and the question of the 'decline' of capitalism. The title of the magazine refers to an approach which is open to others rather than a structure with a membership, and so on. The term '*Aufheben*' has no precise English equivalent. In popular German it normally has two meanings which are in opposition. One is negative: 'to abolish', 'to annul', 'to cancel', and so on. The other is positive: 'to supersede', 'to transcend'. Hegel exploited this duality of meaning and used the word to describe the positive–negative action whereby a higher form of thought or nature supersedes a lower form, while at the same time 'preserving' its 'moments of truth'. The proletariat's revolutionary negation of capital, communism, is an instance of this positive–negative movement of supersession, as is its theoretical expression in Marx's method of critique.

The project of those involved in *Aufheben* draws inspiration from,

but ultimately seeks to go beyond the limits of, the most recent
high points in proletarian theory and practice, such as the Situationist International and the Italian *autonomia* movement.[4] Most
of the people involved in *Aufheben* magazine came together during
the anti-poll tax movement of 1990. The magazine grew out of a
reading group we began around that time. We were reading Marx's
Grundrisse and *Capital*, with a view to developing our ideas in order
to contribute to the class struggle.

The present chapter is part of this contribution. In writing it, we
didn't claim to have a complete understanding of the anti-roads
movement. Rather, we were in a similar situation to many other
people taking part in the struggle at the M11: passionately involved
and seeking to understand in order to struggle more effectively.

Direct action is necessary but direct action alone is not enough. It
is also necessary to develop a theory adequate to our radical actions.
Otherwise all we have to comprehend and legitimise our actions are
the existing off-the-shelf ideologies. These ideologies are grounded
in, and function to reproduce, the very social relations we wish to
overcome: the social relations of alienation, exploitation, state
oppression, meaningless and soul-destroying work, endless economic expansion and everyday misery. In other words, the social
relations of capital.

'Politics' intended and unintended

Roads and capital

The anti-roads direct action movement in the UK can be said to
have begun with the struggle over the building of the M3 extension
in Twyford Down, Hampshire, in 1991–92. Both this campaign and
that at the M11 extension in north-east London served to make
roads into a political issue for many people for the first time. But
whereas 'rural landscape' issues were to the fore at Twyford, the
M11 was an urban development scheme, and so raised issues of
housing, pollution and use of 'community' space. This engendered
a politicisation among participants and onlookers on a greater
scale and of a broader quality ('social' as well as 'natural') than
occurred at Twyford.

However, it is not as if roads were non-political before they became a topic of national controversy. Roads have always been deeply implicated in the maintenance of class relations. In the first place, capital – as both a national and a supra-national subject – requires an efficient transport system in order to move raw materials to factories, and to move finished products to retail centres where they can be sold. Commodities need to be moved about, usually over long distances, to have their value realised in the realm of exchange.[5] In order to compete with other capitals, each transport system must be continually upgraded. Hence the attempt of the various states that make up the European Union to constitute themselves into a single viable economic entity in order to compete with other blocs requires a transport system allowing quick, efficient movement across the whole continent (and between this bloc and others). And hence some of the major road 'improvements' taking place in the 1990s have been part funded by the European Union as part of developing the Trans-European Route Network.

In the second place, we need to explain why modern capitalist states have come to prefer roads to rail networks. There are a number of reasons, but the basic element behind the growth of roads is the status of the motor industry as a key locus for expansion. The car is still the pre-eminent consumer product. Quite simply, car sales and all the commodities related to such sales – petrol, insurance, etc., etc. – can generate a lot of wealth for some people! Moreover, with such a large number of linkages to other industries – petrochemical, plastics, steel and road-building itself, of course – the motor industry serves as an indicator for the whole economy. Huge sectors of the economy are dependent upon the continued sale of cars.

Many participants and commentators would agree with us that the anti-roads movement is in some sense 'political'. We want to argue for a particular understanding of the politics of anti-roads struggle, however, and against certain other interpretations which are current.

A moral or environmental issue?

In the not too distant past, opposition to new road schemes was generally understood to be mere NIMBYism: people who probably recognised the 'need for the road', but who didn't want it going through their own patch. The struggle at Twyford Down can be seen as the beginning of the end of NIMBYism and the birth of a new *bête noire* for the state planners and road empire: the anti-roads direct activists. The principled action of these people has allowed locals to understand their own problems in global terms – which in turn has given them a greater feeling of legitimacy. This whole process has snowballed as different groups around the country have taken encouragement from each other's actions.

In moving away from NIMBYism, many of the participants in the M11 struggle characterised their action as essentially *moral* or essentially *environmental*. However, while individuals may be motivated by their personal values, the M11 struggle is not explicable as a 'moral' issue because it is not a simple opposition of good versus bad. The reason that the planners, the state, the contractors, and so on, attempted to impose the road is not because they are 'evil people'. It is because they were acting in the service of capital that they are 'bad', not vice versa. Only if this is taken into account can we understand the logic of what they are trying to do. Why, for example, did the UK government not implement all of the Rio declaration on global warming? Not because John Major was stupid or lazy or malicious (though he may be all those things), but because the UK government feared quite rationally that UK capital would lose competitiveness in the short to medium term if such changes were made.

The struggle cannot be comprehended adequately as being essentially 'environmental' either. In the first place, the struggle against the M11 link road has highlighted many issues which people recognise as essentially social; some participants were motivated by the threat to the 350 houses on the route of the road rather than the destruction of trees and green spaces. There is a deeper point here also: 'the environment' or 'nature' is not some separate and distinct realm, to be contrasted with a separate social or political realm. 'Environmental' and social issues are actually aspects of the same whole; the struggle over the environment reflects our (human/social) needs for green areas, health and resources. We are part of nature, and there is no struggle outside human needs and desires.

Given that a purely moral or a purely environmental perspective is inadequate for understanding the significance of the M11 campaign, we therefore need to find another framework. In left and radical politics – in the broad sense – there are two dominant frameworks in which the struggle against the M11 link road might be understood: labourism and Leninism (the traditional left), on the one hand, and, on the other, eco-reformism.

Traditional organised politics

To the traditional left, whether labourist or Leninist, most struggles (such as the attempt merely to stop a particular road, or even the whole roads programme) are understood *a priori* principally as locations for the recruitment of individuals to a 'revolutionary party' (or even a parliamentary one) which is thought by its supporters to be the *real* agent for the *real* struggle which actually takes place at another location and at another time.

But many ostensibly reformist struggles of whatever nature, depending on how they are fought and their historical context, may become revolutionary in their own right. Particular struggles, such as those of the new anti-roads movement, may connect themselves to each other as part of a practical critique of the whole capital relation, even if their immediate conscious aims are more modest. Such struggles may be both valid in their own right (that is, they satisfy our immediate needs as opposed to those of capital) *and* point directly to a higher level of struggle; a victory may *create new needs and desires* (which people then feel confident to set about satisfying) and *new possibilities* (which make the satisfaction of these and other needs and desires more likely), and so on.

Eco-reformism takes many forms, but is typically characterised by a naive faith in the ultimate tractability of democracy. Thus the Green Party has proposed a no-growth capitalist economy, and recent commentators have suggested that capitalism and 'greenery' are compatible.[6] Arguments for tractability or compatibility are based on the observation that certain green battles have been won, and that certain green indicators (for example, relative absence of sulphur dioxide air pollution) have been known to co-exist with growth.

But although particular battles may be won through reform, the whole war will not be won this way, since to stifle the hydra-head of capital in one direction is to have it popping up somewhere else. Imagine, for example, that the anti-roads movement was so success-ful that it not only prevented all new roads being built but permanently closed many existing ones. Without a concerted attempt to deal with the growth needs of capital from which the mania for roads issued, our lives would be ruined in other ways – by a massive growth in information technology, railways, air trans-port, even canals! For example, in Holland and Belgium, oppo-sition is less over roads than over railways, which, due to the high level of industrialisation and development over there, are taking up the few remaining green spaces.

What both leftist and eco-reformist positions have in common is that they both look outside ourselves and our struggles for the real agent of change, the real historical subject: leftists look to 'the party' while eco-reformists look to parliament. By contrast, and despite some of the material and comments put out in the name of the No M11 campaign, by adopting direct action as a form of politics, those of us involved in the No M11 campaign looked to ourselves as a source of change.

The No M11 campaign as an existence of thoroughgoing struggle

Having rejected other political interpretations, we now turn to the actual practice of the No M11 struggle to develop our own perspective on its political nature.

Participants' expectations of what counts as success in the struggle against the M11 link road shifted over the duration of the campaign. Particularly after the fall of Wanstonia (February 1994), fewer and fewer people believed we could stop the M11 link road being built. But people were prepared to continue this long war of attrition because they could see that the delay and money the campaign cost the construction companies and the government (through the occupation of squats, invasions of sites and other actions) were having some impact on the ideas of many people and on government priorities.

However, compared to even a traditional labourist struggle, such as the signal workers' dispute which occurred at the same time as the M11 campaign was at its height, the amount of money the

campaign cost the government is actually small potatoes.[7] Therefore the key to the political significance of the No M11 campaign
lies less in the immediate aims of stopping this one road and in the
immediate costs incurred by capital and the state (although these
are great achievements and great encouragement to others), and
more in our *creation of a climate of autonomy, disobedience and
resistance.*[8]

The different acts of creation and resistance that comprise the
No M11 campaign were more or less coherently related as part of
a conscious collective project. What made them radical, subversive
and potentially revolutionary was the fact that the various particular
acts were intended and functioned as parts of a whole way of
existence, a day-to-day existence of thoroughgoing struggle.[9] Much
of the significance of this day-to-day existence of struggle lies in the
fact that a certain way of life is required to maintain the capitalist
system: a life of discipline and conformity, with expression limited
to purchasing power. In order to create the wealth necessary to
maintain itself, this system requires that most of us live in accom-
modation that we pay for, that we pay for our food and clothing,
and so on (and that, as individual purchasers, we aspire to more
and better housing, clothes, etc., etc.) – that we therefore carry out
wage-labour in order to pay for all these things. In order to maintain
itself, capital also requires that those who *do* conform perceive the
lifestyles of those who *don't* as *unattractive and precarious.*

The way of life adopted by many of us in the No M11 campaign
was the very reverse of this – and points to the way a whole society
could live. However, this alternative, subversive form of existence
was born not of idealism but of immediate practical requirements.

Squatting

Day-to-day struggle was not a free choice, but rather a function of
the fact that the campaign was over a large road in whose path lay
a number of houses, trees and other green areas; the best way to
defend these was obviously to occupy them and live in them
collectively. The importance of squatting as a tactic in the radicalism of the M11 struggle was vital, binding together as it did daily
life with offensive resistance: living on the route of the proposed
road allowed easier intervention in the building of that road!
Moreover, a situation without the dull compulsion of rent, work,

bills, and so on, provided the basis for creating and reinventing a community, which, in turn, encouraged other ideas.

Squatting is itself a tremendous act of resistance as well as a material necessity. But we went beyond mere squatting and made the campaign into a more thoroughgoing struggle, and not only through our incursions into construction sites. We went beyond squatting as lifestylism firstly by *barricading* our squats; secondly by *taking over the street itself* in Claremont Road; and, finally, and as part of taking over the street, we made it into our actual *living* space – rejecting in effect the imposed division between the privatised domain of the householder and the 'public' (that is, traffic-dominated) thoroughfare.

'The pixies': devalorisation and auto-valorisation

Parallel to squatting were the many acts of damage and theft ('pixieing') that went on against the link road at night (and sometimes in broad daylight). Equipment, materials, structures, offices, vehicles, fences and machinery at link road sites were damaged all the time, sometimes by a large crowd who would outnumber security and disappear when the police arrived, but more often by small groups who operated out of view of security. This added massively to the costs incurred by the construction companies. Even better, lots of material was stolen from link road sites and other sites in the area. This material was then used for *our* purposes – using fencing for barricading, for example. This process had a beautiful roundness and economy about it: turning the enemies' 'weapons' against them! In devalorising these materials from capital's point of view, we revalorised (or autovalorised) them from our own.

For very practical reasons, these kind of activities were not widely discussed within the campaign, let alone mentioned in public pro-nouncements (press releases, leaflets, pamphlets, interviews, etc.): to admit to theft and damage is to ask to be arrested. This led to a rather one-sided, anodyne picture being received in some quarters of what the campaign was about and what people in the cam-paign actually did. So much had to be secret, even within the campaign. People involved in the campaign simply couldn't go around saying that the campaign's continued existence as a semi-permanent site of resistance depended crucially on theft.

Communal life

Those staying at Claremont Road attempted to live communally in many ways. Many of the houses were shared, and there were communal meals, although a degree of semi-commercial organisation also operated in the form of the street cafés. People experimented with different ways of relating to each other and organising. Some of the limits of what can be done communally reflected the problem of new people or outsiders coming in who can't be trusted. The campaign was very open, but the disadvantage of this was that it made it easy for spies and infiltrators to gain access. The only solution to this was not so much to close up as to *expand and generalise the struggle.*

Free activity: reclaiming 'time'

Some indication of the threat our mode of existence posed to the stability of the mainstream was given by the fact that many people who had relatively well-paid jobs in the construction industry preferred to 'work' with us rather than for a wage. Without doubt, we were nowhere near successful enough in appealing to such people. But nevertheless, we must have been doing something right when so many carpenters and other skilled workers came to 'work' for hours on end to take part in the barricading and related construction work that went on in Claremont Road.

Reclaiming space

People took over the tarmac of the street itself, and only part of it was open to vehicles. We tried to ensure that security guards occupying part of the end of the street did not use it to park their cars; rather, any parking spaces were reserved for our people. One of the elders of the campaign initiated the closing of the main part of the street to traffic by building artworks on the actual tarmac. These works of art were made from objects in the natural and artificial environment: tree stumps, chains, bicycle parts, and so on. This was followed by the turning of the street itself into a 'living room' by using the furniture, carpets, fittings and other objects from some of the houses on the street to make actual rooms on the street. Each had its own character. These rooms did not simply operate as art; they were functional as living spaces. This came to be seen as a deliberate echo of (idealised) pre-car communities where children could play in the street, neighbours socialise, and so on, without fear of being knocked down. As more objects filled the street, and more people took over the road, Claremont was also becoming a virtual no-go area for the police. In the early days, a local sergeant would patrol regularly and knock down the artwork each time he went past. But eventually he stopped going down the street at all. At the time, we felt we had excluded the police through our own numbers and power; but in fact part of it was that the police were being diplomatic. When they deemed the time to be right they came in when they wanted – as on 2 August when four of our houses were evicted and demolished with the aid of riot police. Throughout, however, people led the police to believe that all the artwork and other objects in the street were easily movable, when in fact many of them were cemented into the street, or filled with earth and rubble so they could function as barricades.

In sum, this daily existence of thoroughgoing struggle was simultaneously a *negative* act (stopping the road etc.) and a *positive pointer* to the kind of social relations that could exist: no money, the end of exchange values, communal living, no wage labour, no ownership of space.

Contesting the communal identity

Many of the themes of the No M11 struggle resonate with those found in the writings of the Situationist International.[10] Their concerns with pleasure, humour, critique/satire of consumerism, 'self-realisation' and 'wholeness' are all captured in the opposition 'life versus survival'.[11] Survival may actually be no more than a living death of wage-labour, money, routine, bureaucracy, boredom, the state, the police, consumption, town planning, bourgeois discipline, and so on. Survival may also be at varying degrees of comfort; but, however comfortable, it does not correspond to the spontaneity, love, creativity, humour, comradeship, commitment, risk-taking and leaps into the unknown of *living*. Survival is merely existence within the purposes of an alien and parasitic power; living is the very reverse of this – it is the negation of this encroaching power through conscious, joyous resistance.[12]

As well as sharing some of its strengths, the No M11 campaign fell down in some of the places where the Situationists fell down also. A critique of alienation in the realm of consumption and 'everyday life' is necessary, but what about an adequate analysis of commodity production? Those in the No M11 campaign did not produce such an analysis, not because, like the Situationists, they thought that capital has solved some of its contradictions.[13] Rather they didn't think about capital at all, except incidentally. Towards the end of the campaign, more people thought more often about their own activity as a form of antagonism in relation to capital and the state. But, generally, the campaign's theories remained inadequate to its practices; and into this gap of theory dogma often stepped – usually liberal dogma, reflecting both the middle-class backgrounds of many within the campaign, and the nature of the campaign itself, which fitted uneasily into the traditional image of class struggle.

Participants in the No M11 campaign clearly shared an identity, an identity which was deeply political, whether explicitly understood in relation to capital or not. However, the nature of the campaign's politics was sometimes the subject of intense internal struggles. Dogmas did not always go uncontested. Two controversial issues in particular stand out from the Claremont Road period: the question of non-violence; and the arguments over how the free space was created and maintained.

'Fluffing it?'

Just how non-violent was the campaign?

For some people in the No M11 campaign, non-violence was not simply a tactic appropriate to certain situations, it was a principle to be applied to *all* situations. Yet even those who professed to be principled 'fluffies', or adherents of ideological non-violence, were not always consistent. Violence was used *within* the campaign – reluctantly – to exclude people from Claremont Road. And many who thought of themselves as fluffies would admit that in some situations they would use physical force against another person in order to protect themselves. Clearly, unless they are willing to use the same force to protect their comrades, they are guilty not only of hypocrisy but also of selfishness and cowardice. But the point here is to emphasise that it is not particular individuals or groups who should be criticised – this could degenerate into a merely moral or *ad hominem* argument – rather it is necessary to look at the issue at the level of practices. We do not presume complete consistency, and so the critique is therefore against principled-fluffy *practices* not people.

Practical arguments

In the No M11 campaign, the predominance of non-violence as an integral part of the campaign identity was fuelled as much by a fear of media/public opinion response as by the practical question of how a relatively small group of people could continually disrupt construction work in the face of a physically large workforce of security guards. But there were, indeed, strong practical imperatives behind the campaign's adoption of non-violence.

Given that the work on the road was scheduled to last at least four years, and that the most effective way to fight it was to have a permanent and visible presence on or nearby the route of the road, to be able to climb into work sites and disrupt work, and given also the fluctuations in our numbers, using open physical violence to get past security was not a viable strategy. If, for example, we had the numbers on one occasion to beat the guards in a fight, we would face revenge when we were vulnerable – in our squats or next time we invaded a site when our numbers were low. In fact, in numerical terms we were usually evenly matched with the guards during site invasions, but they were mostly much bigger physically than us. We therefore attempted to operate within certain unwritten rules of play, and we attempted to outmanoeuvre the guards within those rules: a crowd of us would run on to a site, many of whom expected to be escorted or dragged out by the guards, while a number managed to scale the cranes where the guards couldn't reach them.

There were many complaints within the campaign over 'violence' from security guards or police, and over illegitimate use of arrest and other interventions by police. But there was hardly any use of batons, let alone horses or snatch squads, by police at the M11 struggle. Arguably, we were able to carry on our war of attrition because, by and large, we did not appear to up the stakes too much, and so the police often adopted a hands-off approach.

Given this context, it was difficult to argue that non-violence could be dispensed with. On the other hand, on many occasions it was clear that the strategy of non-violence had become written in

Worksite action on the M11 Link Road, early 1995. Photograph by Nick Cobbing

stone as a simplistic panacea. During the period when a large number of new people became involved in the campaign, for example, there was an occasion when someone questioned the usefulness of non-violence simply by asking, 'What do I do after they've hit me?' Instead of being given a rational argument, he was virtually shouted down hysterically with rhetoric about non-violence. Similarly, some people in the campaign expressed fear that the demo against the Criminal Justice Bill on 24 July (1994) might not be 'fluffy', as if the tactics of local road protests should automatically generalise to other situations. The tactic of non-violence arises from a position of weakness: it is like people saying, 'We are weak and vulnerable; let's capitalise on this by using it as a method!' – appealing to the *humanity* and *sympathy* of others (see below). But it simply doesn't make sense to assume we'll always be weak or that the method will work with every different potentially confrontational encounter.

In the struggle against the A36 superhighway just outside Bath, a protester was nearly killed when a tree surgeon apparently deliberately cut the ropes securing him to a tree. After this, protesters took rocks with them into the trees to use in case another such life-or-death situation arose. If methods vary across different anti-roads campaigns, then they will obviously vary across different types of struggle. Non-violence *can* be very persuasive in certain situations; it can discourage security and police from being more violent than they might otherwise be on certain occasions. But what about when the stakes are raised, when the powers that be think we're being too successful? Police and security on the ground will be under orders not to be disarmed by politeness and non-violence; they will be thinking simply of getting people out of the way by any means necessary, and if you can't get away quickly enough you will have to try to defend yourself. At the demo against the Criminal Justice Bill on 24 July, a leaflet was distributed advising people that one tactic they might try if the police started getting heavy was to 'lie down and be a doormat'. This advice was naive, inappropriate and dangerous. *The forces of the state will wipe the floor with 'doormats'!*

Non-violence as part of democracy

A second rationale for non-violence arises from its heritage. Linked as it is with all the historical baggage of campaigns to gain civil rights, the strategy of non-violence was articulated within the No M11 campaign on a number of occasions as a way of bringing us more into the democratic fold. The demand was made that our non-violent protest be recognised as 'part of the British democratic tradition', that we should be able to exercise our 'rights', and that non-violent direct action (NVDA) be seen as a necessary part of citizenship. NVDA was said to be legitimate because it is consistent with certain principles in the law. Organisations allied to the No M11 campaign, such as Alarm UK, Road Alert! and the Freedom Network, made explicit the ideological linkages, citing the Suffragettes as an example and precedent for such integration and inclusion. Michael Randle, the well-known peace campaigner, in his recent book on civil resistance,[14] follows the philosopher Ted Honderich and the sociologist Sheila Rowbotham in seeing certain forms of protest such as non-violent direct action as *enriching* rather than challenging democracy.[15]

But let's be clear about this. What they refer to by the term 'democracy' is the alienated politics that got us into this mess in the first place. Do we want to see this system achieve full ascendancy – with a bill of rights to make explicit the guarantee of our paltry 'freedoms' in exchange for our duty to obey a law which maintains the dull compulsion of capital – or do we want something better? In the No M11 struggle, many of the activities we took part in or witnessed are not at all part of the miserable democratic exchange of representation, rights and duties; they went far beyond this, and were both adequate and satisfying in themselves.[16] These actions point to a type of social form which embodies freedom in a way that democracy simply cannot. Honderich and Randle might regard such activities as roadblocks, barricading, site invasions, and so on, as 'ultimately good in the long run'. But what about resisting arrest, criminal damage and theft in the fight against the road? What about *generalising* what we did to tube-fare dodging? These don't and cannot enrich democracy – they can only subvert it – and so much the better for that.

'Use' of the mass media

The importance of non-violence became consolidated in the beginning of the No M11 campaign because it was good for public relations: a lot of 'respectable' residents got involved because they

liked non-violence as a moral position. They were concerned with
the campaign's image in the mass media, thought to be the
determiner as well as the reflection of (middle-class) public opinion. A concern with getting ourselves into the media continued,
although many people became cynical about this through their
experiences of the press.

Of course we needed to let people (all people?) know that a
force of active opposition existed to the road. But this should not
be conflated with relying on the needs of the mass media to
disseminate our message. The problem with relying on the mass
media is that of colluding with the very prejudices you're trying to
subvert.[17] The more that people like us get our more 'fluffy',
middle-class face accepted by the media and the *Daily Mail* readership, the more we may be agreeing to marginalise our 'darker' side
– our clothes and jewellery, opinions and arguments, drugs and
language – to send it deeper underground. This is the price of
cuddling up to them. If the struggle is indeed about a whole way of
life, the aim should be to change or confront 'public opinion', not
appease it.[18]

Humanism

Perhaps the most deeply ideological of all the justifications for non-
violence was the humanist argument. On one occasion, an experienced eco-campaigner at the No M11 campaign angrily denounced
some people on one of our site actions as 'scum' because they had
apparently been violent towards some security guards. As already
mentioned, the danger of being violent towards security is that,
because we were usually relatively vulnerable, such actions put us
all at risk. But, on the other hand, to call people 'scum' for fighting
security guards displayed an utter confusion. Just who were the
'scum'? The police and private security who attempted to physically
impose a road upon us ultimately by any means necessary? Or some
people who wanted to resist this process? Our relations with police
and more so with security were problematic, changeable and
contradictory. But it was naive to argue that the basis of our non-
violence towards them should be a kind of humanism. The humanist argument claims that all violence is the same since it is all done
to 'human beings'; the argument therefore blurs the qualitative
distinction between the violence that maintains alienation and

exploitation (that is, the violence of the state) and the violence which seeks to liberate us from this alienation and exploitation.

Drawing on the humanistic argument, some of Alarm UK's literature evoked the spirit of Rogerian therapy when it invited us to remember that 'security guards are capable of change just as much as we are'. It is true that security guards are 'human beings too', but they are certainly not '*only* human beings'; they are paid to enact a particular *role* and if they do not do this properly – by being too human, for example – then they will be fired. As Vaneigem says, 'It is easier to escape the role of a libertine than the role of a cop, executive or rabbi.'[19]

How was our free space created and maintained?

Claremont Road was a free space. But there were arguments over which activities were claimed to be the most important in creating and maintaining that free space.

A dilemma over 'hard work' versus 'hedonism' was present in the No M11 campaign from the beginning. Again, the dilemma over this question faced by each individual, the arguments and accusations within the collective, and the waxing or waning of a particular emphasis within the campaign reflected the exigencies of the situation itself rather than a purely intellectual debate. Many of those taking part in the campaign did so consciously as part of a whole way of attempting to resist and avoid the dull compulsion of work-discipline, conformity, and so on. This was certainly true of the Dongas-types who for many people personified the campaign, at least until the Claremont period. Sitting round a tree to protect it was not simply a duty – it was a pleasure in itself. But, particularly when houses were threatened with eviction and demolition, it was necessary to carry out some kind of physical activity in order to slow down the contractors. During the Wanstonia period (January–February 1994), when a block of Wanstead houses was defended, the question of whether the barricading should be total as opposed to selective was a source of persistent and heated argument. The same argument was revived in Claremont Road.

In Claremont Road, barricading was never assiduously done by everyone on the street. Instead, there was a hard-core crew of barricaders who worked incessantly (often inside the houses where

no-one could actually see them) and a large pool of more
occasional barricaders who worked on particular projects, either
on the houses they were staying in or in the street as a whole.
Windows were tinned up from the inside, attics fortified, doors
reinforced, ground floors filled with rubble, and towers built on
roofs, and so on.

But if our struggle was simultaneously a fight to live rather than
simply a grim, dour attempt to slow the road-building down, then
it would have been counterproductive making the houses so well
barricaded that they all became uninhabitable. For one person or
a small group to devote themselves single-mindedly to barricading
is laudable and certainly produced some highly useful defences;
but it could also be a kind of self-sacrifice that conflicts with the
desire for pleasure. It could also exclude the very people who
might otherwise have been defending the house on the day of the
eviction.

But if the special ambience of our free space was not guaranteed
simply by single-minded barricading, nor was it guaranteed by its
opposite – pure hedonism. The tarmac in Claremont Road was full
of armchairs and art, enabling a leisured way of existence. But
resentment built up among both the hard-core barricaders and
others who put a lot of effort into the street. They saw that things
needed to be done and that some people were doing nothing and
yet enjoying the benefits of the street, such as the subsidised meals.
These do-nothings were called the 'lunch outs', and drinking
strong lager came to be associated with parasitic laziness, internal
violence and making a mess of the street. The solution to this was
deemed to be forced expulsion from the street, and during just
one month that summer about twenty people were thrown off the
street in this way.

Was this a return to a primitive work ethic? The old disciplines
of alien bourgeois society reimposing themselves in the height of
the siege? In fact, a level of balance was struck whereby a number
of lunch outs came to be more or less tolerated (as long as they
didn't actually hinder other activities), and more people joined in
the barricading – albeit intermittently. Even though some of those
expelled were a menace to others, there was also a recognition
among some people that there was an element of scapegoating in
the response to the lunch outs. For one thing, drinking alcohol was

'Munstonia', the last house on the route of the M11 Link Road in Leytonstone, London. Photograph by Nick Cobbing

an unreliable indicator of doing nothing and parasitism. For another, the apparent do-nothings were part of a vital reserve army of resistance in the event of big evictions. They also helped maintain our control of the street at night, simply by being there, in the face of encroachment of space by security, and did other things that may have gone unnoticed by the hard-core barricaders (such as some of the 'pixieing') to make the street 'ours'. Moreover, since few on the street were 'always working', the quasi-hysterical revulsion against lunch outs was in some ways a reflection of dilemmas within each of us. Such questions as 'Am I doing enough?' and 'Am I spending too much time taking drugs?', instead of being problematised themselves for being leftovers from old-style work-discipline, became displaced on to an obvious target.

Beyond the M11

Claremont Road was evicted at the end of 1994. The eviction saw the end of the No M11 campaign in its form as an existence of thoroughgoing struggle. However, other, related, campaigns were just beginning. In this section, we discuss some of these developments, the existence of which allows us not simply to apply the analysis we produced during the No M11 campaign, but to elaborate this analysis further. First, we discuss tendencies within the anti-Criminal Justice Bill movement, and second the current state of anti-roads direct action.

Kill or chill the CJB?[20]

In the summer and autumn of 1994, the national campaign against the Criminal Justice Bill (CJB) was riven by the same arguments over non-violence taking place in the No M11 campaign. Importantly, however, whereas at the No M11 campaign there was consensus, more or less, over the necessity for non-violence (if not the rationale for it), in the anti-CJB campaign there was no such consensus; and indeed the struggle over methods became quite bitter at times. The 'spiky' counter-offensive, not only against the CJB but also against the domination of 'fluffy' ideologues, forced the latter to develop and make explicit their arguments in order to defend their position more robustly. This has enabled us to look more closely at the nature and social conditions of 'fluffyism', which we show here to be an expression of the worst kind of liberalism.

The world view of the fluffy

Many who went on the national demonstrations against the CJB may be under the illusion that the fluffies are simply the pacifists of the 1980s re-emerging from the woodwork. There are, however, important differences between fluffyism and the pacifism of the old peace movement. Pacifists at least recognised the state as a social force of violent coercion that needed to be confronted for 'freedom' to have any meaning. Fluffyism, on the other hand, takes liberalism to its logical extreme (and is even more incoherent as a result). The fluffy view of society as an aggregation of *individuals* denies the possibility of recognising the state as a *social* force: below their suits and uniforms the bailiffs, police, property speculators, industrialists, and even Michael Howard and his cohorts, are just individual human beings. Fluffies assume, therefore, that all individuals have a common human interest. Any conflicts which arise in society can, by implication, only be the results of misplaced fears or misunderstandings.

This view underpinned the fluffies' conception of how the campaign against the CJB needed to proceed. As the CJB could only be the result of prejudice, the best way to counter it would be to demonstrate to those nice men in suits that they really had nothing to fear: that beneath the dreadlocks and funny clothes, strange ideas and new-fangled music, the marginalised community was really made up of respectable and honest human beings making a valuable if unorthodox contribution to humanity. The way forward was to overcome prejudice by demonstrating to the rest of society their reasonableness and 'positivity'. Thus, in comparison to the liberalism of the pacifists, fluffyism is characterised as not only fundamentally unconfrontational, but also supposedly apolitical.

As the purpose of the campaign was to provide itself with a positive self-image, the representation became more important than that which was to be represented. Attracting media attention and getting 'positive coverage' became the be all and end all of the campaign as far as the fluffies were concerned. Indeed, were it possible to get positive TV coverage of a demonstration without the hassles and risks involved in actually having one, the fluffies would no doubt have done so. The fluffy is the Situationist's nightmare come true, the rarefied thought of the postmodernist personified – virtual politics.

Liberalism and social positions

The influence of fluffy ideology within the anti-CJB campaign can be understood by a closer examination of the current positions of the fluffies themselves within capitalist society. The CJB was an attack on marginal elements rejecting the conformity of the 'traditional working class'. Within the Bill's scope, therefore, including as it did a clamp-down on unlicensed raves, were hippie entrepreneurs who had a material interest in adopting a liberal position of defending freedom (to make money in their case, to dance in fields, etc., in the case of their punters); adopting a class position would expose the tensions between those who sell and those who always buy, the personifications of the opposing extremes of commodity metamorphosis.

By far the majority in the movement, however, were young unemployed who had no material interest in obscuring class divisions. But this very position of unemployment reinforces the apparent truth of liberal ideology, as the claimant exclusively inhabits the realm of circulation and exchange (rather than production), experiencing only one facet of capitalism. Many in the movement relate to money only as the universal equivalent, as purchasing power, not as the face of the boss. Their income is not payment for exploitation as a component of a collective workforce, but apparently a function of their individual human needs.

Whilst the claimant's pound coin is worth every bit as much as that of the company director, the *quantitative* difference in the amount they have to spend becomes a *qualitative* one that becomes recognised as class inequality, especially if the claimant has not chosen the dole as a preference, has family commitments, or lives in a working-class community. But 'young, free and single' claimants who have chosen to be on the dole, particularly if they have never worked, more so if they come from a middle-class background, and if the housing benefit pays for a flat in an area shared by students, yuppies and other claimants alike, and especially if the higher echelons of a hierarchical education system have increased their sense of personal self-worth, will tend towards the one-sided view of the world they inhabit that is liberalism.

Such a tendency is, of course, transformed by experience. For the individuals who engage in the collective struggles of, say, anti-roads protests, there is the possibility of moving beyond liberalism towards a critique of capitalism. To the extent that such activities remain the domain of dedicated 'cross-class' minorities, however, it is more likely that a liberal viewpoint will be retained in the modified form of militant liberalism – that is, an approach which takes collective action against the state but which still fails to understand the state in class terms.

On the other hand, no such modification can be expected through the world of DiY culture. The collective experience of the rave, simultaneous movement to a pre-determined rhythm with spontaneous outbreaks of cheering or mass hugging, offers the illusion of unity but, once the E has worn off, leaves the individual little closer than before to becoming a social individual with meaningful bonds. The experience of defending a rave against the police, on the other hand, does lend itself to the development of proletarian subjectivity;[21] but our 'fluffy friends' do not seem to have involved themselves with this most positive aspect of the rave scene, preferring the 'positive vibes' of versions of paganism, Sufism, Taoism or some other mysticism.

The failure to recognise the need to overcome the atomisation of individuals through collective struggles in which they can become social individuals becomes not a failure but a virtue in the world of DiY. As a result, the liberalism of the fluffy is far worse than that of any of its predecessors.[22]

Fluffy ideologues attempted to police both the reality and the image of the anti-CJB campaign, but certainly didn't have it all their own way. On the final demo against the CJB, in October 1994, conflict between crowd and police generalised such that hundreds if not thousands who came to the demo with fluffy intentions found themselves rioting – or at least cheering the rioters on. For hours people held the park, despite the best efforts of the cops, who were hilariously pelted with missiles at each one of their ineffective charges. Those in the crowd had time to look around and reflect, identifying friends and familiar faces beneath hoods and masks; and it became clear that this crowd was demonstrating that the contradiction between a class position and liberalism was not simply one of different people – 'militants' and 'liberals' – with different ideas. It was also one of proletarians who had reflected their relative atomisation in their liberal arguments now reflecting the extent to which it had been overcome in the collective activity of rioting: bourgeois ideology and the active negation of bourgeois society as dialectical opposites within the same individual subjectivity.

Reclaim or retreat?

The anti-roads movement came together over the No M11 campaign. Events at Wanstead and in Claremont Road were treated as a *national* focus for struggle. Even those who hated being in the city and professed to care more about trees than about houses defended the buildings of Claremont Road; and people who were concerned essentially about the 'political' aspects of the road (lack of consultation, destruction of a 'community') defended green spaces on the route as a necessary part of the campaign.

To some degree, the different tendencies that came together in a practical unity at the M11 have now come apart. Despite the overlap in personnel, and the range of positions within each campaign, such struggles as the Reclaim the Streets (RTS) campaign in London and the recent campaign against the A30 in Devon display certain crucial differences overall.

Reclaim the Streets events have taken place in many towns around the country, but the London street parties have undoubtedly been the largest and most subversive. Certainly, this is the view of the police, who felt that the ante was upped at the street party in July 1996 when a pneumatic drill was used to dig up the M41 and plant trees. What is even more worrying for those in authority, London RTS has made conscious and practical links with other struggles not previously regarded as connected to the anti-roads movement. Reclaim the Streets wanted to attack not just road-building but the way of life associated with it; RTS activists located this way of life as part of capital. They therefore came to support workplace struggles against capital, such as the strikes by the signal

workers and tube drivers – as evidenced by the banner on the 1995
street party in Islington and the RTS-related Critical Mass 'picket'
of London Transport in August 1996. The latest development is
the link RTS has made with sacked Liverpool dock-workers. Many
were heartened by travelling troublemakers from RTS boosting the
dock-workers' presence in a mass picket-cum-occupation in September 1996.[23] This was followed by the 'Social Justice' demo,
called by supporters of the sacked dockers, which was organised to
coincide with one of the street parties, in the hope, again, that one
of London's main arteries would be disrupted.[24]

The tactic of tunnelling as opposed to mere barricading to hold
up evictions on anti-road camps was first used at Claremont Road
but reached a wholly new level of ingenuity and dedication at the
A30 protest. In the demands tunnelling makes on activists, and in
the effectiveness of such tactics in delaying the eviction and the
smooth functioning of capital and the transport infrastructure, the
A30 struggle was undoubtedly radically anti-capitalist *in its effects*.
But whereas a significant tendency in RTS has pursued the trajectory of anti-capitalist *consciousness* which burgeoned at the No M11
campaign, the A30 campaign has seen the resurgence of some of
the worst features of liberal ideology that flourished at Twyford but
which were superseded to some degree at the No M11 campaign.
Where there has been a tendency for those involved in RTS to talk
of the state, capital and class, there was an equal tendency among
A30 activists to romanticise trees and to evoke mysticism.

The contrast between the two faces of the current anti-roads
movement is perhaps best illustrated by their respective reactions to
recent changes to the benefits system. Certainly, there were practical
imperatives at the A30 campaign operating to discourage people
from signing on – such as the distance of the camp from the dole
office. Yet there also seems to have been a tendency for the A30
campaign to attract the very people who need the dole yet don't
(wish to) recognise their own dependence on – and hence antagonistic relation with – the state as a social force. This was perfectly
encapsulated when two of the A30's media stars were challenged on
TV about their eligibility for the dole. The recent changes to the
dole, in the form of the Job Seeker's Allowance (JSA), make more
explicit the duty of the claimant to be 'actively seeking work'. When
the interviewer pointed out, rightly, that by spending all day down

tunnels they were not seeking work, they proudly responded that they didn't need to sign on because they were very resourceful. Even if it were the case that most people at the camp were not signing on (which we doubt), their response was a terrible cop-out; it accepts rather than challenges the logic of work-based rights and duties institutionalised by the JSA, and it implies that there are viable individual solutions to the problem of the new, harsher benefits regime. The JSA is essentially an attack on the whole working class, intended by its Tory makers to bully claimants to accept low-paid jobs (on pain of losing all their benefits) and to force them to compete with those already in work, thereby driving everyone's wages down.[25] Individual 'solutions' to this are no solution at all: are we all supposed to sell beads at festivals or go busking? Assuming that we've all got the talent to make beads and busk or whatever, such activities would soon parallel the official labour market they seek to avoid, as the drop-out entrepreneurs fight to compete.

By contrast, more of those involved in RTS have been ready to recognise the dole as the 'activist's grant'. As right-wing commentators correctly deplore, direct action campaigns against roads have benefited from a population of activists on the dole, on site and available for struggle twenty-four hours a day: you can't defend a tree, tunnel or squatted house if you have to go out every day to work to get your means of subsistence. The JSA and related measures represent an attack on that grant and hence on an activist 'career'. More RTS activists have therefore been more ready to recognise the necessity of defending the activist grant through collective action against the state.

However, it has to be said that neither RTS nor any other anti-roads campaign has made the JSA a central focus. A vital opportunity has therefore been missed to forge a practical, everyday unity in antagonism to capital, not only between the different aspects of the anti-roads movement but between the movement and the rest of the working class as a whole. In the absence of such a practical unity, fragmentation predominates.

The anti-roads movement served to smash what the then government boasted was 'the biggest road-building programme since the Romans'. By causing disruption and disorder, refusal and resistance, campaigns of direct action against road-building rendered roads a political, and deeply controversial, issue. In the face of

wider economic pressures, it then became easier for the government to make cuts in this area: the legitimacy and inevitability of
endless road-building was no longer assured. The national roads
programme is now dead, therefore, but the future of the dole is
not yet settled. While there are still people keen to fight and so
much to struggle over, there remains the possibility of overcoming
the present fragmentation and reclaiming our class unity in practice and hence perhaps in theory.

Postscript

> In the beginning was the deed.
> Slogan of the revolutionaries taking to the streets of
> Germany in November 1918

In the name of the working class, social democracy drowned the
German revolution in blood. In the name of proletarian revolution,
Stalinism crushed the May Days in Spain. Direct action, self-activity,
autonomy: features of the class struggle that always posed a threat
to the left's representation of the working class; tendencies that it
has had to crush or discredit whether they appeared in Berlin
(1918), Barcelona (1937), Budapest (1956) or Brixton (1981).

By successfully imposing its definition of class on the graves of
revolutionaries, social democracy and Stalinism spawned the 'counterculture' and 'new social movements' – the struggles of those
who didn't conform. The left asserted the primacy of class; those
who felt that they didn't fit in with the left's definition asserted the
specificity of their own needs. But the left's definition went
unchallenged. Thus those who did not wish to reject the question
of class entirely merely appropriated it as a category of oppression
– that afflicting the manual worker – alongside those afflicting
women, blacks, gays, animals or the environment, an eclectic
approach forever implying fragmentation and the impossibility of
real unity.

The counter-revolution of 'neo-liberalism' and the fall of the
Berlin Wall have significantly altered the parameters of our
struggles, however. Stalinism is dead and social democracy is in
retreat. The way is open for a redefinition of class politics that can

embrace what the left suppressed and allow the ghosts of past revolutions to guide us from our nightmarish slumbers. But the forces which have seen off the left have also fragmented our class. With the working class defeated and divided, recent struggles, particularly those referred to in this book, have attempted to develop class consciousness.

Our contribution to this book is a contribution towards that process of developing class consciousness, to be read by those who have engaged in these struggles and who seek to go beyond their limits. As such it may sit uneasily alongside some of the other articles. This is because the very category around which this book is compiled – DiY Culture – serves to obscure the connections and possibilities which our actions anticipate.[26] Culture is the hook with which journalists and academics are trying to recuperate our struggles.[27] There is a world of difference between attempts, whatever their limitations, of people involved in struggle to reflect on it, to theorise their practice, and the efforts of academics and journalists to write about such movements. Whether hostile or sympathetic, as expressions of the fundamental division of labour in capitalist society – that between mental and manual labour – these specialists in writing and in ideas are forcing a praxis that is escaping this division back into it. For those of us engaged in the collective project of getting out of this world and into the one we all feel and know is possible, a critique of the category of DiY Culture and the recuperative project which lies behind it is becoming imperative.

5

The art of necessity: the subversive imagination of anti-road protest and Reclaim the Streets

JOHN JORDAN

> The new artist protests, he no longer paints; he creates
> directly . . . life and art make One.
>
> Tristan Tzara, Dada manifesto 1919

Since the beginning of this century, avant-garde agitational artists[1] have tried to demolish the divisions between art and life[2] and introduce creativity, imagination, play and pleasure into the revolutionary project. My argument is that the DiY protest movement has taken these 'utopian' demands and made them real, given them a 'place'. Inspired by and following in the footsteps of the protest movements and countercultures of the sixties, seventies and eighties, the DiY protest movement is finally breaking down the barriers between art and protest. It seems that at the close of this century new forms of creative and poetic resistance have finally found their time.

With the ecological crisis leading to what some have called a 'biological meltdown'[3] and a social crisis that is demolishing what little local democracy or equality that exists, it seems that only radically creative and *passionate* strategies that bring into question every aspect of our industrial society will avert catastrophe. Ecological issues have been looked at predominantly through a scientific frame, a frame whose language tends towards the objective and arcane. DiY protest is lending poetry to this language and impassioned engagement to the science. Unlike previous eras, where there was a sense that social change would arrive eventually as a natural historical process, things are now very different. Many predictions suggest that at some time around the year 2040 the planet's ecosystems will have lost any ability to renew themselves; this leaves us a few decades to turn things around. It is increasingly clear that there is no time to be dispassionate, that there can be no limits to the subversive imagination.

I could have chosen any of the inspirational campaigns and actions of the nineties to illustrate my thesis: the breath-taking tunnels at Manchester Airport, the extraordinary Trolhiem fort at the A30 in Devon or the monumental tree house villages at the Newbury bypass, to name but a few. The reason I am concentrating on the No M11 Link Road campaign in London and Reclaim the Streets is because of my personal involvement with them. I don't pretend to be objective; in fact the whole gist of my argument is against the notion of objectivity and calls for a society where the personal and the political, the passionate and the pragmatic, art and everyday life, become one.

Separating art from politics and everyday life is a relatively recent historical phenomenon and one that has been very much located in societies that have taken on western cultural values – the same cultural values that are at the centre of the global ecological and social problems. American Earth First! activist, film maker and medievalist Christopher Manes believes that

> the biological meltdown is most directly the result of values funda-
> mental to what we have come to recognize as culture under the
> regime of technological society: economic growth, 'progress', prop-
> erty rights, consumerism, religious doctrines about humanity's domin-
> ion over nature, technocratic notions about achieving an optimum
> human existence at the expense of all other life-forms.[4]

If the problem is one of values – a cultural problem – it therefore requires a cultural response. It is not simply a question of science but also one of art, the process of value finding and aesthetics. Interestingly enough, the Latin root of the word aesthetics – *aesthesis* – means *noticing* the world. It's not difficult to notice the state of this world, yet so many artists immured in their enclosures of studio, gallery, theatre or museum seem blind to it. Those who attempt to push the boundaries of the revolutionary project are rapidly recuperated, neutralised, their political ideas forgotten, their work turned into commodities. Even those with the most revolutionary cultural agendas – the Dadaists, Surrealists and even the Situationists – have become impotent figures in an apolitical art history; all three movements' radical political dreams were destroyed because they still clung on, if half-heartedly, to the question of *art*: its arguments over definitions, its non-participatory relationship with audience and many of its traditional contexts.

Art has clearly failed historically as a means to bring imagination and creativity to movements of social change.[5] Present political conditions require a shift away from such a category; indeed a movement away from all categories, be they art, politics or science. What makes DiY protest powerful is that it 'clearly embodies a rejection of the specialised sphere of old politics, as well as of art and everyday life'.[6] Its insistence on creativity and yet the invisibility of art or artists in its midst, singles it out as a historical turning point in the current of creative resistance. By making the art completely invisible, DiY protest gives art back its original socially transformative power; as Dubuffet said: 'Art . . . loves to be incognito. Its best moments are when it forgets what it is called.'[7]

The poetics of direct action against the M11 Link Road

Poetry is an act which engenders new realities: it is the fulfilment of radical theory, the revolutionary act *par excellence.*

Raoul Vaneigem, *The Revolution of Everyday Life*[8]

The M11 Link Road will stretch from Wanstead to Hackney in east London. To build it the Department of Transport had to knock down 350 houses, displace several thousand people, cut through one of London's last ancient woodlands and devastate a community with a six-lane-wide stretch of tarmac – at a cost of £240 million, apparently to save six minutes on a car journey. It has now been officially admitted that when it opens it will already be full to capacity. Which suggests the need for another road.

For over thirty years the M11 Link Road had been opposed by conventional political means – demonstrations, planning inquiries, lobbying and petitions. Despite the dedication of local residents the bulldozers arrived in the autumn of 1993. So it was time to develop new creative political methods, using direct action, performance art, sculpture and installation and armed with faxes, modems, computers and video cameras. A new breed of 'artist activist' emerged whose motto could well have been creativity, courage and cheek.[9] Their art was not to be about representation but presence; their politics was not about deferring social change to the future but about change now, about immediacy, intuition and imagination. Within the imagination of such activism 'anything is possible': you can give an old chestnut tree a letter box and an address and make legal history by transforming it into the first tree dwelling to be recognised by the courts, thus conferring squatters' rights on its inhabitants;[10] or you can climb on to the roof of the Houses of Parliament to make a statement about the Criminal Justice Bill,[11] and get on to the front pages of every national newspaper.

Theatre director and performance theorist Richard Schechner defines performance as 'behaviour heightened, if ever so slightly, and publicly displayed; twice-behaved behaviour'.[12] The No M11 campaign was a non-stop performance. Nearly every day, we were invading work-sites and using our bodies in direct action, as tools of resistance against the cold steel of pile-drivers, cranes and bulldozers; often these acts were accompanied by the sound of drums, penny whistles and singing.

Unlike the courageous yet futile aesthetic gestures of so many performance artists who have used their bodies in acts of endurance and danger – Chris Burden nailed to a car, Linda Montana handcuffed to her lover for three days, Stelarc hanging from a crane by hooks embedded in his skin – direct action is performance where the poetic and the pragmatic join hands. The sight of a fragile figure silhouetted against a blue sky, perched dangerously high on a crane that has to stop work for the day, is both beautiful and functional. Direct action is by nature deeply theatrical and fundamentally political. The performance of climbing a crane on a building site has many different functions – pragmatism, representation, theatricality and ritual coalesce in direct action.

The pragmatic political function is that it stops work on the road and holds up the contractors. This can cost vast amounts of money; it's rumoured that a whole day of work stopped on one of the

ANTI-ROAD PROTEST AND RECLAIM THE STREETS

major sites can cost in the region of £50,000. The extra security
needed to keep activists off the machinery adds to this cost, as does
the policing bill. All of this leads to delays and hits the road-
builders where it hurts, that is, in their pockets. Its representational
function is that these acts provide powerful news images, images
that have enormous audiences and can bring the issues to public
consciousness. Its theatrical function is that it is enacted in front of
an audience, not only the media, but for local passers-by, who are
often awestruck by what they see and are thus brought into dialogue
about the issues. Its ritual function is that the inherent risk,
excitement and danger of the action creates a magically focused
moment, a peak experience, where real time suddenly stands still
and a certain shift in consciousness can occur. Many of us have felt
incredibly empowered and have had our lives fundamentally radicalised and transformed by these feelings. Direct action is praxis,
catharsis and image rolled into one.

Direct action introduces the concept of play into the straight,
predictably grey world of politics. People being chased by a bunch
of uncoordinated security guards through thigh-deep mud on a
construction site; figures jumping on to the machinery, laughing,
blowing kisses to the digger drivers and D-locking[13] their neck to
the digger arm; driving the security off a piece of land, re-squatting
it, climbing to the top of a tree and singing at the top of your voice.
It's all fundamentally playful, a fantastic game: a game of cat and
mouse, or, rather, David and Goliath.

Anthropologist Victor Turner wrote that

> Most definitions of play involve notions of disengagement, of free-
> wheeling, of being out of mesh with the serious 'bread-and-butter',
> let alone 'life-and-death' processes of production, social control,
> 'getting and spending', and raising the next generation. ... Play can
> be everywhere and nowhere, imitate anything, yet be identified with
> nothing. ... Yet although 'spinning loose' as it were, the wheel of
> play reveals to us the possibility of changing our goals and, therefore,
> the restructuring of what our culture states to be reality.[14]

The playfulness of direct action proposes an alternative reality but
it also makes play real; it takes it out of western frameworks of
childhood or make-believe – and throws it in the face of politicians

and policy makers. The state never knows where this type of playing ends or begins; it seeps from construction site into the television screen, from the company director's office to the roof of the Transport Minister's house. Its unsteadiness, slipperiness, porosity and riskiness erode the authority of those in power.

To engage in direct action you have to feel enough passion to put your values into practice; it is literally embodying your feelings, performing your politics. The body has been marginalised by our technocratic culture. This is dangerous: it further reveals a society completely out of touch with itself and its environment; a society which prefers to use the metaphor of the machine – hard, unconnected parts – rather than the body – interconnected, fluid and soft. Direct action makes visible the devastation of industrial culture's machinery and returns the body to the centre of politics, of cultural practice.

Direct action on the construction sites of the M11 put the vulnerable body of 'nature' and the powerful machinery of 'civilis-ation' together in conflict. Placing your body directly in the cogs of the machine, as a point of resistance in the flow of power, transforms your own body and forces industrial society to explain itself, to justify its actions.

But direct action is not just about theatrical expressions of high energy. During any typical action on the M11, there were many moments of calm. Often after site invasions when work had been stopped dialogue would occur between activists and people work-ing on the site, issues would be discussed, feelings shared. At the same time as these face-to-face exchanges occurred, distant com-munication was taking place as politicians and others with vested interests in the road viewed the images of direct action on their TV screens – images which influence and affect their agendas. Direct action thus merges the intimate personal body of dialogue and the aggressive social body of action.

Many non-industrial societies use their bodies in ritual perform-ances as symbolic analogues for thinking about personal and social issues. Direct action highlights the body's ability to signify both self and society. Direct action takes the alienated, lonely body of tech-nocratic culture and transforms it into a connected, communicative body embedded in society. Taking part in direct action is a radical poetic gesture by which we can achieve meaningful change, both personal and social. Direct action is the central strategy of creative resistance, a strategy that, unlike the rationality and objectivity of most politics, revokes the emphasis on words and reason and demands the acknowledgement of intuition and imagination.

Space invaders: the transformation of Claremont Road

> Are we who live in the present doomed to never experience autonomy, never stand for one moment on a bit of land ruled only by freedom?
>
> Hakim Bey, *TAZ*[15]

If the direct action on building sites was a transformation of the personal and social body, the mutation of Claremont Road into a phenomenally imaginative theatre of creative resistance[16] was a transformation of personal and social space.

Claremont Road was a street of thirty-five terraced houses, directly in the path of the link road. Resisting the bulldozers with the campaigners on this street was 92-year-old Dolly, who had lived there for her entire life. Leaving Claremont Road was inconceivable to Dolly. In defiance of the Department of Transport she remained there till the final minute.[17] In Claremont Road every house apart from Dolly's was taken over by the campaign. One of the first acts of resistance was to close the road off to traffic and open it up to the art of living. In a superb act of *détournement*,[18] the road – normally a space dominated by the motor car, a space for passing not living, a dead duct between *a* and *b* – was reclaimed and turned into a vibrant space in which to live, eat, talk and sleep.

Furniture was moved out of the houses into the road, laundry was hung up to dry, chess games were played on a giant painted chess board, snooker tables were installed, fires were lit, a stage was built and parties were held. The 'road' had been turned into a 'street', a street like none other, a street which provided a rare glimpse of utopia, a kind of temporary microcosm of a truly liberated, ecological culture.[19]

Some of the most aesthetic aspects of Claremont Road were the barricades, built to resist eviction by the Department of Transport.

Sunk into the tarmac, large swirls of sculptural steel cabling were juxtaposed with the carcasses of transformed cars. One with 'RUST IN PEACE' meticulously painted on its side had grass growing all over it; another was turned into a zebra crossing by being painted black and white, cut in half, each half being placed on the kerbstone with a crossing painted between them. These were not just ephemeral monuments to the end of car culture but also beautiful and effective barricades.

Many of the barricades inside the houses echoed conceptual artists' installations of the past. Yet these creative constructions were not just site-specific sculptures which resonated with and reflected the architectural structures of the houses, they were creative social transformations, imagination rigorously applied to real situations, art embedded into everyday life. These houses were not only frames for art, they were homes, real places which could have been renovated and rehoused some of the thousands of homeless young people who end up on London's streets every year.

The 1970s saw artists like Gordon Matta Clarke cut a hole through the side of a house and Walter de la Maria fill a whole room with earth. More recently Turner Prize-winner Rachel Whiteread cast in concrete an abandoned terrace house, due for demolition in nearby Hackney. In Claremont Road a hole was cut in the connecting walls of the row of thirty-five houses to create a stunning tunnel that linked several homes: a strategy to evade the bailiffs, but also a metaphor for communal living; an intervention that cuts through the isolation of individual domestic units. In some houses rooms were filled with earth, often lit by the eerie brightness of a single hanging light bulb. These earth-filled rooms disguised entrances to bunkers which held activists during the eviction. Not knowing the whereabouts of the bunkers, the bailiffs when they arrived would be forced to search with shovels, instead of tearing through the houses with a bulldozer: a much more time-consuming activity, and, at £20,000 per hour for an eviction, expensive! Other houses were packed not with concrete but with rubbish, the detritus of urban decay: washing machines, old mattresses, broken furniture and, most symbolically, old tyres;[20] yet more ingenious engineerings of the imagination to slow down the eviction.

These barricades were accompanied by slogans hastily daubed in bright paint and colourful murals: horses galloping, a daisy chain across the front of every house, a large spoof billboard proclaiming 'WELCOME TO CLAREMONT ROAD – IDEAL HOMES'. Hanging from the defended trees were shop dummies, ribbons, old televisions – a fusion of found objects each hung purposefully as symbolic statement and obstacle for the tree surgeons. A whole house was turned into 'the art house' and more traditional 'artists' filled every nook and cranny with representative images that critiqued car culture.[21] Two cafés were opened up and in the middle of the terrace a stark banner asked passers-by to: 'IMAGINE THIS PLACE, AS A HOME, A WOOD OR THE M11 LINK ROAD.'

A final symbol of contempt for the DoT's plans to evict Claremont was the extraordinary 100-foot scaffolding tower[22] nicknamed Dolly, which broke through the roof of one of the houses. Made from hundreds of 'found' lengths of scaffolding, joined together in a complex and chaotic lattice-work and looking like a cross between Tatlin's monument to the Third International and a NASA launch pad, the tower could be seen from miles away. For its short life Dolly became a local landmark which competed with the Babylon blandness of Canary Wharf on the horizon. This insane piece of crazed, brightly painted and greased scaffolding not only provided the most effective defence against the bailiffs, but also became the most powerful image for the final showdown.

For four cold days in November 1994 Claremont Road and the quarter of a mile of sealed-off streets became the site for a final operatic battle. To the sounds of rave music[23] blasting from the top of the tower, 1300 riot policemen and bailiffs trooped in and out of the area as if in a fine choreographed routine. Activists were hanging in nets suspended across the road, locked into the tarmac and on to chimney pots, sitting on the roofs, buried in the bunkers and welded into a cage at the top of the tower. Enormous 'cherrypickers' completely surrounded by dozens of security guards moved their aerial platforms through the air like mechanical dinosaurs attempting to extract the wriggling activists from their stupendous backdrop. At night bright arc lights illuminated the enclave and an eerie silence fell. Suddenly the place felt like the film set of an apocalyptic movie. Every now and then a firework would shoot out of the tower, and a chorus of 'Power to the tower!' would ascend from the street below.

This was theatre like you'd never seen it; theatre on a scale that

'Dolly', the scaffolding tower, and an activist relaxing in the nets above Claremont Road. Photograph by Gideon Mendell

would not fit in any opera house. It was a spectacle that cost the government over £2 million to enact; a spectacle in which we were in control, for which we had set the stage, provided the actors and invited the state to be in our play; to play our game. Eighty-eight hours later the last person left was plucked off the tower; all that was left to do was destroy the street and with it not only a hundred years of local history but also an extraordinary site of creative resistance.

No sign, relic or trace of Claremont Road remains. We always knew that one day all this would be rubble, and this awareness of impermanence gave us immense strength – the impossibility of failure – the strength to move this Temporary Autonomous Zone on to somewhere else. Our festival of resistance could never be evicted. We would continue to transgress the distinction between art and everyday life. We would continue to make every political act a moment of poetry. If we could no longer reclaim Claremont Road, we would reclaim the streets of London.[24]

Reclaiming the streets from E11 to WC1

> If you want to change the city – you have to control the streets.
> Reclaim the Streets, poster for first street party, May 1995

Claremont Road had provided us with a taste of a free society. Tasting such fruit is dangerous, because it leaves a craving to repeat the exhilarating experience. Within three months we re-formed the group Reclaim the Streets[25] and began planning the first street party.

The idea of the street party was to take over major roads in London and transform them into ephemeral festivals of resistance. The street party itself was a form 'reclaimed from the inanities of royal jubilees and state "celebrations"'.[26] Turning to proactive, instead of defensive, direct action enabled us to expand our remit into a wider cultural critique. Activist Paul Morozzo from Reclaim the Streets and the M11 campaign clarifies this expansion:

> We are basically about taking back public space from the enclosed private arena. At its simplest it is an attack on cars as a principal agent

of enclosure. It's about reclaiming the streets as public inclusive space from the private exclusive use of the car. But we believe in this as a broader principle, taking back those things which have been enclosed within capitalist circulation and returning them to collective use as a commons.[27]

The M11 campaign had already placed the anti-road and ecological arguments of Twyford Down in an urban, social context. This merging of social and ecological principles into a wider cultural critique was to become key in Reclaim the Streets' later alliances with striking public transport and dock workers.[28] For Reclaim the Streets, just getting rid of cars from the streets was not enough. Activist Del Bailie explains:

Won't the streets be better without cars? Not if all that replaces them are aisles of pedestrianised consumption or shopping 'villages' safely protected from the elements. To be against the car for its own sake is inane; claiming one piece as the whole jigsaw. The struggle for car-free space must not be separated from the struggle against global capitalism for in truth the former is encapsulated in the latter. The streets are as full of capitalism as of cars and the pollution of capitalism is much more insidious.[29]

The first stages of uprisings have often been theatrical and carnivalesque, 'a revelatory and sensuous explosion outside the "normal pattern of politics"'.[30] The street party would become a revolutionary carnival in the spirit of

great moments of revolutionary history, the enormous popular festivals of the Bastille, the Paris Commune, Paris '68. From the middle ages onwards the carnival has offered glimpses of the world turned upside down, a topsy turvy universe free of toil, suffering and inequality. Carnival celebrates temporary liberation from the prevailing truth and the established order; it marks the suspension of all hierarchical rank, privileges, norms and prohibitions.[31]

Raoul Vaneigem wrote that 'revolutionary moments are carnivals in which the individual life celebrates its unification with a regenerated society'. But the Street Party can be read as a situ-esque reversal of this assertion; as an attempt to make Carnival *the* revolutionary moment. Placing 'what could be' in the path of 'what is' and celebrating the 'here and now' in the road of the rush for 'there and later', it hopes to re-energise the possibility of radical change. . . . It is an expansive desire; for freedom, for creativity; to truly live.[32]

Imagine a busy high street, Saturday afternoon. Shoppers mingle on the thin strip of pavement that separates the shops from the busy road. Suddenly two cars career into each other and block the road: the drivers get out and begin to argue. One of the drivers brandishes a hammer and starts to smash up the other driver's car. Passers-by are astonished; time stands still. Then people surge out of the anonymous shopping crowd and start to jump on top of the cars, multicoloured paint is thrown everywhere. An enormous banner is unfurled from the roofs of the two destroyed vehicles – 'RECLAIM THE STREETS – FREE THE CITY / KILL THE CAR,' it proclaims. Five hundred people are now surging out of the tube station and take over the street. As the Surrealists might have said, everyday life has been penetrated by the marvellous.

Thus began street party number 1, in Camden High Street in May 1995. All afternoon 500 people danced to the sound of the mobile bicycle-powered Rinky-Dink sound system. Free food was served up from long trestle-tables that stretched down the middle of the road and children played on a climbing frame placed in the middle of a now liberated crossroad junction. As evening fell and people drifted off, riot police moved in and tried to reassert their authority, having spent the entire day without it!

Once again we were introducing play into politics, challenging official culture's claims to authority, stability, sobriety, immutability and immortality by cheekily taking over a main traffic artery. The road became a stage for a participatory ritual theatre: ritual because it is efficacious, it produces real effects by means of symbolic causes; participatory because the street party has no division between performer and audience, it is created by and for everyone, it avoids all mediation, it is experienced in the immediate moment by all, in a spirit of face-to-face subversive comradeship. The street party when it is in full swing – when thousands of people have reclaimed a major road and declared it a 'street now open'; when music,

laughter and song have replaced the roar of engines; when road
rage becomes road rave, and tarmac grey is smothered by the living
colour of a festival[33] – fulfils Lautréamont's desire that 'Poetry must
be made by all. Not by one.'[34]

Two months later and the street party reappeared,[35] this time
with 3000 people dancing to two sound systems in the middle of
Upper Street, Islington.

Imagine: it's a hot summer's day, four lanes of traffic move
sluggishly through the grey stinking city haze, an airhorn pierces
the drone of cars. Suddenly several groups of people appear running out from side streets carrying 20-foot-long scaffolding poles.
In a perfectly choreographed acrobatic drill, the scaffolding poles are
erected bang in the middle of the road in the form of tripods[36] and
people climb to the top, balancing gracefully 20 feet above the
tarmac. The road is now blocked to traffic but open to pedestrians.
Then that spine-tingling peak experience occurs. Drifting accross
this extraordinary scene is Louis Armstrong's voice singing 'What a
Wonderful World' – this wondrous sound is coming from an
armoured personnel carrier which is now standing in the car-free
street. Within minutes thousands of people have filled the road.
Huge colourful banners are stretched from lampposts; some are in
support of the striking London Underground workers, others just
say 'BREATHE' or 'STREET NOW OPEN'; one that simply says 'CAR
FREE' is made of numerous strips which stretch down to the tarmac,
like tendrils, creating a soft fabric curtain across the road. During
the party these tendrils are tied together to create huge bouncing
swings for people to play on. Soon the street is a riot of colour; a
band turns a bus stop into a stage and plays folk music; people
dance; a choir sings; and a ton of sand is poured on to the tarmac,
turning it into an instant beach for children.[37]

Official festivals, displays and entertainments[38] are arranged in
neat rectangles and straight lines: trooping the colour or a traditional march, for example. The street party, however, is vortexed,
whirling; people dance on anything, climb lampposts, move in
every direction: an uncontrollable state of creative chaos. The
street party breaks a cultural obsession with linearity, order and
tidiness, epitomised by roads and cars; as a flyer for the Upper
Street party declared 'CARS CANNOT DANCE: When they move they
are violent and brutish, they lack sensitivity and rhythm. CARS

CANNOT PLAY: When they diverge from the straight and narrow, they kill. CARS CANNOT SOCIALISE: They privatise, separate, isolate and alienate.' Schechner writes that

> to allow people to assemble in the streets is always to flirt with the possibility of improvisation – and the unexpected might happen.... Official culture wants its festivals to be entertaining and ordered. When entertainment is really free, when it gets out of hand, when there is no fixed calendrical conclusion to the celebration, then the authorities get nervous. Such festivals reverberate through the population in unforeseen ways.[39]

Later that evening the authorities did get nervous. Riot police appeared on the scene, and this time they closed off both ends of the road, closed down the tube station and aggressively pushed people down side streets. When asked why they had sealed off all exits a policeman replied, 'Because we want people to disperse.'[40] And people did, but not in the way the state expected; by the time London Reclaim the Streets threw its third party in July 1996, nine more street parties had taken place across the country, each one different, each one rooted in its locality and transforming the traffic-filled space into pleasure-filled place. All over the country people were enjoying taking to the streets and celebrating life's fertile possibilities.

The street party had caught on, and the next one in London would be difficult to organise due to increased police surveillance. For the few days running up to the party activists were constantly followed and the Reclaim the Streets office was closely monitored from a house opposite. When the day came on Saturday 13 July 1996, and we saw thousands of people arriving at the meeting point, we just prayed that the location had not been found out by the police. Ten west-bound Central Line tube trains filled with people sped off into the unknown, and we waited with baited breath.

Imagine: thousands of people emerge from Shepherd's Bush tube station, no-one knows where they are going – the mystery and excitement of it all is electrifying. Shepherd's Bush Green comes to a standstill as people pour on to it; up ahead a line of police has already sealed off the roundabout and blocked the way. A man takes off all his clothes and starts to dance on the roof of a stationary car. The crowd knows this is not the place: where is the sound system, the tripods? Then, as if by some miracle of collective telepathy, everyone turns back and disappears around the corner; a winding journey through backstreets, under railway bridges and then up over a barrier and suddenly they are on an enormous motorway and right *behind* the police lines. People run into the fast lane yelping with joy; up ahead they can see the sound system and tripods surrounded by police. The police line at the end of the motorway is completely confused; they turn around and start to chase after everyone. Their line, their order and control, has been broken. For a few interminable seconds it looks like the thin line between festival and riot is about to be transgressed – but thousands of people are now pouring on to the six lanes of baking hot tarmac, hundreds of white frisbees start to fly in the air. The police try to regroup but everyone is just breaking through their attempts at blocking the way. The ecstatic crowd gravitates towards the truck carrying the sound system which is parked on the hard shoulder. People start banging on the side of the police van guarding it. The truck is now swarming with people. The police van decides it has lost control of the situation and starts to drive off; as it does so the sides of the truck are lifted and the gut-shaking thump of techno blasts out of the sound system. The crowd roars – we've liberated a motorway through sheer numbers, through people power!

Until early the next morning the M41, Britain's shortest stretch of motorway, played host to the largest festival of resistance yet. Ten thousand people danced, chat, ate, met friends and made new ones. The hard shoulder was taken over by stalls and a café, the central reservation became a picnic site and a stage for fire jugglers and performers, and the fast lane another children's sandpit. Stretching across the six lanes were huge, vivid banners: a giant yellow sun, a burst of Matisse-inspired 10-foot-high flowers, 'SUPPORT THE TUBE WORKERS', 'DESTROY POWER' and the Situationists' 'THE SOCIETY THAT ABOLISHES EVERY ADVENTURE MAKES ITS OWN ABOLITION THE ONLY POSSIBLE ADVENTURE.' The unbounded creativity was so catching that even a scrap-metal yard that overlooked the motorway decided to hang up a wrecked van using its crane, a creative gesture to join in the carnivalesque spirit of fun, irony and subversion.

The M41 festival of resistance, July 1996. Photograph by Julia Guest

Some of the most striking images were the two huge carnival figures, 30 feet high with 10-feet-wide hooped skirts, with bagpipe players wearing Restoration wigs installed at the top of them. These seemingly innocent figures were wheeled up and down the motorway all day and night, but hidden under the skirts, away from the eyes of the police, and drowned out by the sound of techno, people were busy drilling into the tarmac with Kanga hammers and planting saplings rescued from the path of the M11 link road, which was still in the process of being built.[41] The next morning, finding tarmac pock-marked with freshly planted saplings, the Highways Agency was forced to close the motorway for several days and resurface it.

Schechner writes that 'the difference between temporary and permanent change distinguishes carnival from revolution',[42] yet in this act of insurrectionary imagination carnival became revolution, real trees were planted, real transformations occurred. Real people, in a real space, in real time (that is, not framed by a calendrical festive date), underwent real change as they developed a new sense of confidence and an awareness of their individual and collective power; for a rare moment they had experienced the breath of the possible touching them – they had transformed the world. They had had experiences that would remain with them permanently.

This street party was the perfect propaganda of the possible – it was a day full of those priceless moments where everything slips away and immense cracks appear in the façades of authority and power. Ten thousand people had enjoyed collectively committing the offence of obstructing the public highway, held an illegal party in contravention of the Criminal Justice Act and caused substantial creative criminal damage. To quote Abbie Hoffman, 'Revolution is anything you can get away with.'

Green and red make black

Who are these lunatics?
Specialist car magazine article about Reclaim the Streets

The M41 street party was to be a difficult act to follow. A few weeks later the Reclaim the Streets offices were raided, computers impounded and an arrest made for conspiracy to cause criminal damage, to a motorway.

Yet integration of social and ecological issues which began on the M11 was further developed after the M41. Following an action in support of the striking tube workers, one of the 500 sacked Liverpool dockers contacted us and asked us to help them in their campaign for reinstatement.[43] This provided us with a priceless opportunity to bring greens, socialists and anarchists together.

In Liverpool for three days in October 1996, hundreds of dockers, their families, DiY activists, environmentalists and trade unionists took part in a moving street party/carnival, a mass picket and the occupation and closing down of the port, where the Reclaim the Streets' black, red and green 'lightning bolt' flag made its first public appearance, as it fluttered defiantly from the roof-top of the occupied Merseyside Docks and Harbour Companies offices. Despite extreme over-reaction, intimidation, assaults and arrests by the police's Operational Support Division threateningly dressed in Darth Vader-like gear, the three days marked a historic meeting point of ecological and social action. It was a powerful confirmation that the 'separation and presentation of the ecological crisis as unconnected to other forms of exploitation only serves the interests of business and state, and needs to be overcome if society is to survive'.[44]

Things can only get better[45]

Don't be a cog in the machine – be a spanner in the works!
Never Mind the Ballots poster, March 1997

As general election media mania was hitting fever pitch in March 1997, posters showing an image of Charlie Chaplin lying on an enormous cog, spanner in hand (a scene from the film *Modern Times*), and proclaiming 'NEVER MIND THE BALLOTS,[46] RECLAIM THE STREETS' started to appear around London. Reclaim the Streets had linked up with the dockers, the Hillingdon hospital and Magnet strikers to create a special event that was to coincide with the March for Social Justice, which had been called for 12 April.

This march, three weeks before the general election on 1 May, was called to signify the need for radical social change.

For Reclaim the Streets this was a chance to highlight direct action as a positive, direct democratic strategy, an alternative to the disempowering ritual of making a cross on a piece of paper, and voting for someone you have never met to 'represent' you, every five years. As one of the flyers for the event put it, 'RTS believe that ... change will be brought about, not through the mediation of professional politicians, but by individual and collective participation in social affairs. In short – by direct action.'

The plan of action was as follows: rush hour Friday, the eve of the march, 10,000 copies of a spoof of the London newspaper the *Evening Standard*, entitled *Evading Standards*, with the headline 'GENERAL ELECTION CANCELLED', and with articles celebrating radical ecological and social alternatives to representative democracy, are handed out free to commuters. Saturday 1 p.m., Kennington Park, the march sets off towards Westminster; 10,000 more *Evading Standards* are handed to marchers. Lambeth Bridge, 2 p.m., fireworks are heard in the near distance, flares shoot into the air ahead of the crowd – following a mass of a hundred RTS flags, people break off from the designated route of the march and run down Horseferry Road. They turn a corner and there in front of

NEVER MIND THE BALLOTS...
RECLAIM THE STREETS!

'With the increasingly meaningless ritual of the general election drawing near and with the main political parties committed to 'more of the same' or 'tinkering with the details' at best, what can be done by those with a vision of a liberated, green society? 'Vote for the lesser evil?' Work for change 'inside the system?'

Reclaim The Streets believe there is another way: take direct action in the streets, in the fields and in the workplace, to halt the destruction and create a direct democracy in a free and ecological society.'

TWO DAY FESTIVAL
OF RESISTANCE!

STARTS SATURDAY 12TH APRIL
MEET 12 NOON
AT KENNINGTON PARK, LONDON
To coincide with The March For Social Justice
RECLAIM THE STREETS: 0171 281 4621

them is the Department of the Environment; hanging from one of its three colossal towers an enormous banner reads 'RECLAIM YOUR ENVIRONMENT'. The crowd rushes towards the tower, which is half-empty due to the relocation of the department the following year, the main doors fly open, people rush inside and occupy the building – the Department of the Environment has been squatted. A two-day festival of resistance is held – workshops take place, music is played, an Internet facility sends images of the event around the world, and Tree FM[47] sets up its pirate antenna on the roof and broadcasts from the 'REAL Department of Environment'. That was the plan!

On the eve of the event, minutes after the 20,000 copies of the spoof *Evening Standard* had been delivered to the central distribution point, the police swooped in, impounded every single copy and arrested three of us for 'incitement to cause affray and incitement to cause obstruction of the public highway'.[48] This was before they had even read the paper! During our interviews, which were held conveniently during the march so we could be kept off the streets, we were told that phrases such as 'direct action encompasses a whole range of activities, from organising co-ops to engaging in resistance to authority' were inciting people to affray; riot in other words. Two weeks later we managed to reprint the paper and distributed 20,000 to amused and confused commuters, without any police intervention.

On the Saturday 20,000 people met in the park and the march set off in celebratory spirit, but when it reached Lambeth Bridge row upon row of riot police made sure the march never deviated from its straight and narrow path. Plan B was set in action: a full-scale street party had to take place in Trafalgar Square instead.

As the march passed the gates of Downing Street, red smoke bombs were thrown and someone climbed up into an open window of the Foreign Office and appeared seconds later throwing hundreds of documents out on to the crowd below – an astounding filmic image, reminiscent of some archetypal revolutionary movie. Eventually the crowd reached Trafalgar Square, ringed by tooled-up riot police, and listened to the speeches of the Rally for Social Justice. At 3 p.m. the official rally began to disperse, but everyone knew that something was going to happen. Reclaim the Streets was determined to have its day.

Suddenly a commotion occurred at one of the entrances to the square. A truck carrying the sound system was steaming towards the police lines in an attempt to get into the square. The line gave way and the sound system was in; the crowd surrounded it and protected it as it made its way to its eventual position outside the National Gallery. Up went a banner proclaiming 'NEVER MIND THE BALLOTS, RECLAIM THE STREETS', accompanied by a massive cheer almost instantly drowned by a shuddering kick drum emanating from the sound system – the party could begin. What followed was a hybrid of party and riot: as police fought protesters with baton charges at one end of the square, others danced the afternoon away under the neo-classical columns of the National Gallery.

Reclaim the Streets saw the event as a bit of a failure, not the creative development of the street party form that we had hoped. Front-page headlines in the mainstream media saw the event as 'RIOT FRENZY – ANARCHIST THUGS BRING TERROR TO LONDON', or 'RALLYING CRY OF MOB ATTACK ON DOWNING STREET – DON'T VOTE, MAKE TROUBLE'.[49] The rave scene, meanwhile, saw it as 'the best illegal rave or dance music party in history',[50] and 'one of the most remarkable free parties since Castlemorton in 1992'.[51]

The Latin root of the term 'art' is *ars*, meaning to join, to fit, to put together. The 'Never Mind the Ballots' event certainly did this. It brought together dockers and ravers, environmentalists and trade unionists, anarchists and socialists. It joined the celebratory spirit of a party with the rebellious release of a riot. It juxtaposed the living, thumping beat of a sound system with the cold classicism of the National Gallery. And it placed two bits of graffiti on the wall of the National Gallery: 'FUCK THE ELECTION' and 'ART FOR ALL OR NONE AT ALL'.

This final street party left Reclaim the Streets dazed and confused, unsure of its next step. The summer of 1997 passed without a big London event and we are searching for a way to develop the idea of the street party, to root events more in community, to build on the budding international street party movement and to bring carnival and revolution one step closer together.

But outside London successful street parties are popping up all over the place – since the first Camden party in 1995 there have been thirty separate street parties. From Hull to Sheffield, from Oxford to Leeds, from Brighton to Manchester, from Amsterdam to Helsinki, from Freiburg to Sydney, the street party is applying radical poetry to radical politics. The party, which, unlike most political parties, does not encourage the endless deferral of the revolutionary moment, is spreading.

The subversive imaginations of the M11 campaign and Reclaim the Streets have suceeded in creating acts of resistance which are both powerful poetic gestures and effective political strategies. Art, politics and everyday life have merged into a fluid, shifting and surging spirit of imagination – an imagination which undermines the bland, linear development of corporate capitalist culture – a spirit which, as written on countless walls during the M11 campaign, 'will become more powerful than you can possibly imagine'.

Ernst Fischer began his book *The Necessity of Art* with Jean Cocteau's paradoxical epigram: 'Poetry is indispensable – if I only knew what for.'[52] To me it seems the DiY protest movement knows exactly what for: to 'visualise industrial collapse'.[53] Perhaps this movement has sown the seeds of new forms of struggle for the twenty-first century. Perhaps the twenty-first century will see the end of industrial capitalism and the return of some sort of social and ecological balance. Perhaps, as Mondrian said, 'Art will disappear as life gains more equilibrium.'[54] Perhaps even the art of necessity will no longer be necessary.

6

Earth First!
Defending Mother Earth, direct-style

ALEX PLOWS

I should emphasise before I go further that I am speaking as *a* voice of Earth First!, not *the* voice. Also I'm aware that the tone of my writing oscillates from assumed objectivity in the third person to saying 'we are this', that is, speaking more as a voice of the movement than a commentator on it. I am both subjectively involved (as an activist) and objectively commenting (as a researcher).[1] What I am aiming to do in this chapter is to identify a political/ethical perspective which I believe is a central theme within the movement; I would expect the majority of committed protesters to agree in general with the position outlined in this chapter, whilst individually disagreeing over specific emphases, for of course there is a great diversity regarding all of the issues I intend to address here. And again, this reflects the nature and structure of the movement: ideology is autonomous, autonomy is the ideology.

Late in 1996, a group of experienced campaigners including myself relaunched the North Wales Earth First! (EF!) group and in doing so posed the question: 'What *is* EF!?' It was pretty strange that a movement could succeed so well in avoiding definitions, in its anarchist principles, that the people who form a part of it found it hard to quantify. In a sense, EF! does not exist at all – certainly not as a 'traditional' campaign group such as Friends of the Earth, with paid membership and policy-making bodies. Instead, EF! is an egalitarian, non-hierarchical 'disorganisation', relying on grass-roots networking and local/individual autonomy rather than centralised policy control. EF! publications, pre- and post-action discussions, workshops and gatherings are the forum for debate.

EF! has no law, no hard-and-fast policies, but general principles which are reached through democratic debate and consensus.[2] EF! as a disorganisation exists through the people who actively make it up at any given time, who come together for a mass action and then dissolve away; EF!'s most tangible element in Britain is the existence of its (predominantly urban-based) local groups. This duplicates the structure of the vision of the original American Earth First! movement, formed around 1980, as Rik Scarce explains:

> Earth First! was to be like a Plains Indian tribe, existing in autonomous groups which shared the same beliefs. There would be no bureaucracy, no lobbyists, no organizational spokespeople, just a force of devoted, unpaid, grassroots activists occupying a niche they had created for themselves in the environmental movement – in short, an anarchy. . . . Perhaps most telling, there was to be no membership. The closest things to membership cards are T-shirts with [the] clenched-fist logo and the motto, 'No Compromise in Defense of Mother Earth'.[3]

The translation of an alternative value system into political action constitutes the agenda of American EF!, the forerunner/counterpart of British EF!. But there are significant differences. The American EF! stance is informed by the philosophy of Deep Ecology, a term and concept developed by Arne Naess. I may be accused of over-simplifying here, but the basic philosophy is as follows: concurrent with Lovelock's Gaia theory – the earth perceived as a living entity – nature is seen as sacred/special. The survival of the planet – the continuation of 'nature' – is paramount; the survival of humanity is not. Thus the American EF! campaign for the preservation of human-free wilderness – for 'nature'. This perspective has been termed 'biocentric', that is, nature, the biosphere, is given precedence over people. This stance separates environmental from social issues and gives absolute rights to the former. The belief that 'nature' must survive even if humanity doesn't, that nature is sacred while humanity is profane (Green Puritanism?), implies that rather than humans being an intrinsic part of nature, nature is somehow 'other' – apart from, only now superior to, us. This is what differentiates British EF! from Deep

Ecology-informed American EF!. As I hope to show, the British
protest movement identifies the interdependence of social/human
rights, and accords them equal value. People, as part of nature,
have the right to be free from exploitation and oppression, too.
What is not questioned here is that humanity has – and is –
embarked on a course of environmental destruction. Where British
and American philosophies (and hence direct action strategies)
part is on the question of humanity's place in nature.[4]

British EF! strategies and philosophies, the focusing on social
issues, the emphasis on the decentralisation of power, the localising
of food/energy production, and so on, have much more in
common with the 'social ecology' perspective championed by
Murray Bookchin.[5] Like Bookchin, EF!ers identify hierarchical
structures and values as being part cause, part manifestation of
'progress culture'. EF! groups were being set up in Britain during
1990–91, inspired by the ten-year-old EF! movement in the United
States. Groups in London, Oxford, Brighton and Reading began
disseminating information about, and undertaking non-violent
direct action (NVDA) against, the government, construction companies, industries, which were seen to be pursuing socially, economically and environmentally destructive and exploitative policies.
Perhaps the earliest – certainly the best attended – EF! actions
targeted Whatley Quarry in Somerset, where ARC were (and still
are) busily turning the Mendip Hills into a vast lunar crater; and
TIMBMET in Oxford, a firm importing mahogany that had been
illegally cut from the Brazilian rainforest. Collective NVDA is swift,
cheap and in yer face: EF!ers enter the office or the work-site and
stop work; machines are climbed on, in the office phone lines are
switched off (or even better answered by protesters) – it costs
companies time, and time is money ... Actions are undertaken
collectively. EF! does not condone, but neither does it condemn,
the individual acts of 'pixieing' which often take place during
actions, for example the removal of disks and documents from
offices, the disabling of machinery on site. Collective NVDA is as
varied and inventive as the protesters themselves, and over the
years techniques have diversified and improved (tree houses above,
tunnels below the earth). The tried and tested technique of people
putting their bodies in front of machines to stop them continues to
work a treat. This is especially so if a few people manage to 'lock

on', that is, use a bicycle D-lock to attach their neck to a machine or fence – one D-lock can hold up work hours after other protesters have been forcibly removed. In 1992 EF! groups visited, and some individuals stayed at, Twyford Down in Hampshire – helping to form the Dongas Tribe which tried to stop this Site of Special Scientific Interest being destroyed by the construction of the M3. It was at Twyford in December 1992 that security guards (Group 4) were first hired to evict protesters, and it is highly likely that the very violent actions of Group 4 helped to kick-start (*sic*) EF! and the NVDA protest movement – Twyford was the catalyst for a raising of our profile (and hence numbers). Being attacked, we lost the 'eco-terrorist' label and gained the moral high ground; and the real terrorists – the state – had let their mask slip. EF! and direct action roads protest mushroomed; at Twyford, and subsequently at the M11 (London) and Solsbury Hill (Bath), protests got the *active* support of hundreds of locals, and of the general public. Good going for a bunch of eco-anarchists.

The rapid growth of NVDA can be linked to the movement's fluid, decentralised structure. From 1992 onwards EF! groups were being rapidly established throughout the country, and campaigns (on local, national and global issues)[6] were researched and initiated independently by these local groups, and networked nationally via EF! mailouts and Road Alert! (an office set up by Twyford Down activists to network direct action) newsletters. From the start EF! has embraced the potential of information technology and has an impressive website.[7] Information is readily and freely available in a variety of forms – the Internet, the flyer, newsletters (Action Updates), 'underground' publications such as *SchNEWS*, *SQUALL*, EF!'s own journal *Do or Die: Voices from Earth First!*. The fluidity of structure allows actions to happen rapidly and spontaneously, without the limitations of the 'top-down' approach that characterise the establishment green groups. A letter in *Do or Die* emphasises the importance of 'the principle of decentralisation and local group independence ... in this way we avoid the hierarchical structure which has broken the militancy of other eco/revolutionary groups'.[8] Thus an initially small and local campaign has the potential to become the focus for a large-scale national protest site in the time it takes to network the information – Newbury, Fairmile and Manchester Airport are the most recent examples.[9] This 'rapid

response' networking technique is highly effective, and links back to anarchist methodologies and philosophies – there's a reliance on cooperation between autonomous groups, and a mistrust of traditional hierarchical or centralised structures and strategies, which are considered as 'part of the problem'. An open letter in *Do or Die* to the then Minister for Transport, Brian Mawhinney, states plainly why EF!ers refuse to negotiate with the state, on the state's terms:

> Let's pretend for a moment that we could suppress our feelings of nausea and rage and sit down to negotiate; what in fact could you offer us? The end of the industrial system – can you offer us that? An end to the assault against the life support systems of the earth . . . can you offer us that? Of course not! . . . Why should we debate, we know what you are going to say, you've said it countless time before, we are bored of listening. The modern ecology movement is over 30 years old; in the bowels of your office there is a whole forest of reports on the ecological stupidity of what you are doing. You know the situation.[10]

In other words, EF! will not negotiate with the system because what is needed for *real* sustainability is the end of that system – and the powers that be know this. Therefore the methodologies (top-down, hierarchical bureaucracy) which perpetuate unsustainability are to be rejected along with the structures and policies themselves.

Yet EF! walks an often precarious line between a justifiable 'no compromise' position and political realism. Pragmatically the machine of modernity is not going to be switched off overnight. So, in the short term, changes in the law, the introduction of green taxes, the banning of arms sales, and other issues are achievable goals to work towards. There are those who regard such policy shifts as merely 'tinkering with the machine'. I see it more like the 2001 computer Hal, a machine dying in stages as its vital components are switched off. Direct activists can set – are setting – the pace for this agenda. At the same time it is vital that others do engage (some would say compromise) with the government and the law to work out the details and ensure the implementation of more sustainable policies. Thus we need to accept that groups like Friends of the Earth, Transport 2000, environmental lawyers, have a complementary role to play to that of direct activism. Dave Foreman, co-founder of EF! in the United States, reminds us that

> it is so easy for radicals to get this holier than thou attitude and to not appreciate the hard work that the more mainstream groups do. . . . By pushing that edge out there, we have given the mainstream groups a lot more room in which to operate. We make them look credible without them having to compromise more.[11]

That EF!'s anarchist principles and structure are effective is clear – five years ago EF! was an unknown minority. Now, in the late nineties, direct action campaigns are well-attended, high-profile media events. (Of course, this brings its problems, and, of course, it's right to question how much of the message behind the hype goes in. But let's not knock ourselves down before we've even stood up: hundreds of people attending evictions, transport policies being challenged not only by protesters but by the public, is a massive achievement, and has been a significant factor in recent U-turns on government policy which have seen hundreds of road schemes dropped since NVDA took off. And we've only just begun . . . !) Decentralisation of power and individual autonomy may also be pragmatic anti-infiltration devices.[12] Without a hierarchical structure there is nothing to infiltrate, no opportunity to seize control, incriminate or destroy from within. And then again, the movement is in a continual state of flux and change – people come and go, an action can be networked by anyone anywhere at any time. Over a weekend a couple of hundred people could arrive at a quarry in Scotland or a board meeting in London, cause chaos, cost the company money and bad publicity, and melt away again . . . until the next time.[13]

As I said at the start, EF! is defined by the people who make it up at any one given time. It is very, very hard for the authorities to keep a check on. Go on an EF! demo at Whatley Quarry and you're part of EF! After the demo you're, well . . . what exactly? Resting? This is true for the movement as a whole: road protester beomes airport protester becomes The Land is Ours urban squatter becomes rave-goer becomes EF!er *ad infinitum*, simply through her/his presence on that particular campaign or demo. It is impossible, then, to talk about (for example) EF! and the roads protest movement as if they were separate entities: individuals flow in and out of both and in many cases would not define themselves in terms of either group. So, often, more than affiliating with other groups/campaigns, we *are* – we *become* – those other groups.

On its Action Updates, EF! defines itself as 'a convenient banner for people who share similar philosophies to work under'. This 'similar philosophy' is an appreciation of a shared ethical/political agenda with a fundamental target: while groups tackle, for example, intensive farming, the arms trade, road-building, these are the effects of a more insidious cause – 'progress culture'. Capitalism, modernity, call it what you will – EF! challenges this dominant paradigm, the structure/values/structure spiral which promotes and perpetuates exploitative unsustainability, and terms it 'progress', 'development'. 'Progress culture' is ironically seen itself as 'only natural', the only viable method of doing things, as Bauman has noted: 'This "development" [has been] "naturalised" into something very close to a law of nature by the modern part of the globe.'[14] Such 'progress' is linear, rigidly defined and parasitic in that it depends on social/environmental exploitation for its perpetuation and – significantly – *fails to quantify the costs of these effects*; 'progress', 'by undermining narrowly defined political and economic goals, rarely encourages attention to the complex patterns of feedback that our actions set in motion'.[15] EF! aims to expose these 'complex patterns of feedback', the long-term, hidden social, environmental and economic costs of 'progress'-orientated structures and policies:

> Capitalism – and its petrochemical/car-making economy – must keep moving. The need for transport infrastructural development is the need of the multinational corporations. The economy ... must expand or die. We have consistently argued that to build more infrastructure simply creates more traffic ... a disastrous spiral down into ecological collapse. You must maintain the demand for cars and petrochemical byproducts as an end in itself. You must preside over the ever-increasing centralisation of production and consumption ... making it progressively more difficult to get by in this society without a car.[16]

It's been a common criticism of EF!ers that we are 'anti-progress'. To which, of course, the response is 'And you call *this* progress?!'

Modern definitions of 'progress' are intrinsically related to the way in which we perceive time. Time, as archaeology confirms, was initially calculated by the observance of natural cycles (the moon, the seasons), and this brought a sense of continuity, a link to the past. Today time is no longer calculated in a cyclical way – it is seen as linear, a future stretching out to infinity in front of us. This evokes a perception of time running faster, away from us as we scramble to catch up, to move on, to 'progress' (Bauman's 'juggernaut' of modernity;[17] literally the human race . . .). Thus the past is rejected as inferior – new ideas and inventions are seen as progressive, as being better than their predecessors, simply because they are new. Any technological 'advance' – nuclear power, intensive farming – is evaluated and privileged as progressive, without considering the unsustainability, the environmental destruction, this technology introduces into the equation. Looked at logically, this is ludicrous: in part because of the lack of value ascribed to the environment (something I'll discuss more fully shortly), in part because 'progress' is still promoted in an unquestioned manner, and in part because of this linear conception of time. Industrial society seems hooked on 'linear progress' and is unwilling to give it up; sustainability, or the relinquishing of some of these 'developments' (the car, the supermarket), is seen as regressive – and this perception is perpetuated by those whose vested interests lie in maintaining the status quo. (As is the myth that sustainable development – organic farming or low-impact rural housing, for example – is economically unviable, as if the present system was somehow a cost-effective one!)

The appreciation of the interrelatedness not only of cause and effect, but of effect with effect – those 'complex patterns of feedback' – leads EF! to campaign, and to affiliate to other campaigns, across a spectrum of related issues. The following is a list of campaigns the North Wales EF! group is currently involved in (and I've probably missed a few):

    locally   the proposed A55 Euroroute though Anglesey
                the proposed housing development on Brewery Fields
                Critical Mass (highlighting problems experienced by cyclists
                    and pedestrians)
                permaculture projects

the local 'No Hawks' group (Anglesey is an air training base
for Indonesian pilots . . . allegedly . . .)

nationally   information and actions networked on the following
campaigns:
genetic engineering
The Land is Ours
land mines and other arms sales
Forest Action Network

On top of these individuals take time out to protest at Manchester
Airport and other direct action camps around the country. The
group liaises with groups including Women's Environmental Network, Transport 2000, Friends of the Earth, Corporate Watch.
Leaving the tired arguments of the 'red vs green' (social vs environmental issues) debate behind, EF! argues that issues of social justice
and human rights are intrinsically linked to issues of environmental
destruction, and that to protest against one is to protest against the
other. Pull a solitary chain – a 'single issue' – and the whole complex
mesh starts to unravel.

For instance, anti-roads protest at (especially) the M11 in
London and the Pollok Estate in Glasgow placed community needs
at the heart of their campaigns. Issues of bad housing, the roads'
impacts on residents' health, safety and quality of life, the fact that
both road schemes affected predominantly lower-income neighbourhoods, were priorities. Social issues, linked by protesters to
the environmental debate, merge into the 'complex patterns' of
the grid of modernity: start a conversation with an EF!er about
roads and you'll inevitably (some say infuriatingly) end up talking
about something different – from roads to road transport, local
food production and consumption, subsidies/pesticides, organic
farming, genetic engineering . . . *there is no such thing as a single
issue*. Similarly, EF!ers are often criticised for putting the environment before jobs, for the fact that, by campaigning, for instance,
for an end to road-building we are sacrificing working-class jobs on
the altar of middle-class environmentalism. Bollocks! These 'development' projects are the most inefficient, the least cost-effective,
methods of job creation going. To offer a reformist rather than a
revolutionary argument for a moment, how many NVQ places and
teachers could be created for the cost of the average road? The

same goes for any of the environmentally damaging industries – nuclear power, toxic waste incinerators – where calls for their closure evoke the response, 'But it'll cost jobs!' Yes, perhaps – but free up the billions of pounds of subsidy money and far, far more jobs could be created. Added to which, of course, there would be the unquantifiable bonus of an end to the knock-on economic losses (the cost of cleaning up after industries, the health bills, and so on) – never mind a safer, cleaner environment. And, just as in the Third World, it is no coincidence that these health-damaging, soul-destroying industries are situated in the middle of Britain's poorest areas – Teesside, for example, has one of the country's highest unemployment rates and is also home to an ICI complex of nightmarish proportions (but it brings jobs to the area, you know!). Another example: 'Travellers are excluded from large parts of the country by virtue of the legislation and guidance of the planning system. . . . Too often official Gypsy sites are in locations adjacent to industrial estates, "between the sewage works and the railway tracks", and often on polluted land which no one else wants.'[18] Those most socially/economically disadvantaged are those who are also most exposed to the harmful effects of environmental destruction. Green *is* red.

EF! is a 'multi-issue' new social movement – that is, we have a holistic (and only intermittently conspiratorial) appreciation of how any particular issue fits into the wider picture.

> [W]e cannot campaign successfully on single issues without address-
> ing the social problems that cause them. In order to improve our
> quality of life we have to fight the present system in its entirety – and
> demonstrate viable alternatives. . . . If we don't fight against the
> totality of the system by understanding a campaign in the context of
> the wider struggle, capitalism will just rear its ugly head elsewhere.[19]

One current academic position is to criticise new social movements as being 'single issue', that in some postmodern isolationist way they 'confirm the principle of insularity . . . corroborate the image of the world as composed of issues that can be pursued and resolved in separation'.[20] In fact (as Bauman might appreciate if he got out of the ivory tower of academe occasionally), EF! does exactly the reverse of this. EF! aims to bring to the public's attention the 'hidden' socioeconomic/environmental costs, the knock-on effects: 'progress' can only be defined as such because *it is itself* presented and evaluated in a 'single-issue' way. The iron cage of progress, of which these different bars, those 'single issues', are constructed, is the centre of EF!'s challenge. But of course EF! is in a bit of a Catch-22 situation. Yes, EF! has a holistic 'multi-issue' perspective, but what are we supposed to do? Split ourselves into an infinite number of molecules and campaign about everything everywhere, all at once?[21] Pragmatically, to stand any chance of changing policies, issues have to be focused on – transport, food production or whatever. In any case, as I've outlined above, groups run themselves ragged by having several campaigns ongoing at any given time, and by actively supporting many others.

It's important to emphasise that EF!'s aim is not only to campaign against unsustainable 'development', but to *proactively* set an agenda of sustainability, to highlight pragmatic alternatives which are not only environmentally friendly but are also socially just and economically viable. Thus, for example, the This Land is Ours campaign is actively supported by EF!ers. Reforestation projects, inner-city community schemes, putting on 'green' plays in schools, LETS schemes, are promoted in EF! publications and initiated and supported by direct activists. Tree planting and permaculture projects (for example, 'Plants for a Future' in Cornwall) are full of EF!ers and protesters taking time off from (of necessity) reactive campaigns to do something not only more proactive, but more *relaxing*, goddamnit!

> Environmental restoration is proactive – whereby we set our own agenda. ... Restoration is less dramatic ... than the preservation battles, but it does establish a vital new paradigm: humanity as creator and healer – one who adds value or makes reparations to nature.[22]

Collective direct action is the framework for change at the macro/structural level – crucially, though, the emphasis is also on individual responsibility: 'Do It Yourself! ... If not you, who?' are common EF! slogans. This collective/individual thing is an important dialectic – for EF!ers, 'institutional changes are not enough ... such macro levels of reorganisation need to be supplanted with changes at the local and most importantly the micro level of individual citizens'.[23] Individual actions – boycotting products, living on the land, growing organic vegetables, cycling, recycling – are seen as complementing direct action, and these are interdependent strategies. In many ways this is obvious: it is impossible to imagine, for example, that someone could attend an animal exports blockade and then go home and eat veal. Similarly, individual actions are undertaken with the aim of having a collective, macro impact, such as forcing companies though economic pressure into adopting green strategies.

In discussing EF! direct action philosophies and strategies, an examination of EF!'s commitment to NVDA is crucial, especially because at the time of writing a few voices within EF! are questioning the effectiveness of non-violence. EF! was established as a non-violent movement, and is defined and motivated by this strategy. At the 1996 summer EF! gathering in North Wales the majority view of those attending was the confirmation and reaffirmation of NVDA principles.[24] Quite what constitutes violence is of course open to debate – damage to machinery ('trashing' Hawk jets, bulldozers, and so on) is not violence but (for the authorities) criminal damage or (for EF!) a potentially effective way of stopping or at least highlighting the destruction of the earth, of innocent people. Self-defence is again another matter. I am discussing both the moral issue and specific protest tactics here: should direct activists undertake action with the belief that *all* life, all human beings, have intrinsic value, or are private security guards, bailiffs and sheriff's officers, and officially employed tree-climbers and potholers validly to be viewed as 'the enemy', as 'legitimate targets' for aggression? For me the use of violence, even in the face of frequent gross provocation, reneges on agreed EF! principles – very socially aware isn't it to want to beat up some anonymous ex-miner-turned-security guard forced off the dole. Clearly there are pragmatic reasons for non-violent strategies, in particular that the public is far more likely to listen to the arguments and support the protests if they can sympathise and identify with protesters. NVDA campaigns currently enjoy the support of much of the general public, not least because campaigners are seen to be creative, peaceful and articulate, the David to the state's violent and over-the-top Goliath. More than pragmatism, though, NVDA touches the core of EF!'s agenda, its long-term goals. Means must be conversant with ends; a truly democratic, socially just society will never be created through violent strategies.

I'll take this opportunity to point out that most EF!ers and direct activists have been arrested, assaulted and given criminal records as a result of our peaceful protests. Many people have been sent to prison; something I narrowly avoided myself, simply for ignoring court orders that ban you from returning to protest sites. Friends of mine got sent down for three months because they broke bail conditions and returned to Twyford to put on a play. Most of us have been subject to injunction/bail conditions more stringent than those they give to many rapists. We all have MI5 files, have our mail opened and our phones tapped; we are classed as terrorists, which would be funny if it weren't so frightening. And all this is simply because we exercise our right to protest – a right made much more difficult to exercise by the 1994 Criminal Justice Act, which included sections specifically targeting direct activists.

EF!s challenge to 'progress' needs now to be put in the context of current thinking on environmental ethics, or ecophilosophy. EF! links western 'progress' to an anthropocentric (human-centred) value system. That is, society perceives itself as being separate to, and better than, nature, rather than an intrinsic part of it. This ethos has been reinforced by Enlightenment philosophies, revolving around the inherent belief in the superiority of man's (yes, man's) rationality over the inferiority of his natural environment. This scramble to dominate and conquer nature, and nature seen as 'other' to humanity, is a schism which opened 'the way for a relationship [with nature] which is primarily exploitative and manipulative'.[25] EF! not only challenges this anthropocentric value-system with direct action, but posits an alternative, holistic ethic as a replacement. Thus, NVDA not only challenges structure and policy, but is also viewed as a strategy for promoting what Denis Goulet calls an 'ethics of respect for nature's diversity'.[26] The perception of nature – *and human beings as part of nature* – as being worthy of respect informs all EF! actions, and is seen as crucial to the agenda of sustainability. This appreciation of self in nature, a sense of symbiotic connectedness, informs values of cooperation rather than competition, the desire to nurture rather than to exploit. It transcends the (post)modern sense of dislocated isolated self and by doing so highlights the importance, the interconnectedness, of

EARTH FIRST! SUMMER GATHERING

WEDNESDAY 9th - TUESDAY 15th JULY 1997
SCOTLAND
FOR MORE INFORMATION CONTACT 0115 202 9365

"CONSTANT EFFORTS TO PROTECT NATURE WITHOU

WHAT IS EARTH FIRST!?

Earth First! is not a cohesive organisation or a campaign but more a convenient banner for people who share similar philosophies to work under. Earth First! operates as a network of autonomous and non-hierarchical groups who use direct action to confront, stop and eventually reverse the forces that are responsible for the destruction of the Earth and its inhabitants.

WHAT'S HAPPENING?

This year Earth First! will have its Summer Gathering in Scotland from Wednesday 9th to Tuesday 15th July. The Gathering is an opportunity to learn new skills and techniques that are of use to direct action struggles and to introduce new people to direct action. It is also a chance to discuss some of the important issues that are of relevance to us all. The following a brief example of what will be covered.

WORKSHOPS AND TRAINING

There will be a huge number of workshops over the course of the week. These will cover subjects such as squatting, wild foods, maintaining health, prisoner support and legal issues. In addition to these there will be other ones for learning and practicing physical skills including climbing, tunnelling, blockading, breaking security cordons and self defence. If there is a workshop that you would particularly like to see happen, or you could offer to do one on something relevant get in touch.

DIRECT ACTION REPORTS

During the Gathering there will be a chance for all individuals and groups present, both those from the UK and overseas, to give a brief talk on their actions, the ideas behind them and some background information. From resisting the construction of roads, airports to fights against biotechnology, from reclaiming streets to liberating captured animals, these and many more will be reported on by some of the people actively involved.

DISCUSSION FORUM

These are likely to happen every afternoon and will involve larger group discussions which will try to address some of the important debates within the radical ecological direct action movement. These will include topics such as what has happened over the past year, ways of moving the struggle forward, dealing with informal hierarchy and cliques, gender, class and race issues and the perennial violence/non-violence debate.

ENTERTAINMENT

In the evenings there will be a variety of things going on including a cinema showing videos on struggles from around the world. There will also be poets, sketches, comics, acoustic music and, of course, plenty of opportunities for anybody to get up and do their own thing!

"WHY PARTICIPATE IN THE RUIN OF CREATION W

The leaflet cover (left) and text for the Earth First! summer gathering in Scotland, 1997

)VING THE CAUSES OF DESTRUCTION ARE POINTLESS."

ACTION!
The Gathering will finish on the Sunday night and on the Monday there will be full training and briefings for an action on the Tuesday. This action will be organised in conjunction with a local direct action group. More details will be available at the Gathering.

WHAT WILL THE SITE BE LIKE?
Next to the entrance there will be a reception area where programmes of what is happening will be available. Additionally there will also be a space provided for leaflets and information ... with a Dead Trees Earth First! book stall selling books and pamphlets at cost price.

... site there will be marquees, large domes for workshops, a crèche at the ... a quiet camping space, toilets, showers and a healing area. Cheap, organic ... available all week from Rampenplan - a group of people from the ... at various actions and gatherings all across Europe.

... a festival. It is a Gathering of those interested in, or involved with, ... of the earth. There will be no sound systems and commercial stalls are ... to get off your face and listen to music all week let us know and we ... a list of festivals to go to. Part of what this Gathering is about is trying ... community amongst us, and any threat to this community through ... harassment or theft will be taken seriously and dealt with by us all.

WHAT TO BRING
Come ... for a weeks camping in Scotland. Bring shelter, warm and waterproof clothes, cutlery and plate... the food and anything you think may be useful for the action on the Tuesday ... bring any information, such as leaflets and displays, about what is happening in ...

You will need money for the food or alternatively you can cater for yourself. Additionally the Gathering is asking for £10 per person to cover the costs of organising this week.

HELP!
We need help to make this Gathering happen; both now during the planning stage, and also during the week itself, so any offers of help would be very welcome. If you can do either of these things contact the address overleaf.

Earth First! has no central office, no members, no paid workers and also no money. Any donations would be useful in trying to get this Gathering together, so if you can afford it make any cheques or Postal Orders payable to Earth First! and send them to the same address.

OU CAN PARTICIPATE IN THE CREATION OF RUINS?"

cause and effect. The crucial point here is that *value is given* to those effects; because the environment/social groups/the global poor are valued as important, as vital, then the ethos becomes one of sustainability, not destruction/exploitation.

For many direct activists the value of nature and self can be described as a spirituality, literally an awareness of spirit, of life force. I need to stress that this is a very personal thing. Many in the movement will identify this sense of connectedness as something that motivates their actions, but would not describe it as a spirituality, simply as a socially committed and environmentally aware attitude. Others do perceive this web of life as something sacred – nature and our relationship within it, the wonder of its chaotic diversity, is celebrated, danced to. Paganism perhaps, but, as I have stressed elsewhere, practical paganism;[27] first and foremost as an approach which has solid foundations in informing our attempts at radical change. Belief in 'earth energy' does *not* prohibit political realism. On the contrary, it is an added incentive. Neither, as I will shortly discuss, can this be descibed as a 'New Age' ideology. While I do not wish to wallow in the mythology of some hunter-gatherer Golden Age, or to go overboard on the wisdom of the world's native peoples (many of whom promote a savagely patriarchal and hierarchical structure), none the less this ethics of respect concurs with Rolston Holmes's observation that 'Traditional views . . . may render perceptible something authentic in nature to which science blinds us. . . . traditional cultures . . . have world views in which they are meaningful residents of a meaningful home . . . [they] have a global ethic that we have not yet attained.'[28]

Or have lost. This knowledge, these belief-systems, have profound implications in terms of healing the schism in our relationship with nature. To appreciate that we have lessons to learn, or relearn, from native world views is not a regression from civilisation to primitivism (again that linear perception of time influences such critiques), but the application of old knowledge in a modern context. The perhaps irrevocable damage done to the planet's resources has been sanctioned and morally justified by a value system which perceives nature as something to abuse and exploit. A society whose values and policies were based on an appreciation of the innate value of nature would not sanction its exploitation. The Celts left gifts for the water spirits; water was worshipped not out of dumb ignorance, but because they were aware that water was a life-giving source. Animism is poetic symbol, a metaphor for the facts of life. Modern, 'civilised' men and women do not believe in water spirits. In our 'Enlightenment' we have poisoned and polluted water, filled our seas with radioactive waste and our rivers with pesticide.

To re-emphasise, the focus on the need for a shift in values is seen as an interdependent complement to forcing change at a structural level. There is no 'either/or' duality, in itself a very western approach. Visualise instead a 'yin–yang' symbol. Black and white comprise a unified whole in which one becomes, and is part of, the other; black within white, and vice versa.

Ethics need to be put into action, and the action will promote the ethics. As Goulet has pointed out:

> Ethics cannot exorcise evil from the realms of political power simply by preaching noble ideals. . . . An ethic of social justice and equity needs to harness concrete instruments . . . build . . . social structures which foster human dignity.[29]

I am suggesting that this is what EF! does, and thus the values/ ethics/spirituality which inform our political action cannot be categorised as a 'New Age' philosophy. You won't find many New Agers on protest camps for the simple reason that the New Age perspective is one of 'social change through individual change'.[30] To be frank I feel I have more in common with the security guards on site forced by social and economic presures into taking crappy low-paid work many of them don't agree with, than with twee hippies who believe that all the world's problems will be solved if we sit on the ground and go 'om'. This individual quoted in David Pepper's *Communes and the Green Vision* sums up this extreme New Age approach:

Don't worry about unemployment. This and other problems will go
away when people tune into their spiritual benignness. They must not
view poverty as a drudge but as a gift. Some of the best things in life
are learned when you are poor.[31]

On the other hand (yin and yang again), maybe there's nothing
wrong with going 'om'. Solstice celebrations, drumming, dancing
round standing stones, are all expressions of the 'holistic ethic' I
am identifying (and my personal belief is, yes, I'm sure sympathetic
magic works!).[32] To clarify the distinction I am making: thinking
positive, creative visualisation and changing one's own lifestyle
('the personal is political') are unfairly criticised by Pepper,[33] since
individual responsibility has a vital part to play in achieving
sustainability. It is, however, politically naive to believe that this *by
itself* will bring about social justice and environmental stability. *It is
the translation of ethics into political action that goes beyond the personal
which differentiates EF! values from those of New Agers.* To reiterate this
I'll give another example. A friend was telling me recently about a
Rainbow Circle gathering in Ireland, where many people sat in a
circle, held hands and announced that 'Patriarchy is dead'. Well
yippee. Small problem, though – it isn't, is it? I was told by my
friend not to 'engage with the energy' of admitting the reality of
patriarchy – that you create your own reality and therefore by
saying 'Yes, patriarchy exists' I was actually *contributing* to its
perpetuation! (Outrageous enough, leaving aside the hilarity of a
man telling me that patriarchy was dead.) New Age? New Ostrich
more like. (Again, I must qualify this with differentiating between
this attitude, and thinking positive – for example, saying, 'I believe
patriarchal structures are being challenged and this motivates me
to help make this belief a reality.') It absolutely infuriates me that
protesters, EF!ers and so on, get tarred with the New Age brush. If
we *were* New Agers then there wouldn't be protest camps. Instead
we'd be on £300-a-week courses in 'Changing Transport Policy
Through Colonic Irrigation'. Patriarchy itself is also seen as intrinsically linked to environmental destruction, which is to say that the
domination of women by men is an extension of the domination of
nature by humanity. This is an ecofeminist perspective that women
(a) are more liable to suffer the effects of environmental exploitation, and (b) are identified more with nature, are seen as being

more 'earthly', and therefore social attitudes to nature (still heavily influenced by Puritan notions of disgust, guilt and rejection) also reflect social attitudes to women.[34]

I hope to have done justice to EF! in this chapter, highlighted current areas of debate within the movement, and laid to rest a few misconceptions, in particular the continuing misuse of the 'single-issue' label: EF! is, consciously, a multi-issue new social movement. It's the view of many direct activists including myself that EF! rejects the dualisms which continue to dominate the political/sociological debate – red vs green, individual vs collective strategies, values vs structure. As Jonathan Purkis has noted, 'political thinkers tend to locate green politics in some sort of either/or dichotomy between these two positions, without fully understanding the context within which radical environmentalism is occurring'.[35] Evidence of the maturity and the sense of ambition of the movement is seen in the fact that it can ask the following question in 1997's book-form *Do or Die*: 'Do we want to build a mass movement or are we content to remain a small band of young, noisy, white, middle class, unemployed, physically able "extremists"?' I want to conclude by responding to that question.

Yes, we need to broaden our base, so that our direct actions are increasingly attended by many different people (as they have been since Twyford, don't forget: Quaker women up the machines, late-middle-age professionals diving through the razor wire on the Dongas!). But we've also got to face the reality that the specific form of direct action which EF! focuses on makes the social group identified above inevitably the best equipped to undertake it – that is, young, fit, no ties, few responsibilities. We can overcome this limitation by devising more inclusive action strategies, but this is only part of the solution. Most importantly, EF! has to ensure that it connects with other social groups and their strengths, that we take the time to affiliate and cooperate with the communities around us. Using our initiative and creativity for proactive grass-roots activities, contributing to our local communities, is essential, which means anything from talks to Women's Institute groups to devising environmental plays in schools, and so on. We do a lot of talking, but we need to stop and listen to what our neighbourhoods are saying, too. At a local level, people are far more likely to listen to us, and actively support our campaigns, if we do the same for them. There needs to be mutual understanding and respect before people will seriously consider ideas like car-sharing, LETS schemes, to see that these are viable practices, not just the antics of weirdo hippie and neo-hippie outsiders.

In terms of the future EF! would like to see, and what sustainable development really needs to be – local production and consumption of alternative energy, for instance – I feel that EF! needs to be the mediator, to initiate and engage in dialogue with society at grassroots level, and talk these issues through. This goes to the heart of an issue that increasingly concerns EF!: 'reform or revolution?' Guess what? We want it *both* ways: with pre-emptive tactics such as ensuring that 'reforms' like alternative technology, sustainable dwellings, green taxes, and so on, are already in place, and that the general public is amenable to and part of these changes, then 'revolution' could be a relatively painless transition. The obvious example is of course car culture: unless public transport becomes the truly viable alternative (reform), cars will continue to pollute our environment, but while attacking car culture we attack central and intertwined aspects of capitalism itself (revolution). For me, reform *and* revolution are symbiotic strategies, and the movement is developing both its proactive and reactive tactics.

But without dialogue we can only build a head-in-the-sand utopia. And we cannot just waltz in and start telling the people what's good for them. I'm not advocating compromising our principle, just tact, listening to others, and an open mind. Grassroots dialogue, EF! as mediator – and still at the cutting edge of radical direct action, forcing the pace of change by hitting the multinationals where it hurts, in the pocket, and peeling off their PR gloss. These are the challenges now facing EF!, and ones I am sure the movement will rise to. To finish with the British EF!'s own answers to its own recent question, the one about building a mass movement:

Enough whingeing – here's some positive ideas
1. Learn how to agitate – successful movements like the Civil Rights movement, trade unions etc, spent lots of time out in communities talking to people and offering solutions. . . .
2. Remember 'the Earth is not dying, it is being murdered and the people murdering it have names and addresses'. . . .

3. Create a movement that people want to join and stay in. . . . We need to create a system that reduces our dependency on capitalism and destabilises it. By working closer with LETS schemes etc. we could create a parallel economy that would make the capitalist one irrelevant. . . .

4. Counteract the media backlash by pointing out our successes more.

5. Criminal damage must be talked about! You don't have to say you do it, but always say that it is understandable, given people's frustrations. . . . Sometimes it is inappropriate and we have to have the intelligence to know when this is.

6. Learn from current 'successful' organisations like The Land is Ours and Friends of the Earth, who score by being well connected, wealthy and strategic. But let's not allow them to set the agenda – use their networks and work with them on local issues. . . .

7. Should EF! develop itself? A difficult one this. We are, by nature and necessity, shy of centralised structures, but could we do with a little more centralisation for fund-raising, resource gathering, concentrated outreach, access to expertise, etc? . . .

Think About It![36]

7

Reclaim the fields and country lanes! The Land is Ours campaign[1]

GEORGE MONBIOT

The Land is Ours (TLIO) campaign emerged from a discussion following a conference on direct action in Oxford in December 1994, at which several people expressed the need to go on the offensive – to start demanding what we did want rather than concentrating on protesting against what we didn't. The campaign began with the occupation of a disused airfield and set-aside land near St George's Hill in Surrey, which the Diggers had seized in 1649, as part of their effort at claiming common land for the common people following the English Civil War. Around 600 people built a village and gardens, performed a play and distributed information in the neighbouring towns. They succeeded in starting a national debate on land, with favourable coverage in all the broadsheets and most national TV and radio news programmes.

Soon afterwards, Land is Ours campaigners occupied the property of the Earl of Macclesfield, at Shirburn Hill, near Watlington, Oxfordshire, in support of people trying to get access to his 2000 acres and to try to stop him neglecting one of the county's last areas of chalk downland. Oxfordshire County Council adopted a motion supporting them and calling for land reform. Hertfordshire County Council has also embraced some of their aims. Two of TLIO's recommendations have been incorporated into government planning policy guidance and the Green Party has adopted its objectives as policy.

In May 1996, five hundred Land is Ours activists occupied thirteen acres of derelict land on the banks of the River Thames in Wandsworth, highlighting the appalling misuse of urban land, the lack of provision of affordable housing and the deterioration of the

A 'yurt', one of the many structures put up on formerly derelict land in Wandsworth, south London. Photograph by Nick Cobbing

urban environment. The site was destined for the ninth major superstore within a radius of a mile and a half. They cleared the site of rubble and rubbish, built a village entirely from recycled materials and planted gardens. The activists held on to it for five and a half months, until they were evicted by bailiffs acting for the owners, Guinness. It was visited by thousands of people, many of whom had come from abroad to see it. It attracted publicity all over the world, and pushed the issues it highlighted up the political agenda.

Also in 1996, TLIO launched its first competition for Britain's best and worst landowners. Nominations from the public were assessed by a panel of independent judges. The Duke of Westminster was voted worst landowner (he has got a special dispensation to inspect tenants' homes at any time, while excluding walkers from thousands of acres of his Forest of Bowland estate, on the basis that they are intruding on his privacy) and Daphne Buxton of Norfolk was voted best landowner, after she established the first common in England this century. In 1997, the Queen was voted Britain's worst landowner, having persistently used Crown Immunity to prevent land on her estates from being registered as Sites of Special Scientific Interest or Special Areas of Conservation, and damaging the rare and remarkable habitats in these places.

In April 1997, The Land is Ours adopted a constitution, largely in order to prevent the emergence of hierarchy. It produced a statement of principle ('The Land is Ours campaigns peacefully for access to the land, its resources and the decision-making processes affecting them, for everyone – irrespective of race, age or gender'). Anyone subscribing to this principle can set up a Land is Ours group and act in TLIO's name. Since then, the movement has proliferated, with fourteen local groups and several special interest groups setting themselves up. A broader and more representative structure should make the movement more capable of mobilising against destructive and exclusive land use and in favour of a rights-based public control of our most fundamental resource.

A personal journey I: from global to local

October 1996 ... Five days ago a bunch of goons in Darth Vader costumes dragged me out of the splintered wood and rubble of

London's only sustainable village. Even as we were being removed, the earthmovers were moving in. They destroyed the wooden houses and the gardens we'd made, and returned the site to the dereliction we'd discovered when we first arrived. Sitting on the pavement in Wandsworth nursing a bruised head, this seemed to me a rather odd place for someone with a special interest in rainforest ecology to end up.

Nine years ago, as a rather naive and gormless natural historian, I went to work in the far east of Indonesia, in the annexed province of Irian Jaya. Until just a few years before, the forests there, and the tree kangaroos, birds of paradise and birdwing butterflies, had been more or less left alone. But now the forests were being pushed back fast, and I wanted to find out why. The answers weren't slow in coming. The government was trying to integrate Irian Jaya into the rest of the nation. To this end, it was flying tens of thousands of Javanese people in, establishing settlements for them and giving them the lands of the native Papuan people. The Papuans were being moved into prefabricated model villages and used as labour for logging and planting oil palms. The forests they had used to supply all their needs – food, fuel, shelter and medicine – were seen by the government as sources of single commodities: timber, for example, or land for planting oil palms. Control of the forests had been taken over by bureaucrats and army officers who lived far away and were not likely to suffer the consequences of the forests' disappearance.

I became interested in the issue of who was pulling the levers of rainforest destruction and, with that in mind, I moved to Brazil when my work in Indonesia had finished. At the time, in 1989, the received wisdom was that the Amazon's forests were disappearing because the colonists moving into them believed they could make themselves rich there. Ignorant of rainforest ecology, they were, we were told, convinced that moving to the Amazon and farming or mining the forests was a better economic option than staying at home.

My findings were rather different. First I found that a rapacious trade in mahogany, driven by consumer demand in Britain and the United States, was laying down the infrastructure and providing much of the economic incentive for further exploitation. Then I found that many of the people moving down the roads the mahogany cutters were opening up had not so much jumped as been pushed. I went back to the places they were coming from, and found that, backed by armed police and hired gunmen, the big landowners were expanding their properties by tearing down the peasant villages, killing anyone who resisted, and seizing the land the peasants held in common. Many of those who moved into the Amazon left their home states because they had no choice. Destruction took place at both ends – where they came from, as absentee landlords destroyed all the different resources they had relied on, and replaced them with just one resource, grazing for cattle, and where they arrived, as the peasants found themselves with little choice but to do to the Amazon's indigenous people what the landlords had done to them.

In East Africa, I came across a rather similar situation. Through both government policy and massive institutional fraud, the land held in common by pastoral peoples such as the Maasai and Samburu was being divided up and moved swiftly into the hands of businessmen. The woods, scrub, grasslands and flowering sward of the savannah were being ripped up to produce wheat. The remaining herders were concentrating into the hills too steep to plough, leading to soil compaction, flooding and drought. The situation was exacerbated by East Africa's conservation policies, which excluded herding people from many of their best lands, ostensibly to protect the game, but in truth to avoid offending tourists. The herders were both set against nature conservation and forced to overuse their remaining resources, while both tourists and corrupt state bureaucracies inflicted, in some cases, far greater damage on this protected land than its inhabitants had done.

Painfully slowly, the penny began to drop. All over the tropics, I had seen environmental destruction following land alienation. When traditional landholders are dispossessed and either private businesses, large proprietors or state bureaucracies take over, habitats are destroyed. I came to see that rural communities are often constrained to look after their land well, as it is the only thing they have, and they need to protect a diversity of resources in order to meet their diverse needs. When their commons are privatised, they pass into the hands of people whose priority is to make money, and the most efficient way of doing that is to select the most profitable product and concentrate on producing it. I saw that, without security of tenure and autonomy of decision-making, people have no chance of defending the environment they depend on for their livelihoods. What Brazil needed was land reform; what Kenya and Indonesia needed was the recognition and protection of traditional land rights. By themselves, these policies wouldn't guarantee environmental protection, but without them you could guarantee environmental destruction.

All this, as well as the appalling social consequences of land alienation, shouldn't be very hard to see, and liberal-minded people in the North have for a long time supported calls for land reform in the South. But, like nearly everyone else, throughout these travels I remained obtuse about the relevance that these ideas might have for Northern countries. In Britain, had anyone asked me, I would have said that land alienation was a done deal, and what we had to concentrate on was urging the government to keep its promises and enforce environmental standards. That was until Twyford Down, Hampshire, scene of the road protest against the M3 motorway extension and birthplace of the Dongas Tribe, in 1992.

At first, I didn't really understand what was going on, or how it related to me. It took a lot of persuasion by some insistent friends to get me down there. But when I arrived, it blew me away. I began to see that this was far more than just a struggle over transport policy. Building the road through Twyford Down was not just bad transport decision-making, but also bad land use decision-making. It was only possible because of a suspension of democratic accountability so profound that the decision to build the road was taken before the public inquiry began. What the protesters were fighting was exactly the same sort of remote decision-making, by people who didn't have to suffer the consequences, that I had seen in Indonesia, Kenya and Brazil.

What had foxed me was that, in Britain, land passed into the hands of a tiny minority of owners and decision-makers centuries ago. The enclosures and the clearances were the culmination of a thousand years of land alienation, but they were as traumatic as those confronting the peasants of north-eastern Brazil today. In England, tens of thousands were forced into vagrancy and destitution. In Scotland, people were packed on to ships at the point of a gun and transported across the ocean to the Americas in conditions that resembled those of the slave ships. Others crowded into the cities. It is no coincidence that London was the world's first city with more than a million inhabitants, while Glasgow remains both one of the poorest and most violent cities in Western Europe.

It is so long since we had a grip on land use that these struggles, scarcely recorded in mainstream history books, have passed out of our consciousness. What happens to the land, we imagine, the transactions and changes it suffers, is no longer our concern. It's a matter for the tiny number of people who control it. Yet it is for the very reason that these changes took place so long ago that they are so important. Their significance has seeped into every corner of our lives. The issue has been invisible to us not because it is so small, but because it is so big. We simply can't step far enough back to see it.

A personal journey II: relations with DiY Culture

In piecing together the history and development of the contemporary direct action movement – from my own experience, that since Twyford Down in 1992 – the editor has asked me to write about my own role, which has been the source of some conflict and controversy. Aside from the usual student protests, my first contact with direct action was my involvement, in 1987 and 1988, with the Operasi Papua Merdeka, the rebel movement in the occupied territory of Irian Jaya. After that, I worked with the Movimento Sem Terra and a couple of indigenous rights campaigns in Brazil, then with the Maasai and Turkana people trying to retain their lands and fight off government-sponsored banditry in East Africa. I learnt from these disparate groups a good deal about organisation, anarchy and efficacy, and, once introduced to it, responded to the British direct action movement with wild enthusiasm.

Loud, bossy and incapable of holding my tongue, at the same time articulate and extremely excited by the issues it raised, I became, for many of those concerned about the emergence of leadership, an object of suspicion. Largely because of my rather colourful and visible past, and because I already knew many of the journalists who covered our actions, I was often singled out for comment by the press. This swiftly led to accusations that I was a 'media tart': a self-seeking publicist. When one of the papers revealed that I had been to public school and that my father was an industrialist and an active member of the Conservative Party, people's worst suspicions appeared to be confirmed. I was, some believed, hijacking the movement, trying to replace its radicalism with a reformist, even collaborationist, agenda, using my contacts and access to the media to launch a hierarchical coup.

I was roundly condemned by publications such as *Green Anarchist*, *Oxfiend*, *Contraflow* and *Class War*. Some of the coverage was pretty nasty – I should, I learned, be guillotined or lynched – some was poorly informed. I was once sitting on a barricade in Islington High Street with hundreds of other Reclaim the Streets protesters, facing off the police at the beginning of an action, when I was handed an issue of *Class War*. 'You'd be more likely', it claimed, 'to find the Pope at Ibrox than Monbiot on a barricade.' I wrote to *Class War* to find out how they knew about the Pope.

But much of what was written had a point. All personality cults are dangerous, divisive and destructive of a coherent radical movement. While I did not set out to encourage one, and tried to steer journalists away from talking about me and towards talking about the issues, I became far too visible. Repeatedly, to my frustration and everyone else's, I was dubbed 'the leader' of this or that action, largely because I was the only person the journalist had seriously spoken to. Some of this was my fault. Knowing that I'm good at talking to the media, at delivering sound bites and summing up a situation, I put myself forward too often. Some of it was the fault of lazy journalism.

Bearing all this in mind, I've tried to put things right by the following means. At The Land is Ours, I now confine my activities to a few backroom tasks. I've been organising interview and public speaking workshops, to pass on any skills at dealing with the media to other people. I've avoided the first day of any direct action – when the press are most likely to be present – or any action that lasts for one day only. I've concentrated instead on my journalism, much of which supports the theoretical framework within which the direct action movements work, without being seen to be speaking for them. *Green Anarchist* and some of the other publications are right: excessive publicity for individuals detracts from and trivialises the work of everyone else.

Planning and development

Let's look at it, to begin with, purely from the environmental point
of view. Environmental quality is a function of development. In the
world's wilderness areas it depends on the absence of development.
In managed landscapes like Britain's, it depends on the balance of
built and non-built development, and the quality and character of
both categories. This quality and character rests in turn on who is
making the development decisions.

If a decision arises from an informed consensus of the views of
local people and anyone else the development might affect, then
you are likely to see people's vested interest in the quality of their
surroundings, and hence the quality of their lives, reflected in that
decision. If, on the other hand, a decision emerges from an
impenetrable cabal of landowners, developers and government
officials, accountable to no-one but shareholders and the head of
department, who don't have to suffer the adverse consequences of
the development they choose, it is likely to have a far more negative
impact on the quality of people's surroundings. The second way of
doing things has prevailed in Britain. We are *all* the poorer for it,
but I am interested in what we might be able to do to correct it.

As I've explained, the land we occupied in London was scheduled
for yet another superstore in the area. Local people were adamantly
opposed to it, as it would destroy small shops, increase the traffic
burden and make their part of the world more like every other
part of the world. They wanted the land, which had been left
derelict for seven years, to be used instead for what the borough
desperately needed: green spaces for their children to play in,
community projects to replace the ones that Wandsworth Borough
Council had destroyed, and affordable housing. The landowners'
proposal was rejected by the council, but that, unfortunately, is not
the end of it. Developers in this country have the most extraordinary legal powers to subvert the democratic process and impose
their projects even on the most reluctant population.

If ordinary people don't like a local authority's decision to
approve a development, there's nothing whatsoever that they can
do about it. If developers don't like the council's decision to reject
their proposed developments, they can appeal to the Secretary of

State for the Environment. Developers know that an appeal will cost the council hundreds of thousands to contest. Time and again developers use the threat of appeal as a stick to wave over the council's head, and as often as not the blackmail works. If the council has enough money to fight an appeal, however, and if at appeal the Secretary of State rejects the developers' plans, all they need do is to submit an almost identical planning application, and the whole process starts again. This can go on until both the money and the willpower of the council and local people are exhausted and the developers get what they want. If the blackmail and extortion still don't work, however, the developers have yet another weapon in their armoury. Planners call it 'offsite planning gain'. You and I would recognise it as bribery. Developers can offer as much money as they like to a local authority, to persuade it to accept their plans. You don't like my high-rise multiplex hypermarket ziggurat? Here's a million quid. What do you think of it now?

The results of this democratic deficit are visible all over our cities. Where we need affordable, inclusive housing, we get luxury, exclusive estates; where we need open spaces, we get more and more empty office blocks; where we need local trade, we get superstores (and I can confidently predict that in ten years' time there'll be as much surplus superstore space as there is surplus office space today). These developments characteristically generate huge amounts of traffic. Affordable housing is pushed out into the countryside. Communities lose the resources which hold them together.

But if this suspension of accountability is onerous in the towns, it is perhaps even more poignant in the countryside. There the message, with a few exceptions, is clear: It's my land, and I can do what I want with it.

Over the centuries, the concept of property has changed dramatically. Property was a matter of possessing rights in land or its resources, and there were few areas of land in which rights of some kind were not shared. Today it is the land itself which is called property, and the words for the rights we possessed have all but disappeared. 'Estovers' (the right to collect firewood), 'pannage' (the right to put your pigs out in the woods), 'turbary' (the right to cut turf), 'pescary' (the commoners' right to catch fish), have passed out of our vocabulary; now, on nearly all the land in Britain, we no longer even have the right of access. The landowners' rights are almost absolute, ours are effectively non-existent.

This means the landowners can get away with some terrible things. Every year throughout the 1990s, for instance, country landowners have overseen the loss of 18,000 kilometres of hedgerow. Since the war, they have destroyed nearly 50 per cent of our ancient woodlands, and, this century, they have ploughed over 70 per cent of our downlands. Heaths, wetlands, watermeadows and ponds have been hit even harder. Most distressingly, across huge areas they have erased the historical record. The dense peppering of longbarrows, tumuli, dykes and hillforts in what are now the arable lands of southern England has all but disappeared since the war. In response to landowners' lobbying, the government continues to grant special permission – the Class Consents – to plough out even scheduled ancient monuments. Features that persisted for thousands of years, that *place* us in our land, are destroyed in a matter of moments for the sake of crops that nobody wants. Our sense of belonging, our sense of continuity, our sense of place, are erased.

It doesn't matter how well loved these places were. Even if people had for centuries walked, played, made love in the watermeadows, if those meadows are not a Site of Special Scientific Interest, the landowner can simply move in without consulting anyone, and plough them out, destroying everything local people valued. Even where they are SSSIs, this seems in practice to make little difference, as these places are constantly being eroded and destroyed, in some cases with the help of the taxpayer.

Agriculture and forestry are perversely not classed as development, and are therefore exempt from public control of any form. Even the erection of farm buildings requires no more than a nod and a wink from the local authority. By contrast, if people such as gypsies, travellers and low-impact settlers, people from somewhat less elevated classes than those to which many country landowners belong, try to get a foothold in the countryside, they find they haven't a hope. It doesn't matter how discreet their homes are, it doesn't matter whether, like the bender communities of King's Hill or Tinker's Bubble in Somerset, they actually enhance environmental quality, rather than destroying it, they are told the countryside is not for them. You can throw up a barn for a thousand pigs with very little trouble, but try living in a hole in the ground in the middle of the woods, and you'll find all hounds of hell unleashed upon you.

What we're getting in the countryside is not just a biological monoculture, but a *social monoculture* as well. Just as in Kenya, only one product is being optimised, and that is profit. The costs to the wider community count for nothing. This accounts for the familiar sight in Britain today of mile upon mile of agricultural land empty of human beings. It's hardly surprising. Britain now has fewer people employed in farming than any other western nation. In the city state of Hong Kong, twice the percentage of the population works in agriculture as in the green garden of Britain. Yet, though farmers' incomes are rising, we continue to shed farm labour at the rate of twenty thousand workers a year.

These problems are aggravated by our physical exclusion from the land. People fought so hard for Twyford Down because they had a stake in it; they had a right to walk over it and saw it as their own. When excluded from the land we have less interest in its protection; it is someone else's business, not ours, so, with a few exceptions, we let the landowner get on with it. The exclusive use of land is perhaps the most manifest of class barriers. We are, quite literally, pushed to the margins of society. If we enter the countryside we must sneak round it like fugitives, outlaws in the nation in which we all once had a stake. It is, in truth, not we who are the trespassers but the landlords. They are trespassing against our right to enjoy the gifts that nature bequeathed to all of us.

So what are we going to do about it?

Well, it's time that we began to see that an analysis of Britain as a western liberal democracy is no longer relevant. What I have been describing are Third World politics, Third World economics. We need Third World tactics to confront them. And this is what the direct activists, whom I first came across on Twyford Down, saw before anyone else in the country. They saw that we had to take our lead not from our own recent traditions of letter writing and banner waving, but from the anti-apartheid movement and the Brazilian land reform campaigns. Direct action is not the whole answer, nor is it an end in itself; but it is an unparalleled means of drawing attention to issues which have languished in obscurity to the cost of us all.

We need: Land for Homes – low-cost and self-built housing in cities, places for travellers and low-impact settlers in the country-side; Land for Livelihoods – subsidies and planning to support small-scale, high-employment, low-consumption farming; Land for Living – the protection and reclamation of common spaces, reform of the planning and public enquiry processes, mandatory land registration and a right to roam. The land, in other words, must start to serve us, rather than simply those who control it. Development must become the tool of those who need development most – the homeless and the dispossessed – rather than benefiting only the developers.

For the land we tread is not theirs, it is ours. It is the duty of all responsible people to seize it back.

8

Tossed in the fire and they never got burned: the Exodus Collective

TIM MALYON

Midnight on the Woodside Industrial Estate near Dunstable. The warehouses are empty, car parks full. People sit patiently, playing sounds, smoking spliffs, waiting. Up at the roundabout a 10-ton army lorry and two Land Rovers have just arrived, painted green, with red stars. It's Saturday night, and the party's just beginning. Some three thousand people are assembled, mainly from Luton and Dunstable, but also Oxford, Hitchin, north London. Nothing's been advertised, no fliers, just one phone line, and even that's not necessary. Word of mouth passes fast. People know each other, come back here, over and over again, one of the most loyal party posses in the land, and for good reason. Pick a face at random, and ask why:

It's all about the atmosphere isn't it, at the end of the day. You could go to a club, everyone's standoffish. Down here it's like a family, everyone's happy, everyone's chilled. You don't have to worry about people trying to rob you or nothing like that down here. The people who run the show, at the end of the day, they're in charge and everyone respects them. If you respect the people, you're not gonna cause any trouble in the rave.[1]

Horns honk, engines roar, people run for their cars; we're on the move. The people 'who run the show' are the Exodus Collective. They're mostly locals from the Luton and Dunstable area. Many went to school together, which helped lay the roots of Exodus's racial harmony and mix. They're not some party posse parachuting in from afar, holding a 'do' then moving out regardless

of consequences. They're responsible for their actions. Mums and
Dads read all about them in the local press, especially when trouble
drops, as it has done, too many times. But then, I and I survive. A
line from the Twinkle Brothers, 'Tossed in the fire and they never
got burned', is inscribed on one of the Land Rovers.[2] Adversity can
breed progress, if the intention is right, and that's what this chapter
is all about: the Exodus Collective in Luton, north of London.
Their blending of free parties, their development of a DiY community, squatting their own collective housing, farm and community centre and their systematic harassment by the authorities
are all looked at here.

*

Exodus's post-Israelite chapter opened on 5 June 1992. DJ Hazad
('because I'm a natural hazard') was a founder member. 'I'd always
dreamed of a stack of speakers just a bit taller than me, so's me
and all my friends could go into a field and listen to Bob Marley,
or some "do" music, some dance music.' Typical of DiY culture and
what was to come, Hazad heard about three empty speaker boxes
that had been thrown into a skip. 'I took them back to me Mum's
garage – they were a bit tatty – stacked them up one on top of the
other, and there's me stack there.' A couple of days later he
bumped into 'Jack The Stack'. Jack was fitting car audios and
reckoned he could fit speakers into Rich's cabinets. 'And then on
5 June 1992 we took that stack up to a forest on the edge of
Dunstable, went to the two main pubs in Dunstable, told the people
there was a party going on, and up they came. It went from 150
people for that first do to about a thousand by the third.'[3] Money
from the drinks bar and bucket collections was poured back into
extending the stacks. By New Year's Eve 1992 they formed a wall 30
foot long by 12 foot high, and 10,000 had joined the party. One
dancer described the feeling:

> When I'm dancing in front of the stack it feels like my stomach is in
> my heart, like a burst of energy, like a glow. You feel like expressing
> yourself. You can dance however you want. You can turn your back
> and not be afraid, because everyone is free, people can express
> themselves and let themselves out and have no fear. The sound system
> is part of the community. When Exodus first started, more and more

people were coming to the parties. The parties got bigger, the bucket donations got bigger because of the people, and the sound system got bigger. So the people owned it, because they paid for it, everyone paid for it. It was the community's sound system, it was the people's, not owned by Exodus, we just look after it. All them people who come to the dos, they paid for it.

Exodus's musical background is a topical take on much of what has been happening outside of the mainstream industry over the last ten years. Hazad holds the history:

> The early roots came from following a sound system around the country called Gemini High Power, a Luton sound system which played blues dub. It was MCs chatting over dub reggae – this was before the house scene had kicked in full-on in England, maybe 1986 time. We used to go as quite a crew, maybe ten or fifteen, mainly white people. And the MCs, they respected that, so that the lyrics changed over time, instead of 'respect to all the black people in the crowd', it became 'respect to all the black and white people in the crowd'. We couldn't wait for Saturday nights. Gemini was an inspiration. It seemed more prominent with conscious lyrics than other sound systems. Gemini used to come with political and spiritual lyrics. That was what really attracted us, as well as the bass lines.

Some of the lyrics were prophetic:

> Me come to tell you what police can do
> Me come to show you what police can do.
> Me walking down the road minding me own business
> Police boy stop me – say you're under arrest
> We have the evidence so you'd betta confess
> Me say, no officer, lord you must be bad . . .

To this day the bass lines and lyrics of reggae, especially Bob Marley, remain crucial to Exodus. Regular dub nights are held, down at the barn on the farm, at which Malaki, ex-Gemini sound system MC, often chants the lyrics. Exodus's first home-grown music track came out of collaboration between him and several Exodus DJs.

Members of Exodus maintaining the 'stack' (speakers, rigs and other equipment) used for parties. Photograph by Nick Cobbing

Exodus in the land
Big things a' go on
It's a road block
My God
Babylon them come
But they must turn back
It's a road block
My God
Babylon them loathe that.

They work on the Manor
Exodus work on the farm
With the horse and sheep and pony
Peace and Love
And respect for everyone
So whether you are African, Asian, Red Indian or a white man
Ya see
Exodus are in the land.

An important change has happened to the music recently, proof positive of the Collective's ability to evolve. Several of the older generation of DJs had been starting to alter their music: different pace, different styles. So they passed on their record collections to the new up-and-coming generation. That way, the younger DJs could still keep playing some of the old anthems, mixed in amongst their own new music. 'When we're not on the decks, not on the mic, not on the gate, not on the generators, then we know it's working,' explains Glenn Jenkins, who is thirty-four. 'Exodus looks to empower young people, the next generation, rather than clinging on to things.'

*

But the saga's running ahead of itself. It's 1986, and the word's spreading out of a new sound in town. House has arrived and Hazad continues the tale:

There was a sound called Livewire, who were operating for a while in Edgware Road, and what they've done, they've squatted a nice size warehouse, kind of like what we do today, and they'd kick the dance in there. And it would be a wicked, collective, rocking dance. Because this new phenomenal beat just gave young people who was looking for that sort of thing the place to be. But at that time again, when Livewire had that warehouse, they only had that warehouse for about three or four weeks. I remember they had a little kitchen in there, and the only reason they had that kitchen in there was because they had to say they were squatting it and they had to exercise their squatters' rights at the time, to hold on to the warehouse. But on the fourth week we went to go there, this huge warehouse had disappeared, totally, it was gone, demolished.[4]

Of course the culture didn't stay that raw. Whilst remaining underground, a number of systems started operating that would charge substantial entrance fees – the infamous 'M25' raves belonged to this period – a series of unlicensed pay-parties focused around the London orbital motorway which attracted huge press publicity. Not for the last time people started to resent this commercialisation, most prominently travellers. Sound systems like the legendary South-West traveller crew, Circus Warp, started putting on their own parties. Hazad again:

The travellers done some of the best dances because again it took the spirit of the free party totally by the scruff of the neck. All of a sudden you started hearing about traveller dos, traveller festivals. We were getting phone calls telling us this travellers' do was going on in Chobham Common or Lechlade or wherever it was, mainly in the West Country, and obviously, again, you follow your nose. We shot down there, to be very pleasantly surprised. It was a free party. In you went, the vibes were back, the spirit was back, the 'I want all the money out of you I can get then piss you off in the morning' was gone again and it was back into the underground. The travellers took it right into the underground. I don't think the state liked that, because it was opening up the townies' eyes to what travellers are. And of course because the travellers were holding the dances the media were focusing in on the travellers. They had a heavy purge on the New Age Travellers, saying their camps were riddled with hepatitis, really branding them to the public. But then what happened was, all of a sudden you had an influx of thousands of townies going into these travellers' dos and actually realising these travellers were the soundest people you could ever meet. I don't think the state quite liked that. It was a definite bonding of the street youths.

The state definitely didn't like it; neither the underground dance culture nor travellers and certainly not the two together. At the end of May 1992 police tried to block off a free festival near Bristol, the Avon Free Festival, which caused a convoy to move off from there, accompanied by the massed media. Other convoys, of travellers, ravers and free festival followers, started out from all over the country, ears glued to the radio. Eventually a resting place was found at Castlemorton Common, where police estimated 25,000 people gathered. Shortly afterwards the Criminal Justice and Public Order Bill was introduced into parliament, accompanied by a purge on New Age Travellers, who were forced off unlicensed sites and excluded from scarce licensed ones. Traveller festivals again became a thing of the past, with dire economic and social consequences for everybody involved. The underground dance movement was also targeted. Dance focused increasingly on commercialisation – with some notable exceptions. The week after Castlemorton Common finished, Exodus put on their first do. By 1993 they were coming on strong.

   If the state disliked townie and traveller youth bonding together, it equally disliked the dance culture, with its ability to draw together thousands of people, and squatters cooperating. Glenn Jenkins, former train driver and ASLEF shop steward, has referred to the Exodus dances as 'our minarets, gatherings which draw people in from the cold. Music is the calling force which pulls people together so we can make a stand on land, the disgrace that is wasted land.' One of the remarkable aspects of Exodus's parties is the broad range of people attracted, from teenagers to middle-agers; employed and unemployed; politically aware, or just wanting a good time; black and white; male and female;[5] urban and rural youth; old hippies, punks and Hell's Angels; New-Age and traditional travellers; road protesters and squatters. On 4 January 1993, Exodus supported fourteen homeless people who had squatted a long-empty property in Luton, the Oakmore Hotel. Money from bucket collections at the parties helped renovate the derelict property. At this stage a sympathetic Dunstable police officer, Chief Inspector Mick Brown, had already gone public, adopting as his motto 'jaw, jaw, not war, war'. He appealed publicly in the local press for a legal warehouse where Exodus could hold licensed dances. 'The people who were running these unlicensed raves', he said, 'were trying to avoid any opportunities for violence, so I adopted a dual approach: on the one hand risk management for those attending; on the other hand actively looking for a way for Exodus to hold these events legally.' Before initiating this cooperation, Brown had spent many hours talking with the Exodus Collective and had also run an undercover drugs operation to assure himself that Exodus weren't dealing. 'There is no evidence', he concluded, 'that Exodus, in whatever sense one wishes to use that name . . . were selling drugs at the raves.'[6]

Following occupation of the Oakmore, according to Glenn Jenkins, the police attitude totally changed. The next meeting with Chief Inspector Brown was cancelled. On 15 January police raided and severely damaged the Oakmore Hotel in response to an alleged complaint that an occupier was causing criminal damage by shaving the front door. Two people were charged with affray. When their cases came to court, despite six months' warning, police were unable to produce notebooks belonging to thirteen officers involved in the operation. Exodus suspected the notebooks would have shown the raid to have been pre-planned, rather than a response to the alleged 'criminal damage', for which nobody was ever charged. Luton police admitted that a surveillance operation of the Oakmore had been set up. Following non-disclosure of the notebooks the trial judge dismissed both affray charges.

Six weeks after the initial police raid, the Oakmore was evicted during a snow storm, 'Operation Ashanti'. The occupants were given half an hour to leave. St Margaret's Hospice, a derelict old people's home, was immediately occupied. Exodus were eventually granted a lease, and renamed the property HAZ Manor, Housing Action Zone Manor. People pay their rent/housing benefit into a communal pot, which is used to renovate the building. Decisions are reached by consensus rather than majority rule at collective meetings. Space has been created for some forty people to live there now, with their own rooms and a communal kitchen and living areas. Workshops are being built, crafts learned. It's a big miracle, a beacon of Do-it-Ourselves help. In the context of Exodus and HAZ Manor, 'DiO' is more appropriate than 'DiY'. Individuals work away on their own, renovating their rooms. But big improvements like the flagstone patio outside, or the communal kitchen and dining areas, have happened when the spirit of collective endeavour takes over – 'bosh days' as they're called, training and firing people up to intense and skilled labour who sometimes might have been unemployed for years.

*

One of the early party venues was Longmeadow Farm, compulsorily purchased by the Department of Transport in order to widen the M1, then left to rot. Exodus squatted the farm and offered rent to the DoT which eventually gave them a lease. As with HAZ Manor, extensive renovation was carried out on the farm buildings, as well as a bungalow and house where collective members now live. Almost all the wood used was recycled from pallets donated by local businesses. There's a growing herd of animals, including horses, goats, a bullock, sheep, ducks, and several love-struck Vietnamese pot-bellied pigs. The plan is to open the farm up to the public, and especially local schools. 'There are no other facilities like this round here,' commented Rosemary Davis, Headmistress of Luton Ferrars Infant School during an open day. 'It's a unique experience. I'm very impressed.'[7]

Exodus's word-of-mouth access to thousands of people and its history of reclaiming territory for the dispossessed, either short or long term, inevitably attract police interest. But some officers recognise the positive effects of Exodus's activities. On weekends when Exodus were holding dances, Chief Inspector Brown said,

> licensed premises were experiencing a fair amount of loss of trade, loss of customers. People might pop into the pub for a quick drink around ten, but then they'd be off for the rest of the night. Some licensees were starting to get into real financial trouble. As a consequence there was a lessening of alcohol-related offences, gratuitous assaults, bottle throwing, the random public disorder that generally goes with town centres and drink.[8]

Coincidentally the crime rate in Luton dropped by 6 per cent the year Exodus started putting on parties. During the period in 1993 when Exodus suspended the parties as a result of injunctions and police activities, pub takings in the Luton area rose by 40 per cent, this at a time when takings elsewhere were reported to be dropping as a result of reduced alcohol consumption by party-goers.

One of the Exodus Collective dances – this one in a sand quarry which was squatted for the night – in Luton.
Photograph by Nick Cobbing

Then came the big police operation – Operation Anagram. At 8.15 on Saturday 31 January 1993 large numbers of police raided Longmeadow Farm on a drugs warrant and 'to prevent a breach of the peace'. They arrested thirty-six people, who were taken to Luton Police Station. The PA was confiscated. Chief Inspector Brown was not consulted, and said he only knew of the planned raid one hour before. 'I was rather put on the spot. There was no time to question the decision.' By this time the operation was being supervised by County Police headquarters in Kempston. Asked why there had been a change of policy, Brown replied: 'I heard a number of Members of Parliament had written to the Chief Constable saying this should stop, that the police ought to get on the case. At about the time the decision was taken to pull the plug on negotiations, there were some Members of Parliament advocating drastic measures.'[9] Sir Graham Bright, former Parliamentary Private Secretary to John Major, was MP for Luton South until the 1997 election, and responsible for a private member's bill imposing a maximum £20,000 fine and six months' imprisonment on anyone organising unlicensed parties. He was quoted in the *Luton News* at the time of Anagram as saying he hoped people 'would be prosecuted to the maximum'. His fellow former MP, John Carlisle, erstwhile Tory member for Luton North, said shortly afterwards in a Commons speech supporting the 'anti-rave' sections of the Criminal Justice and Public Order Act: 'We have had to ask local forces to be on standby so that police can stop a rave before it takes place or go in and break it up.' Bedfordshire Police have always denied political involvement in their operational decisions.

Despite a warning from Brown, police had not counted on the crowds assembling at the Woodside Industrial Estate. When word of the arrests went out, between three and four thousand people drove down to Luton Police Station, surrounded it, turned on the music and danced their displeasure. In line with Exodus's policy of non-violence the demonstration was 'massive but passive', this despite a local newspaper report that an 'agent provocateur' had been arrested for inciting violence who turned out to be a police officer. Everybody was released that night without charge, save for a couple of cannabis cautions. Police promised to return the PA equipment. According to Chief Inspector Brown, 'the crowd left the demonstration with some panache. They tidied up after themselves and put their rubbish in bags. I thought that was quite a nice touch really.'[10]

Worse was to follow: injunctions to stop the parties; two further huge police operations, 'Anatomy' and 'Anchovy', at a reported cost of £103,000; and an alleged drugs plant on Paul Taylor, a leading black member of the Collective. Taylor is widely respected for his role in bringing together black and white people within Exodus. 'The charge against Paul Taylor was part of a policy to discredit and smash our organisation, because it was capable of organising civil disobedience and standing up for itself,' Glenn Jenkins commented. 'It was a plant. Those charges were part of a package designed to suggest we were actually here to conspire to sell drugs.'[11] Paul Taylor was found 'not guilty'.

Full coverage of the raids, drugs find, alleged plant and Paul Taylor's acquittal was published in New Statesman & Society on 24 June 1994 and 21 April 1995. These and further stories have subsequently been repeated and expanded, in The Big Issue, by Jim Carey in SQUALL and in Mark Saunders's Channel Four film Exodus from Babylon. The police have neither denied nor sued but refused all interviews on the subject. This silence, but more importantly the sheer volume of operations against Exodus, contributed towards a unanimous and unique vote on 27 April 1995 supported by all the political groups on Bedfordshire County Council, calling for a 'full public inquiry into Bedfordshire Police's and others' activities against members of the Exodus Collective and others, chaired by Michael Mansfield QC, the country's leading civil rights lawyer'. This remains the first and only example of a local council voting to investigate its own police force itself, rather than trust the Police Complaints Authority.

*

Summer 1995 saw major riots on the Marsh Farm Estate in Luton, home to many people who attend the dances, and to Glenn Jenkins, Exodus's spokesperson. The riots started on a Wednesday evening with a car being burned and soon engulfed the entire estate; the result of police over-reaction, in Jenkins's view. Thursday and Friday night saw massed stone-throwing and petrol bombing. Saturday night was expected to be the violent climax. Then something strange happened. Glenn Jenkins:

We held a community dance and pretty much emptied the streets of Marsh Farm, from Friday night when there was hundreds and hundreds of people. On the Saturday night, there was virtually nobody.

Asked whether this was because the people who would have been on the streets of Marsh Farm rioting on the Saturday night were at the dance, he replied:

That would clearly seem to be the case. I came back here at five o'clock in the morning to pick up some records with DJ Kay and there was no one here. It was just hundreds and hundreds of police, all dressed up and no place to go.[12]

Exodus's role, denied by the police, in emptying Marsh Farm that Saturday night was criticised in the postbag of *SQUALL* magazine. Under the title 'To Rave or to Riot', Emile Henry accused Exodus of 'basically acting as unpaid auxiliaries to police crowd control methods'.[13] Exodus replied:

If you 'gain freedom' through violence, then you should expect to have to defend it by the same means. We believe in the triumph of reason over will, good over evil. In other words, that our culture, based on sharing and co-operation, is so right and their culture, based on self-interest and competition is so wrong. ... Something deep inside of most people says that violence is wrong. We believe in the building of a non-violent society that values all life, and which has respect, not force as its police. So surely you should begin as you mean to go on. ... We believe it is our duty to be constructive, not destructive, because we are confident that the construction of a new way always signals the destruction of an old one, and that DiY culture is the roots of the new one.[14]

*

It's 1996. Three o'clock in the morning. The convoy has arrived. At one end of the occupied warehouse stands the stack of battered black speaker boxes. The burglar alarm's just gone off and DJ Guy has started his usual warm-up techno set. Since Paul Taylor was found not guilty on the drugs charge Exodus has been continuing with the parties free of police hindrance. There's been ongoing friction with the police in other areas, but the Exodus dances remain the largest unlicensed 'dos' since the 1994 Criminal Justice and Public Order Act banned those infamous repetitive beats. Exodus would like to go licensed, but their attempts so far to locate a suitable building have been thwarted.

Chief Inspector Brown has taken early retirement. Outside the warehouse his old sidekick, Inspector Tony Kimble, is standing in the rain chatting amiably with 'the youth'. He's asked for a comment, obviously wants to give one, but equally obviously is nervous. Since Brown's days, police statements are channelled through the press office. Eventually we find a form of words. 'The people who have arrived here have not caused any problems,' says Kimble. 'They're parked all down the road, quite normally. They're good humoured, and talking openly to me. I've had no personal problems dealing with the people who attend these raves. Obviously this is contrary to what some may have experienced. But I personally have had good relations with the Exodus Collective.'

Nearby there's a group of youths standing around – time for another vox pop, a random take on public opinion at the do:

'If it weren't for Exodus, everyone'd be at home watching videos or getting in trouble.'

'This stops you from getting in trouble?'

'Yeah! It gives us something to do. It's better than nicking cars, know what I mean.'

'What, it's an alternative activity to nicking cars?'

'Yeah. It's either this, or nick cars, get into trouble, do crime. This stops us from getting into crime. Yeah man! It's better.'[15]

Glenn Jenkins expands on this theme:

What we do is accept the fact that we've all got little bits of money. We could all seek to better ourselves personally, individually, and a lot of people do that through crime, and the better the criminal, the more progress, apparently, so that's the problem as it exists now. What we offer, what we try and do is accept the fact that we've got very little. We haven't dropped out, we've been forced out, and then we say, if we all take a little piece of that little that we've got, and put it into the middle, and have it accountable, it's still our money, it's still my fiver that goes into the middle, then all those poor people's money together can start to make something out of nothing. So being part of that, all of a sudden your idea of betterment, your idea of progress changes. You can see a new future, without going in and apparently bettering yourself by stealing a credit card or whatever. So that's what we've done. We've set an example of a different form of betterment, a different form of self-help. We all get better together. It's a community fund that is open to all of us and if it buys a plane we can all get on it. It's not that we don't recognise the need for money; we recognise that people will need to better themselves. It's just that we've replaced the old notion of better with a different notion of better. That's why it's so powerfully effective on crime.

There's powerful examples in our group of people who are reformed criminals, because they don't have to commit the crimes any more to better themselves. They all feel the sense of betterment that I'm talking about, the 'we all get better together' notion. And largely, it came from the fact that some of the people in our group are the people who would feel that first, who would feel this spiral of that having to be bad to survive, that's a spiral where soon people end up getting killed, and America's a good example of that. So we are the people who felt it first, and were moved to act. Because one of our statements is, 'All we want is peace in the ghetto.' We don't want to leave the ghetto, we just want peace in it.

We've had living examples of people who have come to the dances and committed bad acts, and what we mean by bad is preying on the weak, mugging for example. We've had muggers at the dances, and we've had to use reasonable force, like manhandle them out of the place, because they had just terrified somebody and robbed them. What we did was switch off the music, gave a description of the person who'd done it and said, 'Wherever you are, we're looking for you, and you'd best leave the dance.' Because that sort of thing just doesn't go on here. And then a crowd of people started pointing and shouting, 'cause I said the bloke's got a red jacket with a black hat on, and someone was seen whipping a red jacket off really quickly. So everyone started pointing him out and some of the peace stewards, which are voluntary people from the dance, good people in the community who are respected, some of them went over. There was a bit of an argument, obviously, and the muggers, there were two of them, they were grabbed by three or four people and marched out of the dance, to the applause of everybody. So that made everybody feel not alone any more. And that travelled the network like wildfire. Mugging is about preying on the weak, not about going into a strong community, where the whole crowd's gonna turn on you. So the only way you can stop these things is by uniting the whole community, not

by penal measures, not by putting a blanket over the thing and
throwing people in prison.

As it happens, we knew the muggers. And we put word out that
they were barred from the dance. When you consider that there's
nothing else happening in Luton, then to be barred from Exodus is a
bit of a gutter. We didn't say strictly 'You're barred.' We said, 'You're
barred until you can come to the farm and talk to us about why you're
prepared to noise up this vibe that we've got here, 'cause we thought
it was supposed to be in everybody's interests this dance, so why are
you not respecting that?' And within two days the two people involved
had come up to the farm, spoke with us, we had maybe a four-hour
chat with them, a good chat, sometimes heated, but respectful of each
other. In the end they agreed with what we were trying to do and the
principle behind it, because it's about community defence. Now when
those two are at the dances, they've helped us on more than one
occasion with other muggers that we had to reason with along the
way. And there's nothing better than a bloke standing there and
saying, 'Look, man, I did this at Exodus, and now I don't.' It works,
it's powerful. Now muggers at the dance are so rare that it's beautiful.
And you can't fuck with that.

What we're doing is more than replicable. I think the social effects
of it are massive, already, even before we've established the community centre. Just talk to anybody who's involved in Exodus and
you'll see the major achievement it is to make people feel much,
much better about themselves, to leave behind that sense of despair.
So I think this is something that people will demand in their towns
and countries, because it's a solution to all those feelings of coldness
and darkness and despair. And it's those feelings that bring about
crime and suicide and drug abuse, making the distinction between
drug abuse and use. So if we're addressing those feelings, then we're
a possible solution to things we've never dreamed of. I mean, you
start with entertainment, and you end up with the world, a rave new
world.

Dave is seventeen, a powerful example of including the youth, of
bringing in people who are losing hope and heading for prison.

I live at HAZ Manor. I left home when I was fifteen 'cause I didn't get
on with my family. I was homeless for about three weeks, staying with
my friends, sleeping on their sofas. I didn't like school, didn't like my
family. There was a lot of coldness, a lot of bitterness in my life,
bitterness for school, bitterness for my family, bitterness because there

was no way out. I was just a kid who didn't do well at school, couldn't do well at school, so I rebelled against it.

I fucked up at school. I'm not really academic. And my life was falling apart at that time. I ain't too good at English or maths or science. I took ten exams, but I done crap in all of them. Then because I was only fifteen, under law you're not allowed to live on the street, you have to be in the care of your parents or in the care of the government. I moved into care, I went into a children's home, and the kids that were in there, most of them were criminals, either waiting to go to court or waiting to go to prison. So I mixed with them. They asked me if I wanted to help them once and I said yeah. I tried breaking into a place, and got nicked for it. So I was done the first time I ever tried breaking in anywhere.

I became a thief. I was nicking from shops, full on, every day. Either I was sitting about or nicking. And then come the weekends I weren't nicking because I was going to the raves. The raves were something to look forward to at the weekends.

I went to a Youth Training job in a sports shop. I was running up and down stairs doing people's laces up. I wasn't taught nothing. It was a fucking horrible job, running about, looking at numbers, and passing the shoes to someone else. Then I had to make tea and clean the carpet after work. It didn't stop me from doing crime, and I was being treated like a piece of shit. So I left that. I thought, fuck this, I'm a young person, and I want to do something. A lot of kids must think this. I was still going to the Exodus raves at the weekends.

And then I moved into HAZ Manor, after coming to the raves every two weeks. I moved in, asked people who lived here, and started doing something totally different. This is an alternative to working on YT for me, it's an alternative and it's good. And I ain't doing crime no more, because there's no need for it, because I've got a roof over my head, I've got people who love me who I live with, and if I'm hungry I can go and see them. And if I'm bored I can do something, community work, working on the parties, working here at the Manor, working at Long Meadow Community Farm. I can do anything I want. I can create something, and be proud of it. When I do something here, it makes me feel part of something. I get a buzz out of it. And I do it with love as well. My life is warm here now, where before it was cold. I love it.

When we're putting on a party and I lift them speakers, I think of the party, I think of all them people who'll be having a good time. This is for the people, this is by the people, all them people coming together, all them young people, like me when I first went. Sometimes

I remember how I used to be. I think, what would I be doing if I wasn't doing this? The Exodus parties stopped me doing crime at the weekends, 'cause I had something to do.

If I hadn't met Exodus, and hadn't have moved in to the Manor, or gone to the raves, I would be in prison now, because I would have carried on crime. It would have caught up with me in the end. It was catching up. If I weren't here, I'd be in nick, I'd be in prison or on the way to prison. But this is happening, and I'm not in prison and I'm not going to prison. This is a solution to a problem, for me, and for many other people. What's happening here is a solution to crime, because I used to do crime, whereas now I don't.

*

Exodus have a dream, the Ark Community Centre, transport out of Babylon, a warehouse where the dances could happen once a month, towards which everyone would donate £5. This money would go towards the running of the centre. There would be recording studios, cost-price food and Marley's bar, workshops, a craft area, a local radio station and newspaper, so no longer would the community have to rely on outside media interests. In effect the Ark would enable revenue from the dances to be channelled back into the community from which that revenue originated, rather than going out of the community and into a promoter's pocket. As Exodus themselves say, 'It will give this movement a permanent home and a means whereby people who have no voice at present can speak.' But the dream keeps on being blocked. Exodus have identified the perfect warehouse. They even occupied it and started work on it, having offered the owners rent and attempted to enter into negotiations, to no avail. They were evicted. Now (November 1997) the Highways Agency are trying to evict Exodus from Longmeadow Community Farm (subject to a review by the Minister for Roads, Baroness Hayman), selling it over Exodus's head to the highest bidder, even though Exodus put in a bid over the asking price, and have recently finished completely renovating the bungalow.

The catalogue of inaction to assist Exodus, and action to stop the Collective, continues relentlessly. There have been eleven police raids to date, sixty-five arrests and fifty-five charges, but only ten convictions, of which nine were guilty pleas to organising unlicensed parties. All fines have been dropped by the courts. Most recently Dunstable Police have applied successfully to the licensing magistrates to remove Glenn Jenkins's mother's licence. She runs the Globe public house where many of the Exodus posse drink. She is appealing against the decision and is awaiting the verdict at the time of writing.

The outlook, however, is by no means gloomy. Since the general election in May 1997 there have been Labour MPs representing Luton, Kelvin Hopkins and Margaret Moran, and a Labour government running the Highways Agency. Kelvin Hopkins has taken up the case of Longmeadow Farm with the Agency. INURA, the International Network for Urban Research and Action, based their annual conference at Exodus in 1995. The organisation has written to Rt Hon. John Prescott MP, Secretary of State for the Environment, Transport and the Regions, and to Glenda Jackson MP, as follows:

> In our view theirs [Exodus] is an innovative and inspired project representing best practice in the field of social development. We believe this initiative offers a model of self-help which could be replicated elsewhere .... We were concerned to hear that the future of this project [Longmeadow Community Farm] is under threat. Consequently we have felt it necessary to voice our concerns and we would urge you to intervene in this exceptional case.

Meanwhile, Tony Blair's new Social Exclusion Unit has been approached to facilitate establishment of the Ark Community Centre.

Land has been offered to Exodus where licensed summer festivals could be organised, 'to bring back the spirit of the free festival'. The St Albans Diocesan Board for Social Responsibility has recently commissioned a highly favourable report on Exodus, whose author, Malcolm Nobbs, was quoted in SQUALL magazine as saying: 'I actually felt closer to God at Exodus than I have in some churches in the diocese.'[16] Rev. Roger Woods, vicar of Streatley, whose parish includes HAZ Manor, has reprinted the report in the local parish magazine. Bridges are being built. And members of Bedfordshire County Council are renewing calls for the public inquiry, calls which might fall on slightly less deaf ears at the Labour-controlled Home Office. As Paul Taylor says,

'We don't want retribution, we want justice. We want the Ark Community Centre for Luton. And we want to remain at Long-meadow Community Farm.' The man asks for little, but gives much.

Back in 1994 Glenn Jenkins made a statement which rings as true today as it did then:

It's about time the politicians got honest, stopped talking bollocks about green shoots in the economy and told the people the truth about work. We're not drop-outs, we're force-outs, people who are not wanted any more. There's no future for a lot of people in the present set-up, no chance of decent work. So people need something else, a new existence. The system needs to assist us to diversify. Politicians should support this diversification, because it'll have positive effects on their world. We're on a mission. We're at the cutting edge of a way, an answer. It could even be a solution to the decay of Britain PLC.[17]

*

The party's over. The floor is swept. The warehouse stands empty and silent, once more 'a monument to the disgrace that is wasted land'. All that's left behind as a reminder of the joy that was and could be once again is a piece of cardboard leaning up against the wall on which a poem has been written. It's addressed 'TO THE LEASER OF DIS PLACE':

> We hope that you are not too mad
> Coz of the good time we've just had.
> We haven't caused you damage mate,
> Even though the dance ran *late*!
> Three thousand people were here tonight
> Making *use* of this place – right.
> It's not a crime to come together
> In places sometimes *left forever.*
> We come in convoys *five miles long,*
> So many thousands *can't* be wrong.
> So, once again, we're sorry for
> The broken lock on your front door.
> But, being truthful, we can't say
> That we regret, in any way,

Bringing back community
To a town that's lost it totally.
Thanks
Peace, Love, Unity and Respect
Exodus of Luton
JAH LIVE

9

Dangerous dancing and disco riots: the northern warehouse parties

DREW HEMMENT

> no matter how many draughts of forbidden wine we drink,
> we will carry this raging thirst into eternity.
>
> Hakim Bey, *TAZ*[1]

My last memory of a Blackburn party is of an attempt at storming a police station to regain a seized PA. We had followed the convoy for over an hour along motorways and down leafy country lanes to our warehouse destination only to find the PA truck had been stopped by a routine police check and the PA impounded. The driver told us that it was being held in a small village police station a few miles away and this information spread like a virus through the crowd – which then set off marching towards the police station, like a carnival winding its way through the deserted rural lanes, music pumping from car stereos and people dancing and shouting on top of the cars. There was no plan to this spontaneous act of unity and resolve, however, and when the procession arrived at the police station the momentum was broken on its walls. These were people on a mission, but without deadly intent. Radicalised by a winter of confrontation and discontent, some people started throwing missiles, but others in the crowd tried to stop them, and many more just stood around or shouted. At one point a police officer on duty in the station opened the door and rushed out to try to grab someone who had strayed up close. But upon emerging he was stopped short by the sight of the mass of people at his gates. After a second's pause as both sides stood frozen in time the crowd surged forward and the policeman darted back inside, just managing to slam the door behind before being overwhelmed. (If only. . . .) A hail of missiles followed. With iron bars covering all the windows, that fleeting chance turned out to be the only opportunity there was. Pretty soon it became clear that it was futile, and, anticipating what was to come, people started exchanging clothes in order to confound any later identification. Within twenty minutes they arrived: half a dozen riot vans driven at speed into the middle of the crowd. The back doors were flung open and squads of riot cops poured out . . .

This story, dating from 1990, has it all: party progress met by systemic negation, a festive outburst keeps the vibe alive, frustration and transference before the solid walls of state power, and the ultimate imposition of order and control. So what happened to the party? And where did the party heads run when the battle lines were drawn – underground, overground, or somewhere even more secret that exists between the two but which has yet to be mapped?

'High on hope'

we fought the law
but who won?

The north-west of Britain is better known for its urban wastelands and decaying industries than its night life, but between 1989 and 1991 it saw some of the most intense and sustained disco debauchery in the history of house as the otherwise unremarkable town of Blackburn became the centre of a DiY party movement that would spawn two of the country's most successful clubs, Cream and Back to Basics, and culminate in a series of large-scale riots and the arrest of 836 people at a single party.

The warehouse parties took place at the juncture between the unruly excesses of acid house and the development of the dance scene into a cultural phenomenon with global pretensions and mass appeal. Arising before any coherent ideology had coalesced around dance culture, and before its commercial viability had been ascertained, they are both a seminal moment in this history and a microcosm existing on their own terms. Here I look into the rise and fall of the infamous Blackburn parties, with a particular interest in their escalating confrontation with the law. I then look at their legacy by considering the ART LAB, a dance and art collective that arose four years later just down the road in Preston. What they shared was the effort – against adversity – to make art out of life rather than just marking time. Both inspired the sense of unlimited potential that always accompanies a step into the unknown, not to mention the discovery of new worlds of sound and forms of expression. Both survived – for a while – against all odds. And both provided a meaning and focus to people's lives where before – and after – there was none. But while Blackburn took on the whole world (and for a while looked like it could win), the ART LAB offered a small-scale and local solution that gives a valuable lesson in how it is possible to outwit despondency and stagnation in contemporary times.

Fuelled by amplified noise, repetitive beats, relentless rhythms, alien soundscapes, police chases, drugs and late nights, the warehouse experience was something never before seen. What had started with the yuppie economics and laissez-faire lifestyle of the London orbital raves swept like a tidal wave across the country, until it reached the furthest reaches of the northern conurbations. Here it struck a chord with the disinvested bodies of the post-industrial wastelands who had been abandoned by Thatcherite economics and forgotten by global trends. Barriers between races and classes were broken down, a generation of football hooligans tuned in and chilled out, and the inner-city underclasses broke out of the ghettos and discovered a new world of potential and release. At the vortex of the storm was Blackburn (and in particular the underground party collective Hardcore Uproar). The town was renamed Boomtown and took on the feel of an independent state existing in the psychedelic imaginations of the people involved and on the graffitied motorway signs on the convoy routes.

To understand the significance of the parties it is important to grasp the context of cultural desolation and economic death found in northern towns such as Blackburn and Preston. The dour and ugly urban features were mirrored in the hopelessness of the residents' lives. People had little to lose and everything to gain, which explains the immense amount of creative and psychic energy unleashed by the parties. With this the parties helped to build a sense of regional identity and cultural pride: the expression 'It's grim up north' was invested with a new meaning and came to signify the perversely positive pathos of the times.

Music has long been used as a signifier of regional identity in the north-west of England – from Mersey Beat and the Beatles, through Northern Soul and the punk of the Buzzcocks, Joy Division, and the Fall's 'The North Will Rise Again', to indie bands such as the Stone Roses and Oasis. At the time of the warehouse parties Manchester in particular was witnessing a cultural renaissance, reinventing itself as 'Madchester' and selling the indie-dance sounds and narcotic lifestyles of bands such as the Happy Mondays to the world. But this music industry-engineered rebirth was in fact parasitical on the new energy emanating from dance culture – and from Blackburn in particular. Television footage of the Blackburn parties was packaged and sold as a Mancunian export, creating incredulity and scorn amongst the party-goers. Manchester did play a pivotal role in the development of dance culture. The Hacienda did more than any other club in Britain to cultivate the house sound, and tracks such as 808 State's 'Pacific State' and A Guy Called Gerald's 'Voodoo Ray' – both originating from Manchester – are among the most sublime moments in UK dance music. But the warehouse parties arose at a distance from this, and maintained a fierce independence. They were simultaneously a popular-festive outburst from the provinces and the site of a new hybridised cosmopolitanism constructed over and against the rationalised modernism of the city centres, as people from all corners of the country came together and danced to the exoticism of imported sounds and incipient musical styles. And, beyond this, within the dance scene in general, it was less that the music was an expression of an authentic regional identity than that the way it was played and received – especially the do or die attitude – created a unique sense of place and a feeling of cultural empowerment.

An obvious precursor to the warehouse parties was seventies Northern Soul. Inspiring a passionate following, the Northern Soul 'all-nighters' were characterised by an obsession with obscure black American soul records, frenetic dancing and night-shifts that could last an entire weekend. As with dance culture, it was the experience of moving to and being moved by the music that was important, rather than alcohol or sexual conquest. What was to become a national dance phenomenon had its roots firmly in the north-west, and it was only down the road from Blackburn and Preston that Wigan Casino became its focal point. People would travel considerable distances to get there, and once inside they were free to dress and act how they liked, whether they wanted to dance on the tables or get a bit of sleep on the floor: 'At the Casino anything went. . . . A party of blokes could literally have turned up in their underpants and gained admission as long as they had membership cards.'[2] There are many similarities with the warehouse parties, such as the long pilgrimages, the centrality of dance, and the importance of the musical output of post-Fordist Detroit – although whereas Berry Gordy Jr at Motown attempted to construct a new (mass-produced) reality for black Americans, Detroit techno artists faced with the intransigence of structural racism were more concerned with mapping (aleatory) routes out of the everyday. Northern Soul was also deeply underground: there was not the spontaneous, open communal organisation that characterised the early dance scene, and yet it was based on local networks of participants and was spread by small, independent record shops. The difference is that it remained underground because of its conscious quest for the subcultural capital of rare tracks that no-one else possessed. Whilst Northern Soul looked backwards to the past in its quest for 'new' sounds, the postmodernism of house preferred pastiche to nostalgia, combining fragments old and new into its potent sonic cocktail.[3]

Disco damnation

The north-western party scene took its cue from the ecstatic highs and musical adventures of the Hacienda in Manchester, but it was with outdoor parties such as Live the Dream and Joy that it really took off. However, these legal parties held in marquees were easily identified and stopped by a police force wary of potential noise and nuisance. This set the scene for what was to follow – the explosion of illegal, underground warehouse parties that abandoned the bureaucratic structure of licences and health and safety regulations, and instead sought spaces where the penetrating gaze of the law could not reach.[4] Following the arteries of the motorway network, the inner-city breakout found and reclaimed the spaces abandoned by the tide of industrial decline. Left standing empty and unused, derelict factories and brand-new prefabricated warehouses alike provided the perfect venues for the party phenomenon that could appear out of nowhere and vanish without trace in its effort to outwit the police.

By adopting their typically confrontational stance, all the police achieved – initially at least – was to pour fuel on the fire they sought to control.[5] As a result, a culture of criminality and violence developed within a cultural space dedicated to music and dance that was initially peaceful and non-violent. Indeed, Blackburn is one of the rare instances in which crime itself has been raised to the status of an art form.

Equipment was supplied by an ever-expanding cottage industry of thieves and audio technicians.[6] In particular Jules and Fossie formed the hard cell in this campaign of guerrilla sound production, constructing new speaker cabinets in secret locations each week to replace those seized the week before, whilst smuggling the expensive components out through the police lines so that they could be reused. (Jules kept on going despite being banned from the city limits of Blackburn, placed on police curfew and bound over on £10,000 bail – until ultimately he was jailed for noise pollution.) On the night the sound system would be taken to the warehouse shortly before the party was due to start. Then the convoy would be led there – driving through road blocks, the wrong way down motorways, and blocking off police vehicles as required – timed so that it could arrive just as the music was ready to start. Then the people would be directed into the warehouse as quickly as possible, for once they were inside the police were powerless to prevent the party going ahead. It is a testament to the organisers that not once did the police ever get to a venue before the convoy.

Through a collectivisation of resources (auto theft), people who would never have been able to afford a car were able to participate in this high-speed pursuit. A cat and mouse game developed between police and partiers, with the convoy becoming an essential ingredient of the fun. In an interview in 1995, Chief Inspector Beaty – the officer in charge of policing the parties – described to me how he would stand on motorway bridges as the convoy passed beneath and see three rows of white headlights stretch as far as the eye could see behind and three rows of red tail lights disappear into the distance in front. The scale of it was such that it was

possible to drive towards the confluence of motorways surrounding
Blackburn knowing that if you kept searching you would almost
certainly come across cars heading the right way (although this was
also a cause of more than a few misadventures, with many an old
couple followed to their home after a late night at the bingo).

Thousands of urban kids let loose on an unsuspecting land
created a surreal spectacle, as scallies in ski hats and baggy jeans
brought lawlessness and lunacy to neon-lit industrial estates and
motorway services. The hit and run tactics of the parties meant that
there was rarely the luxury to supply much more than the bare
minimum – a PA and a set of decks. The warehouse walls were
decorated not by sophisticated lighting or styled decorations, but
by a few projectors, simple backdrops and the colourful figures of
the dancers themselves, as people scaled the walls and balanced
precariously on the steel girder frames of the buildings. Even the
sound quality – and sometimes the DJing itself – often left much to
be desired. But these inadequacies were easily forgiven, as what
mattered was that there was sound at all.

If there was any musical style to the Blackburn parties it was
Balearic – the eclectic fusion of American house, European hard
beat, Italian garage and UK sampledelia and indie-dance. Flowing
out of the black and gay clubs in the ghettos of Detroit, Chicago
and New York had come a sonic revolution which set the UK alight.
The abstract sounds and minimal rhythms of artists such as Juan
Atkins, Derrick May and Frankie Knuckles took the legacy of disco,
funk and European electronica into new realms of audio mayhem.
Combined with the ambient sounds of the Mediterranean night
this washed up on British shores in the form of a do-wat-ja-like
sensibility and a sonic sensitivity tuned to dancefloor affect rather
than the pop music formula driven by the 7″ single and radio
playlist. Anything could find its way into the mix, from the US
house of the Reese Project to Andrew Weatherall's remixes of
Primal Scream, and from the abrasive sounds of the urban night
on Steve Poindexter's and Mike Dunn's acid excursions to the
evangelical hope of Stirling Void's 'It's Alright' and Jo Smooth's
'Promised Land'.

In tune with the beats aesthetic forged by the early deck pioneers,
this was music dominated by rhythm and texture rather than by
songs. Vocals became disconnected fragments, sounds tactile

shapes, and music an immersive environment in a genre that mixed messages of harmony with renegade frequencies and twisted rhythms. Rather than make a statement or match a trend, the music explored new zones of experimentation whilst always engaging with the body and maintaining the groove. These were sounds that pushed new expressive frontiers, but without lapsing into the intellectual irrelevancy that characterises much experimental music. They both continued and broke with a tradition of black music that was carried from Africa in the secret resistance rituals of the slaves and that infiltrated mass culture (black and white) through gospel, soul and funk. Unlike Northern Soul's obsessive quest for rare, forgotten originals, house substituted studio distortions for the original instance, and celebrated inauthenticity over the real – continuing the tradition of audio abduction that runs from the studios of Lee 'Scratch' Perry, through Juan Atkins's and Rick Davies's 1982 workouts as Cybotron, and forward to the contemporary drum'n'bass of 4 Hero and beyond.

Left with its defiant two fingers stuck firmly up its own arse, punk never escaped the rock 'n' roll swindle it exposed. But dance culture swept the rug from under the music industry's feet by refusing to play the game. Before the cult of the DJ reintroduced passive fixation into the dance experience, the anonymous DJ replaced the pop star and collective dance swept away the crowd transfixed by the spectacle of the rock star jerking his guitar off on stage. Whilst the floors of contemporary dance clubs can at times resemble glammed-up military parade grounds, the Blackburn crowds favoured the arbitrary and impulsive over the ordered and prescribed. Northern Soul, too, had shifted the emphasis towards the action on the dancefloor. But it was still largely about competition and display, and broke the male gaze only by reversing its polarity and maintaining a rigid gender distinction as men became the chief protagonists of the dance. Revealing its debt to gay disco, on the other hand, dance culture introduced a more amorphous and diffuse sexuality that allowed women and gays more scope for active expression without forcing any particular position or orientation upon the crowd. A degree of masculine dominance remained, however, due to this ambiguity remaining non-reflexive and thus existing incongruously alongside traditional gender relations and sexual outlooks.

Beyond these cultural and artistic shifts, the most celebrated aspect of dance culture is its decentralised mode of organisation and revolutionary forms of participation. In this instance more like punk than Northern Soul, early dance events grew from ground level, organised by the participants for their own satisfaction. There was no strict separation between organisers and crowd, with regular party-goers often finding themselves helping in the running of the events. This added to the effect that dancing has always had of loosening social restraints to unite people of all colours and classes – 'equal under the groove', as the saying goes.

However, the truth of the matter with Blackburn was not so simple. Whilst it was possible for anyone so inclined to get involved, and whilst most people dedicated their time and risked their liberty for free, the Blackburn parties were ultimately organised and run by an inner cell of gangsters. Indeed, it was only their tight organisation and undercover experience that made such wholesale mayhem possible. People could be charged up to £5 on the door, which, with up to 10,000 attending every week, meant that some people were making a lot of money – and stories were common of people disappearing into the night with black bin liners full of cash. In contrast to the anti-market ideology that would later prevail with the free parties, here the commodity exchange of late capitalism had been replaced by the covert profiteering of the black economy.

But Boomtown was not just run *by* gangsters – it was run by and *for* gangsters. Until the good times dried up and the in-fighting began, we were all gangsters together: Boomtown was more of a pirate utopia than a hippie paradise. Like the Caribbean islands taken over in the seventeenth century by escaped slaves and disaffected sailors – such as Captain Mission's Libertatia in Madagascar – there was a generalised participation and a communal assent that accepted that the people taking the risk deserved what they got, and that all that really mattered was that independence was maintained and that the dance went on. What can be said, however, is that there was a significant degree of naivete about the ruthlessness of the gangster organisation that lurked beneath the surface. And when the proverbial shit did hit the fan a lot of innocent idealists (including myself) had their fingers burned and their illusions shattered. Many found the comedown too much to bear. And yet others managed to negotiate the wreckage and turn the energy to creative ends. An example is Nathan, who, despite being made a scapegoat and suffering violence and intimidation, continued to work in lighting and sound production, and also Jane, the editor of the Blackburn fanzine *Ear to the Ground*, who went on to build a successful promoting, DJing and production career – without compromise – with the urban down-beat dance collective One Tree Island.

From Boomtown to Doomtown

Collective dance and abstract sounds led to a revolution in the way people related to art and to each other. But it was in the confrontation with the intransigent blue lines of the law that dance culture became overtly politicised. It is always the sight of a common enemy that binds people together most – especially if that enemy wears a uniform and claims a monopoly on violence.

I recall one party in March 1990 – which was later to be the scene of one of the darkest nights of police violence – when I arrived at a warehouse near Nelson at 6 a.m. with the party in full swing. Walking up to the warehouse I heard the deep chords of Kid and Play's anthem 'Too Hype' mixed with the sounds of horns and cheers washing towards me. The doors were wide open and through the haze of the steam escaping into the cool night air my bleary eyes could make out the colourful seething crowd within. With the hairs standing up on the back of my neck I felt like Neil Armstrong on the moon, every step I took one giant leap for (hu)mankind. I don't know if it was hope but I was high on something. But then it was six in the morning.

But later that night when the crowd had started to thin, the doors of the warehouse which had been closed against the rising sun were flung open to a chorus of loud bangs and flashes. Through the smoke came a solid wall of blue moving to dissect, isolate and 'sterilise' the area. DJs and equipment alike were thrown 5 metres off the improvised stage, whilst towards the crowd came a double line of police in full riot gear marching shoulder to shoulder, striking their linked shields in time with the beat of their hobnailed boots – a sinister alternative to the repetitive beats of

Candy Flip's 'Strawberry Fields Forever' which they had inter-
rupted. There were a few isolated screams, and then people started
rushing and pushing towards the back of the warehouse as the
police lashed out at anyone within their reach. With those at the
back hardly aware of what was happening, the crowd became
squashed and hemmed into a corner, terror on people's faces. A
tall Rasta shouted for everyone to stay calm, and then someone
managed to throw open a door at the back. Everyone poured out
into the fresh air – but outside was another line of police waiting
to stop them, and people had to dodge the flying truncheons to
escape. This was in contravention of the need to allow an avenue
of escape, and in blatant disregard for the police's stated concern
for safety.[7]

This event changed the nature of the situation altogether. Stories
circulated about police beating young girls over the head and other
such misdemeanours, and the incident entered the collective
memory not only of the people there, but of everyone involved in
the northern rave scene. It welded people together as a community,
more determined than ever not to lose their way of life. An
entertainment was becoming a movement, and more and more
people were being drawn to a life on the dark side of the law. In
the extreme cases, even violence against the police came to be seen
as legitimate, as self-defence in the face of a threat to both their
physical persons and their way of life. In the resulting climate, new
people were attracted to the parties who went only to fight with the
police. In the face of massive and sustained police pressure there
followed a succession of serious riots – repetitive beats met with
repeated beatings. This situation reached a climax on 22 July 1990
in the mass arrest of 836 people at a single party at Gildersome
near Leeds – one of the biggest peace-time arrests in Europe this
century. I had my records confiscated at this event, and the only
other DJ – Rob 'parasite-electric' Tissera – was sent to prison for
inciting a riot (Section 2 Public Order) and 'dishonest abstraction
of electricity'.

With the events at Nelson, the authorities served notice of their
new policy of zero tolerance, assembling a national party force and
flooding the region with the same policemen who had learned
their bloody trade during the Miners' Strike and against the Peace
Convoy in the mid-eighties. The irony was that even such extreme

measures did not of themselves stop the warehouse parties. It was more the actions of hardcore gangsters who travelled up from places such as Cheatham Hill in Manchester and who were prepared to use violence to obtain a quick profit that put people off. With guns starting to appear on the scene, the parties were no longer worth the risk and became few and far between. When there was enough money floating around for the big cats to have their cream everyone was happy. But with the profits drying up the Blackburn gangsters revealed their true face and in-fighting and mutual recrimination began.

Eventually the sense of purpose that had built up around the parties was destroyed. With them gone, the people in the Blackburn region returned to the hopelessness of economic desolation. The premature end of such high hopes and soaring aspirations brought people back to earth with a sickening bump as the dream died and despair returned – Boomtown became 'Doomtown'. And those who consider this misery a price worth paying in the war on drugs should note that the end of the parties did not put an end to drug use, but turned existing drug users to stronger, life-destroying drugs such as heroin. The next generation of parties lost the utopian flavour of the Blackburn parties. In place of 'Brave New World' (Poole Bank) and 'The Love Decade' (Gildersome) – the last two Blackburn parties – came 'Revenge'.

The ART LAB

> The light that burns twice as bright, will always burn
> half as long. ART LAB we salute you.
>   No Damn Cat[8] (graffiti following police raid)

The vacuum created by the demise of the Blackburn parties was soon filled as the dance virus mutated and spread to all corners of the cultural map. After the introduction of the Increased Penalties Act (1990) and the Criminal Justice and Public Order Act (1994) dance culture split into two parallel universes, as, on the one hand, club culture swallowed the poisoned pill of respectability and built its elegant castles in the sky, and, on the other, the free party scene forged links with a wider countercultural movement with its potent

Flyers before (left) and after a summer of confrontation in 1990 reveal how the utopian rhetoric gave way to animosity. Original Blackburn flyers from the collection of the author

combination of traveller mobility and sound system ampliphonics. These two worlds are invariably presented as polar opposites. And yet they both share the decentralised organisation, loose collectivity and open networks of influence and exchange. The real enemy is the corporatism that enslaves the music to business strategies and the professionalisation that divides and excludes. Whilst clubs can nurture new genres of music and communities of practitioners, they can also become mere supermarkets of style. The apparent deregulation of consumer society which promises unlimited free-dom in fact hides an ever-increasing adherence to the code. With the noose being increasingly tightened around the neck of legit-imate promoters (particularly after the introduction of the Public Entertainments Licences [Drug Misuse] Act 1997, which gives councils sufficient clout to force club owners to bow to their every wish), it is left to the free party organisations to keep alive spaces beyond the 'new deal' of legal asphyxiation – from local sound systems such as the Rhythm Method in Lancashire, to those with an international following such as the DiY Collective and Spiral Tribe.

But the free party formula is not the only alternative to suffoca-

tion by bureaucracy and incomprehension. Often the most interesting events occur where least expected, and a refreshing alternative
to the official history of house as written in the glossy magazines
came from a source isolated from these wider movements and
trends. Four years after the last Blackburn party, in November
1994, an ex-punk called Allan Deaves decided to convert the
warehouse space in which he lived into an audio immersion zone.
He had been involved in the Mutoid Waste parties in London in
the early eighties and had just spent four years as technical director
of the Tunnel club in New York, but he had no experience of the
UK dance scene and no contact with the free party networks. He
was joined by Alison Frith and others, as a collective of interested
people formed around this new space. With its name recalling the
experimental zones of the sixties, the ART LAB was born. Situated
just ten miles down the road from Blackburn in Preston, it faced
many of the same problems and raised many of the same issues as
the earlier warehouse parties. And yet the answers it gave and the
form it consequently took were very different. The LAB was a fixed
space, run by a few very committed artists for a restricted audience.
And whereas Blackburn was covert but in yer face, the LAB was in
the open whilst deliberately low key.

In addition to the mutual effort, collective release and united
confrontation with the law, with the ART LAB it was also the
incredible dedication of those responsible for the evolving art
environment that bound people together. The ART LAB's two
floors were converted into a living sculpture with new touches every
week and a breath-taking attention to detail. Caught between the
riveted steel of our Victorian heritage and the computer components of our technological future, the LAB's walls evolved into an
intricate mix of organic, rusting pipe-work, digital circuit boards
and computer monitors tuned in to constant static. Alien icon-
ography mixed with machines that seem to possess a life of their
own whilst being on the verge of falling apart. And extra touches
would be added that would not even last the night, such as a
different logo painted on the floor each time and worn off by the
dancing feet during the course of the night.

Much more than just a dance club, the whole top floor was given
over to the depraved scene of people lounging around amidst the
sofas, beds and sculptures, their trivial pursuits aided by the cheap

The walls of the ART LAB invoke the hot spirits of post-rave urban paranoia while framing the delirious diversions of the party. Artwork by Allan, Chuck and the rest; photograph by No Damn Cat

Pip and Rich experience some toxic pleasures at the ART LAB. Photograph by No Damn Cat/Cowie/Hemment

coffee and free slices of fruit which were available all night. From the irreverent vision of its Keep Britain Messy campaign (my contribution) to the community spirit of the free DJing and sound engineering workshops it ran for local kids, the ART LAB always pushed the club concept two steps further. Donations accepted on the door allowed the retro-futurist DJ booth to be fitted with state-of-the-art equipment – such as Pioneer CD-J mark II CD mixers – so that this underground space could support cutting-edge sonics even without the megabucks of the big clubs. Until a court injunction closed the LAB down in 1996 there were even plans for a CD of tunes written by some of the regulars and there was a fanzine called *The Daily Rumour* named after the newspaper that was painted on the venue's toilet wall with a new headline each week – such as 'Justin Robertson Abducted by Aliens' the night he was supposed to DJ but failed to show.

What was memorable about the LAB was the energy and enthusiasm it inspired. As admission was by invitation only there was a degree of exclusivity, but this measure – necessary for the space to exist – served also to increase the sense of intimacy. With word spread through local networks, it attracted an unlikely mix of punks, hippies, bikers, bankers, students, crusties and the nouveau-chic – most new to the dance experience, but all able to find a home at the LAB. The DJs, too, were new to the game, and, initially at least, they supplied an unrelenting diet of up-for-it techno anthems with few excursions into eclecticism or depth. Whilst not to everyone's taste – and certainly not for the faint-hearted – this formulaic simplicity meant that what the LAB offered was all the more accessible and immediate, musical sophistication eclipsed by the messy art of dancefloor delirium and the sheer intensity of the tribal stomp. Ultimately it was more than the venue or the sounds that was special; it was the people who went who created the atmosphere and ensured the departure from sanity and restraint.

For Allan Deaves, the high points were the occasions when people voluntarily donated equipment to replace that seized in police raids, notwithstanding the high risk of it also being seized. For others the actions of Allan himself provide the most poignant memories. The resident DJ, Adrian, recalls one occasion when the floor was bouncing and straining so much due to the frenzied dancing (he had earlier noticed his feet leaving the ground every second beat) that one of the struts supporting it from beneath gave way. He rushed over to tell Allan, who, without any sign of panic, proceeded to remove one of the floor panels at the edge of the room, climb underneath the floorboards, wriggle towards the broken strut and fix it whilst people continued to dance above him – oblivious to his impromptu subterranean service.

The space had to be protected against both gangsters and the law. With entrance by invitation only, it avoided licensing regulations because it was the home of those who ran it, and it escaped the attention of the police by staying low key: everyone had to have their invites ready when they arrived so that there would not be people milling around outside, and the numbers were strictly limited to 300 – which also meant that there was never enough money to make it worth robbing. In addition, unscrupulous dealers were kept out, everyone was made to feel safe, and people were encouraged to take personal responsibility for themselves, what they brought with them, and for those around them.

After surviving for almost a year without incident, the LAB was raided on successive occasions, with the cast-iron doors broken down with a hydraulic battering ram and riot cops pouring in.[9] Once inside the police made illegal searches of the premises and helped council officials confiscate equipment under noise pollution legislation without ever even stopping to take decibel readings (which environmental health officers can do under obscure local by-laws, the equivalent of convicting you of drink-driving without testing your alcohol level). Passports and personal effects were confiscated for over a year, £700 in fines were levied, and thousands of pounds' worth of equipment was seized and destroyed. But what finally put an end to the ART LAB (at least in its original form) was a court injunction stopping the building being used for gatherings of more than fifty people on grounds of public safety – on pain of imprisonment.

Even though no effort was spared on the safety of those who entered, the LAB was outside the system of official checks and measures required by law. It had found favour with the police, who were primarily concerned with threats to public order and considered the packs of drunk men who would spill out of local bars at closing time looking for a fight a far greater problem. But in this case it was the local councillors who took offence. As with the

Blackburn parties, this was something not only outside their jurisdiction but also beyond their understanding – and so it was not to be tolerated. The gap in comprehension was demonstrated by the authorities' justification for their first raid, when they maintained that the sweaty, scantily clad bodies indicated that pornographic movies were being shot within. Never was it so true that the actions of those in power reveal more about the workings of their own fetid minds than about what is actually happening on the ground.

Free party sound systems have the luxury of being able to pack up and disappear into the night. This makes them more mobile and harder to combat. But it also means that any liberation they might achieve is fleeting and transient. Whilst free parties and alternative culture in general seek to escape the clutches of modern society by opting out of the game – skirting over the areas they liberate without ever trying to achieve a lasting settlement – the ART LAB sought to open a space that would stand the test of time and weather the attentions of the law (without it becoming the victim of its own success by solidifying into a permanent cultural institution). Rather than just liberating that space for a night, it also freed the material conditions that would allow it to continue and grow. Instead of disappearing from view it stood up to be counted, whilst nevertheless evading the contemporary mechanisms of control and culture of surveillance, allowing people free expression and the chance to create something on their own terms.

The ART LAB was an *interzone* between the non-place of alternative culture and the dictates of bureaucracy and the law. Allan wanted to run a venue without being a club owner – 'Done for the art of it not for the financial side.' For him, when it becomes a business, 'There's neither art nor heart in it.' Even the most hardcore sound systems often find themselves running into the profit imperative as soon as they start dealing with club managers. The LAB showed how a space can be reclaimed and defended without surrendering the purity or the passion: rather than try to overturn the whole world, explore crevices and slip between the gaps. It also shows that if you want to buy in without selling out, use the system against itself: pervert to subvert. This is not something that can be taken for granted, but in Blackburn required a Faustian pact with the criminal underworld, and with the LAB rested on the willingness of Allan, Alison and the others to stand up in the full face of the law and take all the harassment and punishment that could be thrown at them. For them this was a price well worth paying – and they haven't finished yet.[10]

In a way the LAB was like the art works painted on its dancefloor – it was not intended to be permanent, but was an artistic statement that was destroyed as it was consumed. It suffered an untimely death, producing a vacuum that has yet to be filled, and leaving those at the centre bruised and burned out – and yet it achieved everything Allan and the others set out to do: 'I should be happy with this, and use it to build something else.' Even though it was brought to a premature end, the LAB both stood as an example to anyone wishing to set up something similar themselves, and provided a space in which the people who went could experiment in creative expression and thus start to devise artistic projects or political strategies of their own: 'I want everyone to use the lab as a stepping stone to their own next level' (Allan Deaves). The LAB was a breeding ground of renegade art, and a launch pad for autonomous action. Many were able to take the inspiration it offered and go on to do their own thing, some finding work in music or journalism, and others going on to other forms of collective action.

A case in point is that of Roo, a dedicated clubber who had had no real involvement in alternative politics until, in 1995, she met some activists from the nearby Stanworth road protest site at the LAB. She took a group of people down to visit their camp, and ended up becoming converted to the cause. She has since swapped her worldly possessions for a life on the road, and, in the best tradition of DiY protest, is using the example of her own radicalised lifestyle to directly engage in environmental conflicts. It is ironic that the motorway being contested was to link Blackburn and Preston, a trail of asphalt at odds with the highway of excess traced above, one leading to congestion and pollution, the other to both artistic highs and committed political and environmental engagement. Another example is that of Roo's friend Rich Brains, who, when he discovered that he had all but exhausted the artistic limits of his set of Technics decks, traded them in to finance extended stays at various protest sites (although, unlike Roo, he is still occasionally seen around their home town of Lancaster and he still plays at Rhythm Method parties). Just as the further adventures of DiY and Spiral Tribe have demonstrated that the autonomy does not have to evaporate when the party is over, the stories of Roo and Rich reveal how the dance experience can break down barriers and open people's minds, not to the spurious aspirations and conservative politics often found in the New Age movement, but to radical alternatives that take the energy and inspiration of dance culture beyond the comedown and into new zones of autonomous life. 'It was the party that got me where I am today – and I'm still dancing' (Roo, 11 September 1997).

The dance scene itself will continue to flourish not because of the strength of any 'movement' or the truth of an ideology, but simply because of the power of its combination of autonomous art and collective intoxication. If there is a lasting lesson to be learned from the ART LAB it is that such senseless acts of beauty are possible if the mutual endeavour is there and the desire is right, and that even when the cultural horizon appears stale and stagnant there are always forces pushing up from beneath the ground that can confound the subcultural speculators and unsettle expectations.

10

The Great British Ecstasy revolution

MARY ANNA WRIGHT

Over the last ten years many people have changed their attitudes to drugs. A lot have changed the way they spend their leisure time. Some have changed the way they treat other people. They may have changed the music they listen to. Many have altered how they make money. Some have become slaves to the weekend, having the best night of their lives every single week. Some can take it or leave it. Others have tried to build their lives up to the level they learned to cherish. Hundreds of thousands have experienced the Ecstasy revolution.

The Ecstasy revolution is based on a series of profound moments when the baggage of British values was brought out for an airing under the influence of this Class A drug. Packed within the baggage are rules of behaviour deeply ingrained within our society. Rules like the structure of the British class system, the role of men and women and the sanctity of the law have become increasingly untenable. As dissatisfaction with the political system increased and diverse cultures merged, the baggage was unpacked with a questioning of authority. For many, primarily young people, this questioning coincided with an introduction to a new drug and a new social experience.

The Ecstasy revolution took time to gather force. In the beginning a few people took a few pills at a few parties. Now the E-thos of peace, love and unity has become so much accepted into our social lives it can almost be taken for granted. Experiences that were once considered profound became everyday. The Ecstasy experience involved intense insights into the depth of the human psyche that touched on spiritual revelation or metanoia.[1] It is guessed that today a million tablets of Ecstasy are taken every week in Britain.[2] Those who take it are almost always treated with derision by the media, which tend to slant their stories with an inappropriate emphasis on Ecstasy's likelihood to kill. When people who take Ecstasy read about it in the press they tend to dissociate themselves from what they read. For many young people the reporting surrounding Ecstasy prompted their first realisation that the newspapers were not always telling the truth. This mistrust of the media went hand in hand with the questioning of authority and a legal system which outlawed a social life gaining in popularity. When the culture surrounding Ecstasy use came under attack, this disbelief at the moral panic turned, for many, into a more tangible protest. The links with other groups under attack were strengthened in an affirmation of networks.

This chapter will unearth the seeds of the revolution. First it examines the history of Ecstasy (or methylenedioxymethamphetamine, MDMA for short), how it works and how it came by its present legal status. Next the links with dance culture are explored, highlighting the significance of Ecstasy within DiY culture. Finally the challenges Ecstasy presents are outlined. Such challenges are often on a symbolic level yet are so pervasive to the fundamental structures and habits of society that they have attained significance in terms of long-term radical change. The chapter concludes that the Great British Ecstasy revolution started in the brains, thoughts and actions of the Great British Ecstasy user. Throughout points are illustrated with extracts of a series of interviews covering representatives from all areas of the dance scene.

The Ecstasy story

MDMA was invented in 1912 by a German chemical company. This organisation, Merck, still holds the patent for the drug and this still causes problems with the drug's legal status. A drug cannot be patented twice. Costs involved in carrying out safety tests are recouped if a company owns the patent so maintaining exclusive sales rights. Because no-one but Merck can legally profit from MDMA it is unlikely to undergo the rigorous experiments to which medically useful drugs are subjected.[3]

It was American chemist, now cult hero, Alexander Shulgin, who inadvertently brought MDMA to public attention. Shulgin had invented an insecticide for the Dow chemical company who then gave him free rein to research what he wanted. Having developed a keen interest in psychedelics through personal experience, he began work devising new psychoactive compounds. He broke with traditional scientific methodologies, testing new drugs on himself and a group of friends rather than using animals. This work continued in his home laboratory long after Dow found his discoveries unacceptable. Shulgin rediscovered MDMA in the mid-sixties. Along with several other drug researchers, he was particularly interested in its potential for use as a therapeutic agent. In 1977 Shulgin gave the drug to a therapist friend who was so impressed with its effects he travelled around the States introducing thousands of other therapists to it and training them in techniques which would enable them to use it effectively.

MDMA gradually started to gain popularity as a recreational drug and acquired the street name Ecstasy. In America Ecstasy could still be bought legally at this time. The American pattern of usage was different to the one that followed in Britain. While here it tends to be used with big groups of people together at a club or originally a rave, in America it was used with small groups of friends at home in a setting similar to the way marijuana is often smoked. Curiously perhaps, even though house music originated in America, it took the British to combine Ecstasy with music.

British law is unlike American law in that drugs are not treated as individuals; whole families are grouped together. MDMA, along with MDA, MDEA and other related chemicals often found in street samples of Ecstasy, was classified as a 'hallucinogenic amphetamine' in Class A, and it was prohibited in 1977 under an order modifying the Misuse of Drugs Act 1971. In America, Ecstasy remained legal until 1985, when, by attempting to stop the drug being outlawed, a group of drug researchers brought it into the limelight, spreading awareness to masses of new users. After a scare concerning a totally different drug, the Drug Enforcement Agency clamped down and, using new legislation, banned MDMA. This ban curtailed legitimate research into its therapeutic potential. According to Nicholas Saunders, 'the effect of prohibition was to prevent research into the drug without altering the habits of recreational users'.[4]

Ecstasy trickled into Britain from the mid-eighties. Some came with the followers of the Bhagwan Rajneesh cult, a little from club-goers and musicians who had ventured stateside. The snowball effect happened after the Balearic island of Ibiza became popular as a destination for party people. Ibiza already had a well-established drug culture and reputation as a hippie hang-out. In 1987, when the holiday season ended, the unique mixture of seamless DJing and Ecstasy was brought back to London and the acid house phenomenon was born. Over the last ten years Ecstasy use has increased exponentially. Year in, year out, customs seizures increase as more and more people want to take it, often discovering it through their involvement with dance music. Much of the Ecstasy taken is now produced in Europe. For British youth Ecstasy has become a milestone on the road to adulthood like cutting your teeth, riding a bike and losing your virginity:

> I live with two girls who are eighteen years old. . . . For them it wasn't a question of growing up, and going down the pub. It was a question of growing up going to dance clubs and taking Ecstasy. That's what they were leading up towards whereas when I was at school it was totally anti-drugs. I wanted to get into pubs which I did when I was 15; now it's different.

The dance scene provided an easily accessed network in which Ecstasy could be sold. Friends bought in bulk for each other and the old notion of evil dealers preying on the innocent seemed redundant. This pattern of distribution compounded Ecstasy's popularity on the dance scene; it appeared to unlock an understanding of the music and everyone involved seemed to know how to get 'sorted'. It would be naive to ignore, however, that, like most things traded illegally, control of Ecstasy supply is often big business for a few very powerful cartels. They are never too 'loved up' to forget how to use intimidation and violence to maintain their position.

Because it is so widespread within youth culture it is extremely difficult to pin down the revolutionary potential of Ecstasy. A huge number of people now take what could be seen as a trigger to new ways of behaving. It is hard to say for certain whether Ecstasy causes this behaviour or if these people would have been doing whatever they are doing anyway. It seems likely that in a sample as large as the number of Ecstasy users you will find all sorts, from future politicians to anarchists, protesters to conservatives, from the energetic to the apathetic. You cannot say Ecstasy makes you go out and change the world or everyone doing anything significant in Britain today would have taken it. Neither can you say all E-heads (a new derogatory term for the nineties, as smack-head was for the eighties) do little else but hug each other and dance around when they hear a fire alarm or pneumatic drill. To many, for E-head read air-head and file with the other stoners and slackers who cannot hold down a proper job.

The Great British Ecstasy revolution caused a stir because it was not easy to pin a label on the participants. Ecstasy was one of the first drugs that people took across the board; it was not just hippies or schemies[5] or pop stars or yuppies. The dance music scene where most of the Ecstasy is taken epitomises this: when dance music became popular, all the standard social divisions appeared to dissolve. Even though the dance scene has now segregated into distinct genres, the divisions can be put down to musical taste and not the traditionally strict British class structure:

> It obviously works as a very powerful force in terms of people wanting to be together. It fights fascism, it fights racism, it's seen as an all-embracing culture that lets you in no matter what religion or colour you are, so I think it's more than just a hedonistic thing ... it's an attitude of let people express themselves and enjoy themselves no matter what social background or which part of the world they come from.

Ecstasy seems to make people more determined to cooperate with one another. One reason for this is a physical response to the chemical's action in the brain. The subtle changes in behaviour caused by Ecstasy have brought about a revolution, a revolution that is not about overthrowing the government but is a gradual reclaiming of personal power and a realisation that most people would like the space to be able to get on with each other. To some this may seem to be based on narcissism, but for many of the first wave of Ecstasy users a revolution starting with the self is highly significant. Ecstasy arrived in Britain at the end of the 1980s, after years of Tory rule and Thatcher's emphasis on individualism; after her notorious statement that society did not exist, something had to snap.

> It came as a rebellion thing because everyone was bored out of their brains at the end of the eighties when a few people were making a lot of money and a lot of others weren't. I just think for a lot of people [taking Ecstasy] was just a mad new clubbing thing, it was a total new youth culture that adults had no access to and we felt we were totally in control of. Black and white people together for the first time. That really was a prominent feature you know.

The action of MDMA on the brain is to cause the release of seratonin and dopamine. These chemicals are neurotransmitters which alter the messages passed between brain cells and so affect mood. The result is that Ecstasy produces a similar feeling to being in love, and can induce feelings of empathy. Under the influence of this drug the distinct streams of youth merged. The rhetoric of previous popular cultures may have appeared all-encompassing but in the case of dance culture it seemed the actions bore out the sentiment. The history of subculture acting as a zone for racial mixing should not be ignored. In the case of dance culture, however, those involved highlighted this as a positive feature of their culture. For many in the dance scene it felt like the social barriers were dropping; often having no experience of previous subcultures, this unity seemed both remarkable and new. Black or white, male or female, gay or straight, rich or poor, the dancefloor provided an alternative to a divided society, and Ecstasy fuelled the dancing. While the Ecstasy experience was individual, it usually happened in a collective, albeit temporary, situation. Large numbers of people taking Ecstasy together share in what is essentially an ineffable experience communicating non-verbally in ways often related afterwards as telepathic or intuitive. These people are all prepared to cross a legal boundary to take Ecstasy, yet often feel strongly that what Ecstasy offers is more acceptable than the legally sanctioned alcohol-based alternatives:

> Seeing them all happy on E rather than beery leery was really good. I remember on the stage with them just like dancing away and there

was a complete stranger this bloke just grinning at me and dancing
sort of the same and we'd both be dancing almost in a routine and
like look at each other occasionally with the best grins on our faces
and we just knew exactly what each other was thinking. It was fantastic.

The snake-oil effect

In *PIHKAL*, the book he wrote with his wife, Alexander Shulgin
records the chemical construction of new drugs along with qualitative comments.[6] The notes on Ecstasy provide an insight into the
true effects of the drug. The effects of pure doses of MDMA are
recorded from the perspective of a scientist who has road-tested
hundreds of other drugs. We have developed a set idea of Ecstasy
experience now, partly told us by the media and part the mythology
of its use within dance culture. Shulgin's notes paint a picture of
what MDMA would be like without the pumping bass line, the top-
up line of speed, the buzz from the other dancers or the fear that
you will drop dead:

> [With 120 mg] I feel absolutely clean inside, and there is nothing but
> pure euphoria. I have never felt so great, or believed this to be
> possible. The cleanliness, clarity, and marvellous feeling of solid inner
> strength continued throughout the rest of the day, and evening, and
> through the next day. I am overcome by the profundity of the
> experience, and how much more powerful it was than previous
> experiences, for no apparent reason, other than a continually improv-
> ing state of being. All the next day I felt like a 'citizen of the universe'
> rather than a citizen of the planet, completely disconnecting time
> and flowing easily from one activity to the next.
> ... As the material came on I felt that I was being enveloped, and
> my attention had to be directed to it. I became quite fearful, and my
> face felt cold and ashen. I felt that I wanted to go back, but I knew
> there was no turning back. The fear started to leave me, and I could
> try taking little baby steps, like taking first steps after being reborn.
> The woodpile is so beautiful, about all the joy and beauty that I can
> stand. I am afraid to turn around and face the mountains, for fear
> they will overpower me. But I did look, and I am astounded. Everyone
> must get to experience a profound state like this. I feel totally
> peaceful. I have lived all my life to get here, and I feel I have come
> home. I am complete.[7]

Shulgin's work reveals the subtle nature of Ecstasy. It enhances what is already there. Ecstasy will not make you hallucinate, but it might make you appreciate the world around you. Shulgin uses the term 'window' in his notes to describe the effects: 'It enabled me to see out, and to see my own insides, without distortion or reservation.'[8] Most people I interviewed described feeling 'let in on the biggest secret on earth' when they first took Ecstasy. They describe not so much having rose-tinted spectacles, more like discovering they were short-sighted and finding lenses to focus on what had been there all along:

> Es give you an insight into another way of feeling about life and possibly to a certain extent you are never the same again. At the time it was a very underground thing, like we've discovered something and God aren't we privileged. It didn't make you feel cocky. It was more of a lucky feeling.

In *PIHKAL* Shulgin discusses what he describes as the 'snake-oil' effects of Ecstasy. Shulgin writes: 'There was something akin to snake-oil – in the sense of an apparent cure for anything that ails you – about this elixir called MDMA.'[9] Was Ecstasy, then, a panacea for all that was wrong with British culture? Could it allow us to forget our differences and lose our selves in music? Ecstasy certainly holds an important position in doing so and thus bringing into question a lot of assumptions about the way people interact. Ecstasy has been described as making users feel greater ease of self-expression, more caring towards other people, greater happiness and increased spiritual awareness.[10] There are those for whom Ecstasy has become far from this positive experience. Some Ecstasy users feel paranoid or depressed and there have been some highly publicised deaths associated with it. It is still unclear what the long-term impact of Ecstasy use will be; one of the problems with its legal status is that research into such issues is neither mandatory nor financially profitable. However, it seems that many of the Ecstasy users have shared in a personal revolution that indicates an extension of the expressive revolution which has been radically altering our interpersonal relationships since the 1960s.

The Great British dance corporation

The most obvious difference noticeable in a club where Ecstasy is the drug of choice is the dancing: 'Everybody was dancing everywhere. They were dancing on top of speakers, dancing on top of bars, dancing on top of tables, chairs, not just on the dancefloor, and absolutely everyone was dancing.' Since Ecstasy became popular, the gaze was taken from the dancefloor. People did not observe, they participated, in anonymity, in this new-found democratic space. The emphasis was turned away from peacock displays of the latest moves, trying to pull or getting into a fight over a spilled pint, and the music became the reason for being together. Dance music, the culture surrounding it and the use of Ecstasy have a shared history. One interviewee remembers his first experience of taking Ecstasy in a club:

> I just lost all track of time basically and I was just dancing all night. Before I was quite into sticking with my mates because I didn't know many folk there, but then when I was on E we sort of bumped into each other throughout the night and said 'Are you having a good time?' It was when people got into hugging everyone ridiculously and so you felt like everybody was your mate. It didn't matter that your actual mates were elsewhere. You knew that everyone around was dancing away and into the same things but you were in your own little world. I got tapped on the shoulder once and I turned around and it was a 10-foot spaceman up on stilts with flashing lights waving at me and I went 'All right mate?' and he sort of stuck his thumbs up and started doing some mad dancing. It was quite surreal but it didn't freak me in any way; I just thought, 'Nice one.'

From its early days at the end of the 1980s the dance scene has encouraged initiative and enterprise. The organisers of illegal impromptu parties would ask for donations or entrance fees and use the money to cover costs and build up their sound systems. As time passed, the dance scene grew, diversified and evolved. The free parties had largely become an alternative to mainstream licensed clubbing, not simply an extension of it. Originally, however, the two went hand in hand. The effects of Ecstasy do not suddenly stop when licensing laws dictate, after two in the morning.

When the punters were kicked out of the clubs there were plenty willing to travel to continue the party:

> The Hacienda shut at two and it was, 'Where are we going now?', and we'd bomb off to Birch services and places like that on the M62. Everyone would be dancing around on the tables and then the word would come that there was some party somewhere and everyone would go to that.

The peak of the rave phenomenon came in 1991, and there followed a cash-in on the desire to dance all night. Thousands of chemically induced like-minded souls were prepared to pay for the privilege. While many organisers provided value for money, as with any industry there were cowboys. Listed DJs did not appear, facilities were missing, security guards were heavy-handed, some events did not happen at all. Dissatisfaction with the legal alternative spurred on many Do it Yourself enthusiasts. Cobbling together equipment, they became organisers of their own parties. Cheaper than the licensed raves and without the restrictive door policy of a lot of clubs, thousands of people spent their weekends ringing secret phone lines then driving in convoy to party destinations all over the country. A kind of inverse snobbery has developed around the free party circuit. These parties were seen as hardcore; you had to really want to be there and they were highly likely to be raided by the police. Paying to go to a club or licensed party was classed as selling out, buying into the system. If it wasn't free it wasn't good. Even within the legal end of the dance spectrum there is a feeling that some clubs are too 'corporate', succumbing to the lure of money, playing music that is too commercial and attracting a crowd that has 'missed the point'. One successful promoter told me:

> We aren't totally sticking the Vs up to the system because we are working in it. In a way though I guess we are because we've got jobs that weren't around before, jobs that don't fit in with the system. But look at things like Cream and the Ministry of Sound and they have become the system; they are the fucking system.

The more underground a club or party was, the closer it was considered to be to the so-called 'true' feelings of the scene: peace,

love and unity, being in it for the music, not caring what clothes
you were wearing and not having to pay through the nose to be
able to dance with your friends. As time passed it seemed that,
rather than rejecting the Tory ideals Ecstasy's empathy once
challenged, the dance scene had nurtured a nest of Thatcher's
fledglings eager to gobble up the loose change of the chemical
generation. The dance scene split into those who saw an opportunity to cash in, those willing to cough up and those who valued it
as an escape from those priorities:

> There was all these nutters from the inner cities going out and having
> a good laugh. And then there were middle-class kids like me accepted
> into their world and it all became kind of one thing. At first it was a
> massive rebellion to say, 'Yeah, we're going out to have a good time
> even though we've got nothing', and then lots of people started
> making money from whatever they were doing, whether it was from
> the legit things in the business like making their own music, loads of
> people started DJing, there was never any of that before. Then there
> was the illegal stuff, selling drugs or whatever.

There is no doubt some of the new entrepreneurs could be
accused of selling their soul to capitalism, ripping off punters
and pulling off scams. Their job was easy with thousands of blissed-
out unquestioning clients on tap, who had no legal channels
open if they wished to complain. Many others, however, were not
this unscrupulous. Such enterprise created a challenge to the
supremacy of the large-scale corporate structures of our industrial
past. Merging the boundaries of illicit and regulated income, the
'night-time' economy plays an increasingly important role in the
economy of the country as a whole. Producers of dance music are
prime examples of the emerging DiY culture. Affordable technology means they do not have to wait for that elusive record deal.
Studios were set up in bedrooms around the country and the tracks
recorded on these micro-labels were then self-distributed. It took a
while for the major record companies, who had carved their
reputations and wealth out of rock music, to realise what was
happening. The new micro-labels were flexible in response to the
rapid turnover in releases and fluctuations in style of the dance
scene. Such features make them part of a post-Fordist economy.

The Fordist structure of the majors made them unable to keep up with this fluidity, but by setting up specialist sub-labels they are starting to reverse this trend. The implication of the mode of production of dance music is much more significant than it would first seem. Far from being consumers of a culture created for them, or simply exhibiting a response to the social situation that they find themselves in, those involved in dance culture are 'individuals and members of collectives which are at the forefront of creating a new culture and economy'.[11]

This cultural production has a varying impact on the economy of the country. It is often felt that free parties avoid such transaction, but most still involve at least a trip to the cash and carry to stock the bar. Unless the generator operates by wind power, and the party-goers arrive on foot and only drink from a babbling brook, all parties will line the government's pockets in some way. Prompted by public outrage after 1992's massive festival at Castlemorton, there was a clampdown on illegal parties; the Criminal Justice and Public Order Act in 1994 had specific anti-rave clauses. Informal networks were united in protest at the new legislation. These people were prepared to cross a legal boundary, whether to stop a new road, to disrupt a fox-hunt or to take their drugs of choice and enjoy their own brand of entertainment. The latent period of this movement was over, the strands surfaced and cemented together in more visible opposition.[12]

The symbolic challenge

The Ecstasy revolution is based around a symbolic challenge to the codes deeply ingrained within British society. That the challenge is symbolic does not mean it does not have a significant impact, but that it is representative of a fundamental assault on the habits of our culture. The codes challenged are so deep that we tend to take them for granted; unless, that is, we have a powerful tool to bring them to light. For me the most significant code the Ecstasy revolution unearthed was the relationship between men and women. At one of the first dance nights I went to I fumed to myself as I felt the man behind me blowing on my shoulders. I tried to ignore him but he started rubbing ice over me. As I turned he started giggling and moved to do the same to a man standing near, who appreciated the efforts to cool him off. I was geared up to be on the defensive. I was used to clubs where you expected some drunk bloke to try it on, and when the slowies came on at the end of the night you locked yourself in the loo. To me and my friends this was the Ecstasy revolution: you could go to a club, wear what you wanted and be left to dance.

This situation is not so cut and dried any more: from feeling free to wear little in hot clubs, displays of flesh became used for titillation. It is ironic that the early tabloid interest in Ecstasy concentrated on its potential to loosen the knicker elastic of the young ladies that took it. The idea that scantily clad youngsters could spend the night together and only dance seemed too much for the salacious appetites of journalists. To them acid house meant orgy; Ecstasy made you insatiable and rave girls were easy. Years down the line and with increasing competition, dance music magazines have remembered that sex sells. Photographers often zoom in on the babes in high heels and wonderbras. The freedom to behave as you want may not seem like a real revolution to fusty old Marxist men. For those of us, male or female, who have found our signals crossed and warnings ignored, however, the escape from desire was intensely liberating. Such gender-free utopias may only be short-lived, but the memories of the experience are longer lasting. To have the opportunity to forget classification by race, class or gender allows a close examination of what unites us rather than our differences. For many, a symbolic challenge seems the only choice for revolution; the previous government's tactics seem to have privatised radicalism. A generation disempowered and alienated from the political system will not even register to vote because 'all the parties are the same' and it would involve paying a backlog of council tax anyway. The likelihood of a full-on coup is minimal.

A lot of the people interviewed described quite significant changes in their attitudes that they relate directly to their Ecstasy use. In his work on social movements, Italian sociologist Alberto Melucci emphasises the importance of fighting for new orientations of social action: 'They believe you can change your life today while fighting for more general changes in society.'[13] He feels that radical change is possible from a personal gesture. Using his criteria, dance culture can be classed as a contemporary movement which can be seen to demonstrate to society that alternatives are possible. Melucci's work acknowledges the difficulties in translating such action into political effectiveness and avoids judging the merits and disadvantages of gaining political representation. He suggests that when looking at contemporary movements it is important not to separate individual change from collective action. The following quote, from the director of a very well-established independent record label, illustrates how the two relate:

> I was a male chauvinist: arrogant, big-mouthed – well I'm still arrogant, but I was big-mouthed – hated queers, hated women, they were another class to me. Basically I was a proper fucking boy. I guess [Ecstasy's] got its pros and cons but I changed big time.

This may seem an extreme example of the Ecstasy revolution, and of a revolution that is personal, but it is not atypical. It does not matter whether people are in the most corporate of clubs or dancing in a squat, they are all likely to have a fundamentally similar experience. It would be too easy to concentrate on the DiY, free party end of the dance continuum for an analysis of the revolutionary potential of MDMA. You can expect radical people with radical ideas when radical measures have to be taken to get the party off the ground in the first place. The interesting part is when people like the man who made the last quote face up to their own prejudices. Thousands of similar people are constantly overlooked in the search for revolutionaries. They are not especially 'right on', not into any particular causes, not doing much for themselves, like dressing up, dropping the odd pill and 'larging it' on Friday nights after work. Their power to cause change may at first seem pretty limited; they are unlikely to block a road, live up a tree or even write a letter to their MP. The potential power of these people lies in their sheer numbers. It has been said before but it is worth repeating that a revolution starts with a change of heart. Revolution like this is not solipsistic; it is an internal change, but one that can affect every interaction we have with others. Rather than talk of the Great British Ecstasy revolution, it would be more accurate to talk of the Great British metanoia.

Postscript

Nicholas Saunders was an articulate, informed ambassador for Ecstasy culture. He was killed in a car crash on 3rd February 1998. RIP, Nicholas.

Love, Mary Anna

11

Repetitive beats: free parties and the politics of contemporary DiY dance culture in Britain

HILLEGONDA RIETVELD

If I can't dance, it's not my revolution.

Emma Goldman[1]

Today I danced to amplified repetitive beats in Trafalgar Square. On this warm sunny spring day, 12 April 1997, a demonstration to support sacked Liverpool dockers had expanded into a carnival of colourful flags, fire jugglers, stilt walkers, roller skaters, cyclists and samba drums. On arrival at the great central London square, the marchers found a sound system on an old truck, courtesy of Reclaim the Streets, positioned at the top, right in front of the National Gallery. It pumped out a type of 4/4 beat which Manchester DiY collective Network 23 dubs Enema Techno,[2] fast, frantic electronic sequences with a boosted bass that grabs the entrails of anyone who chooses to stand in front of the speakers. The crowd were enjoying themselves in front and on top of the truck, jumping up and down, waving hands and fists.

It's the law

This type of entertainment, encompassing a mobile sound system which produces amplified repetitive beats at a rate of 130 to 180 BPM[3] for a crowd that dances oblivious of a sense of time, has become a common way of spending one's leisure time in Britain 1997.[4] Yet one needs the approval of the legislative authorities to be able to put this into practice. Being a demonstration without a licence for a dance party in a public space, the particular

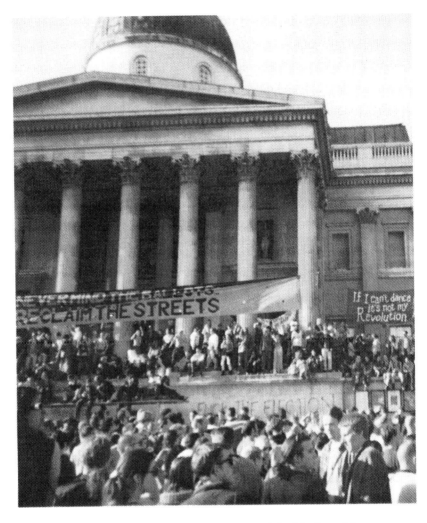

The Trafalgar Square party, 12 April 1997. Photograph by Iain Cartwright

happening above was only possible because the sheer numbers of participants would make the clearing of this party strategically cumbersome for the police. Instead, they stayed on the sidelines, getting involved with sporadic skirmishes and, much later, threatening the truck driver and passengers with a murder charge which could not be upheld.[5]

From this event, where several other sound systems never made it into the square, being impounded by surrounding police forces, one may conclude that samba bands are allowed in public spaces while sound systems are perceived as problematic. An unlicensed, non-tax-paying, loud, rumbling techno sound system could be perceived as profoundly disturbing to those who like to be seen to be in control, especially when entertaining a group of people who seem to be consumption society rejects/rejecters on a Saturday afternoon in the middle of a very busy capital city at its peak of shopping and tourist activities. Having said this, the stray Japanese and Australian tourists loved it; without the presence of smelly buses the grand square provided an excellent holiday atmosphere. Privately, police officers were beaming the occasional smile at the carnivalesque scene in the spring sun. Still, the following day, headlines of various newspapers were not in favour and ignored the positive elements of the day. Instead they chose to concentrate on traditional 'news values', such as the occasional violence off the square that was to be expected from a group of people who feel that current parliamentary priorities exclude their interests:

DON'T VOTE, MAKE TROUBLE[6]

RIOT FRENZY — ANARCHIST THUGS BRING TERROR TO LONDON[7]

VIOLENCE AT DOCKERS' DEMO — POLICE DROP CHARGE OF ATTEMPTED MURDER AGAINST VAN DRIVER ARRESTED AT RECLAIM THE STREETS PARTY — DISORGANISATION THAT LEADS TO DIRECT ACTION[8]

The sound system in itself could not be held responsible for the more violent aspects of that day, yet it added a libidinal energy that made the demonstration a powerful experience for most. The fear of mad, uncontrolled/uncontrollable mobs is a reccuring emotion in the mainstream press and in the discourse of governing authorities. Since 1991, various types of laws have been introduced to curb the pleasures of, first, acid house, then rave and free sound system parties. For example, the most spectacular police action was the arrest of 836 people at an 'acid house party' at Gildersome near Leeds on 22 July 1990.[9] The most sensational in the collection of nineties UK legislation against dancing gatherings is Part V, Section 63 of the Criminal Justice and Public Order Act (CJA, 1994), which is titled 'Powers in relation to raves'. This law gives police '[p]owers to remove persons attending or preparing for a rave'. The latter is defined as 'a gathering on land in the open air of 100 or more persons ... at which amplified music is played during the night', where '(a) ... the gathering extends over several days' and '(b) "music" includes sounds wholly or predominantly characterised by the emission of a succession of repetitive beats'.[10] One could point out that the above dance event is not covered by this law for the sheer technical reason that it did not occur 'during the night'. In fact, raves have taken place in a great variety of spaces, which are not always in the open air, and notions such as 'night' and 'repetitive beats' are rather vague and arguable. The point here is that a British law directly addresses very particular types of music consumption involving house, techno and rave music. In his book on the legacy of the UK acid house parties, Matthew Collin has remarked on this as follows:

> for the first time the word 'rave' appeared in British legislative language. Although other youth movements had inspired new legis-lation, never before, over years of post-war moral panics about activities of teddy boys, mods, hippies and punks, had a government considered young people's music so subversive as to prohibit it. John Major's government, unlike many pop commentators, obviously didn't consider dance-drug culture to be either meaningless or apolitical.[11]

Although Collin gives an excellent account of events, he does not really analyse what these politics entail. This chapter will explore some possible and perhaps less possible options, bearing in mind that an explosion of great dance parties at a time of political disappointment does not equal a critical front. For instance, a recent survey at London dance events by drug agency

Release has shown that music, socialising, atmosphere and dancing were the most important reason to go out, with drugs ranking fifth place.[12] However, it is possible to identify some aspects of cultural politics both internally and in the reactions by the media and authorities in the context of dance parties, free ones in particular.

DiY disco

The DiY scene of which Reclaim the Streets is rightfully part seems to have a particular version of the 'dance-drug culture', mentioned by Collin, which is defined in small press publications such as *POD*, *SQUALL*, *Frontline* and *Dream Creation Inc.* To summarise briefly, it is a story that speaks of how the concept of raves had been adopted by a British mixture of travellers and (ex-)hippies who attend free festivals, as well as eco-activists and urban (ex-)punk or crustie squatters, who all employed certain forms of direct action tactics in a DiY manner during the early nineties. Especially since 1992 it seems,[13] various sound systems have flourished within this very loosely defined cultural space. This story illustrates the fact that the CJA has united previously disparate groups. In his book on cultural expressions of protest groups, George McKay has put this very well:

> Actions against the Act have revived and simplified the whole notion of a politics of pleasure for large sections of British youth. Not only have there been campaigns, demonstrations, publications against it, but also there has been an extension of the 'Party and Protest' side of DiY culture, as a regular column in *SchNEWS*[14] puts it.[15]

In addition various sections within the 'alternative' dance scene, mostly in southern England, speak of altering the world by dancing to repetitive beats, taking thought-provoking drugs and exploring ideas. It is a mixture of self-invented mythology in addition to ideas developed by idealist hippies such as Fraser Clark, who has advocated Shamanarchy for zippies[16] (briefly celebrated in 1993–95 at London club Heaven as Megatripolis) since the late eighties. Some of the more 'fluffy' trance parties, organised by hippie-inspired collectives such as Pendragon and Return to the Source (who do not necessarily operate on a free party basis), are genuinely concerned that their dance nights have a positive vibe; to achieve this they perform rituals to ban bad spirits and to honour the cycles of life and the universe. At the other end of this spectrum, Spiral Tribe profess a more hardcore idea which takes human stamina to its extremes, by living through exhausting nights and days of sleep deprivation, psychedelic chemical intake and very loud techno. Their inspirational spokesperson, Mark, explains:

> Castlemorton (1992) we were going for six days non-stop. Camelford in August '91 we were going fourteen days, twenty-four hours. To experience that you experience a world you didn't know existed. The sun goes down, the moon comes up and you see the world spinning. My record is nine days without sleep. It's a shamanic thing.[17]

Although the CJA was in the pipeline already,[18] the legal description of a 'rave' is closest to the descriptions in the above quote, whereby Castlemorton was attended by various sound systems and over 25,000 people.

The DiY version of events is also a story that talks of free parties and anti-commercialism. Above all, it is a story which stresses a collectiveness: no more hierarchies of star performers and of 'Mr Big' the organiser. Examples of such sound systems are diverse, operating mainly on the basis of free parties with a bucket collection to keep things running. The music played veers towards European techno, with generous helpings of trance on the more hippie-inspired events and gabba (gabberhouse) in the urban squatters' scene. Occasionally one also hears African-American gospel-inspired garage, a genre in which the bicycle-powered, low-volume, day-glo painted mobile system Rinky-Dink specialises.

One of the oldest sound systems is Tonka, which has been around for decades, providing disco and acid house during the late eighties at events such as the rooftop parties on a huge squat in Holborn, London; since the beginning of 1995, when they lost their impressive warehouse squat in Rotherhithe, they have mainly provided the sound for pub parties in south London. Sugar Lump, also from south London, claim they brought the concept of non-stop party to the festival scene at Glastonbury in 1989, where they played for a solid week behind the market stalls; during the nineties

The Rinky-Dink bicycle-powered sound system at a Critical Mass event. Photograph by Nick Cobbing

they adopted progressive house and still mix a great variety of dance music.[19]

The DiY collective from Nottingham has quite a large roster of DJs, providing a varied musical agenda. Together with Smoke-screen and Breeze they have initiated a self-defence scheme (as opposed to a 'hardcore' direct confrontation) for small sound systems (attracting crowds of around 500 people) in the area of Derbyshire and South Yorkshire, known as All Systems; in addition to the three sound systems, currently this also includes Pulse, Babble, Floatation, Rogue, Go-Tropo and Spoof (Sheffield People On One Forever). This larger collective owns a communal sound system called Kamikaze, spreading the cost of losing equipment when busted and helping neighbouring sound systems, such as Black Moon Sound System, who lost their rig due to the CJA. The money for All Systems free parties is made by DJing in clubs through the week.[20]

In similar rural settings such as quarries as well as in caves around the Pennines, Lake District and Cheshire, Rave in the Cave parties have provided memorable small-scale one-night events since 1993, with music ranging from garage to jungle and attracting 200 to 700 people on each occasion from all the surrounding cities and towns. The first parties inspired others to create their own events under the same name, which all worked with a variety of success. These parties attracted a wide range of people, from those who live for festivals to office workers; the publicity relied on a network of faxes, which most only had access to in their (urban) workplaces.

Spiral Tribe have had a lot of publicity, mostly due to their hardcore belief in free non-stop techno dancing, which resulted in serious police harassment. Their story has an epic ring to it, flirting with the British free festival circuit and continuing in mainland Europe, where they were driven due to their uncompromising stance. For the London area they helped out in setting up a CJA self-defence group of sound systems called United Systems who staged The Mother in 1995, an event which was supposed to be as large as Castlemorton, but which ended up being internally split (resulting in two venues on the same weekend) and then prevented from occurring through an increased sophistication in police surveillance.[21] Other British sound systems have gone into exile in Europe as well, joining Teknivals from Paris to Prague, which Amy

Garner dubs 'the travelling circus of the late-20th century';[22] there are some links here with the Berlin squatters and party scene and the annual Berlin Love Parade where thousands of people dance in the street with jovial endorsement from the Berlin authorities. Strengthened by their relative success on the continent, a fraction of the tribe toured the USA with their sound system and mobile studio in the summer of 1997; however, the police were not always sympathetic to their loud presence.[23]

Spiral Tribe's historical importance is that they have inspired several sound systems of a particular hardcore techno format. One of these is Desert Storm from Glasgow, who since Christmas 1994 have taken their free-techno-for-all gospel to war-torn Bosnia several times; according to those who travelled with them, the idea that a party can boost morale seems to have been quite successful.[24] In the UK, however, their presence is not always welcomed by policing forces; their truck was turned back during their attempt to reach Trafalgar Square for the Liverpool dockers' demo, while after a Reclaim the Streets party in Bristol on 21 June 1997 their equipment was seized.[25]

Some of Desert Storm's Bosnia touring crew had also been involved with Demolition Sound in Hulme, Manchester. Its regular Wednesday parties livened up a bohemian and impoverished council estate in the process of dereliction, demolition and rebuilding during the summer of 1994. Their setting was the little council shopping precinct, where people danced to techno and progressive house on top of shop roofs and relaxed on second-hand sofas until the few remaining shops opened the next morning. The Demolition crew also had some informal links with street performance group Dogs from Heaven, the French circus Archaos, the club Megadog and the northern English dance scene.

The Luton-based Exodus Collective, who have received considerable press and police attention for various activities, are yet another example of a successful DiY sound system, though they are much more than this, using their large parties for local people to support their social welfare DiY group. (Exodus are discussed by Tim Malyon elsewhere in this book.) There are plenty more examples, from beach parties on the south coast and ad hoc festivities in Wales to barn parties in Scotland, not to mention the dance scene in Ireland.

Party roots

From the above one can gather that the free sound systems are not run by a homogeneous group of people and do not exist in a cultural vacuum: cross-fertilisation occurs continually in terms of musical styles, chemical intake and format.[26]

Firstly, musical influences can be found in German electronic punk and electronic trance (*Neue Welle*), as well as 'industrial' music[27] associated with inner-city anarchopunk scenes from Berlin to San Francisco; Chicago African-American acid house and wild pitch; Detroit black-futurist techno;[28] Belgian body music, New Beat and subsequent techno; superfast Dutch gabberhouse (or gabba); and also (perhaps to a lesser extent for the hardcore techno scene) disco, electro, garage and deep house music.[29]

Secondly, party chemicals (or body technologies) such as beer, LSD, speed and cannabis met a competitor in the entactogenic[30] empathy-generating drug MDMA, commonly known as Ecstasy or E. This drug made a major contribution to what is now understood as the rave scene of 1988–93, giving its participants a feeling of a shared inevitable importance. Simon Reynolds suggests that: 'Amongst all its other effects, E incites a sort of free-floating fervour, a will-to-belief – which is why the most inane oscillator synth-riff can seem to be radiant with MEANING.'[31] E facilitated a unique passion for parties: 'raving is about the celebration of celebration',[32] Reynolds states, and my earlier findings agree with this tautology.[33] However, as social researcher Sheila Henderson has observed in her study of Ecstasy use amongst young people in Britain between 1992 and 1996, the intensity of dance parties is related to an equal sense of political disappointment and resultant apathy.[34] Having attended a huge variety of dancefloors, it seemed as if the celebration revolved around a great void: void in the direction of energy on the dancefloor, void in the mind, void in articulated politics, with E convincing all that this void made sense, that it was not scary or depressing but a thing to feel good about.[35]

Thirdly, the format of these dance parties has not dropped out of thin air. In terms of hedonism in hard times, the free festivals[36] and British–Jamaican dub sound systems at various blues parties[37] are of historical importance to the British DiY scene. In addition,

Ibiza and Amsterdam, which were once stop-points on the hippie trail, provided particular holiday formats of long nights and days of carefree drug-induced dancing to DJ music.[38] And, of course, the London warehouse parties during the eighties were important. In that decade they provided hip hop and dub sound systems, as well as avant-garde squatters' events, such as those staged by the Mutoid Waste Company.[39] The raw 1988 acid house parties RIP on Clink Street by London Bridge are an example of dance parties influenced by previous warehouse events. Interestingly with regard to the DiY-underground story, one of the RIP organisers had spent her formative years with the anarchopunk Crass collective.[40] Another important model for unbridled fun in the face of political adversity was generated within a predominantly gay African-American and Latino club and party environment in Chicago and New York which revolved around variations of house music.[41] One UK club which successfully used this format together with the Ibiza vibe, the Hacienda in Manchester during 1988–91, inspired a huge crowd of future music makers, including free sound system DJs such as Mark from Spiral Tribe and DJ Danny of Demolition Sound and Desert Storm.

Politics of pleasure 1: the bodice excites the Id

It is important to see the development first of acid house parties and then raves (the most influential models for free sound system parties) against a backdrop of the political climate in Britain during the late eighties. Unbridled Thatcherite enterprise culture (that is, anarcho-capitalist DiY principles) promoted notions of self-help, no reliance on the state and making money off your own bat. In tandem, the same government also put restraints on moral 'excesses'.[42] Not only public pleasure but also the private sphere was affected; for example, selling certain videos ('video nasties') or practising certain types of sex between consenting adults (such as sadomasochism sex) were criminalised during the eighties.[43]

The British state has a long history in regulating pleasures associated with parties. A fear seems to exist of the unregulated body that dances and is intoxicated. By celebrating in large ('vulgar') social groups, this body can be perceived as huge and overwhelming, a threat to a presumed spiritual purity of the nation. During the last couple of centuries, a tightly laced bodice of rules has been put into place to regiment this body. Historically, 'the grotesque body' was once celebrated at carnivals before Lent but is now virtually legislated out of existence,[44] reduced to the impoverished state of Shrove Tuesday in Britain. (Protestant) Christianity seems to have been a big influence on the repression of parties. For example, as a club, venue or pub, one needs to apply for a special dance licence on a Sunday. Other licensing laws which regulate the consumption of intoxicating liquor are also very tight; not many other countries in Europe will close their bars in clubs at 2 a.m. or keep their pubs, which in Britain often close as early as 11 p.m., exclusive to over eighteens.[45]

It is therefore not surprising that the acid house parties, that heady mix of house'n'E dance events in 1988, were followed by various moral panics that involved the regulation of the body. Decisions were demanded and made about the regulation of body technologies such as loud dancing music and dance drugs.[46] A good example of the result of such repression of pleasure can be found in an account by Wayne Anthony of Genesis/Biology, promoters who had successfully staged parties that attracted thousands in 1989. He vividly describes how he and his friends organised a huge New Year's Eve rave for 1989–90. Police were on their tail and doing their darnedest to prevent the party from going ahead. After a mad chase on the motorway, with an estimated 4,000 people in convoy, they arrived at the site, which was surrounded by police. The sheer number of people forced the police to leave, however. Anthony continues:

> The equipment was set up in a matter of minutes. By twelve o'clock, ten thousand people screamed, cheered, clapped, jumped and hugged one another at the turn of a New Year and a new dawn. It was an awesome sight, partly anarchy but we're not anarchists. We didn't originally intend to break into people's property and throw huge illegal parties. It's just one of those spontaneous actions which usually ignites and creates a way of life. But the truth is, the whole dance phenomenon was being oppressed to a level which branded party promoters and people who attended 'evil acid party promoters'.... We're forced into believing we live in a democratic society, yet because of a lack of understanding we are outlawed and thrown to

the vultures. We weren't politicians, criminals or terrorists, nor did we pose a threat to national security. We were just ordinary people lost, with nowhere left to turn. . . .[47]

Sarah Thornton, a self-proclaimed outsider of the rave/club scene, has pointed out that media-led moral panics provided the parties with increased 'subcultural capital' which attracted a huge youth leisure market.[48] For most of the punters, raves provided an escapist hedonist leisure activity in an increasingly commercialised rave scene, which was estimated by the Henley Centre for Forecasting to be worth between £1 and £2 billion in 1993.[49] Dance-drug culture has become very popular within the regulated licensed environment: the 1996–97 *UK Club Guide*, which mostly picks out the clubs on the cutting edge of dance, lists 'over 300 of the UK's favourite clubs'.[50] Clubland is being rationalised according to strategies worked out by lawyers, accountants and marketing specialists; 1997 examples of successful commercial clubs are Cream in Liverpool and Ministry of Sound[51] in London.

The flip side of the legislation game was that unlicensed parties were driven underground, attracting different kinds of promoters. On the one hand, these were the unscrupulous money spinners who operated in a grey economy of (semi-)criminal involvement; people who didn't mind being on the wrong side of the law or at least manipulating the rules in interest of profit.[52] On the other hand, using the relatively simple logistics of a mobile sound system, parties could be held in the open air or in squatted/borrowed premises; without even paying for a licence, these can be run very cheaply and so free parties were enabled.

So, the reactions by outside forces have pushed what initially were apolitical non-manifesto hedonist gatherings into a political mould. Recognisable elements of rave culture, its DJ-driven musics, sound rigs, disorientating light rigs and self-obliterating punters, can now be found at various places on the political spectrum. This may leave the occasional observer, trying to impose a unifying meaning on it all, in a rather confused state of mind. For the purpose of this essay, I will keep the focus mainly on the 'alternative' party circuit.

Politics of pleasure 2: move with the groove

Having discussed some passages from the CJA relating to 'raves', one wonders how especially the notion of 'repetitive beats' entered British legislation. What makes this aspect of a 'rave' so special? One could argue that the phrase was used purely in order to define the raves which caused moral panic. One could also propose that if repetitive beats intoxicate the dancers into a type of trance, then regulations comparable to drug laws and drinking licensing need to be imposed. But it may be fun to toy and speculate with this notion a little longer.

The notion of repetitive beats kept some thinkers occupied well before the word 'rave' ever acquired its current meaning. For example, in 1941, when Hitler's Nazi party ruled Germany and had managed to inspire the German occupation of a large part of Europe, German cultural theorist Theodor Adorno was worried about repetition in music. He argued from a Marxist yet elitist viewpoint whilst in exile in the USA, a new country full of mass-produced popular culture. There he formulated the idea that the consumer of popular music can be divided into 'two major socio-political types of behaviour toward music in general and popular music in particular, the "rhythmically obedient" type and the "emotional" type'.[53] The latter, he argues, can be seen to be the sentimental person who hides from the causes of her/his unhappiness. In most dance music, both emotions and rhythm play a role; the types of consumers cannot always be distinguished. An example of the 'emotional' type may be the 'loved-up' E-taking dancer who gets all overwhelmed hearing the gospel-inspired lyrics of some rave tracks about love and happiness. But there are no laws against emotions as such. However, one could argue that the 'rhythmically obedient' type is addressed in the CJA. This type is also more relevant with regards to the instrumental no-hope/no-nonsense 4/4 150 BPM drone-like techno which seems to be favoured at many DiY events.

Whilst being more than a little worried about the rise of Nazi and Fascist ideologies in Europe and the commercialisation of jazz, Adorno felt that the 'rhythmically obedient' type could be found especially amongst youth:

They are most susceptible to a process of masochistic adjustment to authoritarian collectivism. The type is not restricted to any one political attitude ... repression and crowd mindedness overtake followers of both trends ... as the standardized meter of dance music and of marching suggests the coordinated battalions of a mechanical collectivity, obedience to this rhythm by overcoming the responding individuals leads them to conceive of themselves as agglutinized with the untold millions of the meek who must be similarly overcome. Thus do the obedient inherit the earth.[54]

Obedience to a capitalist culture industry or to the manipulative calls of Hitler and Mussolini were the options that Adorno was presented with. In some ways he seemed to imply that repetitive beats had a regimenting quality. However, he must have been unaware of the fact that the Nazi regime had brought in regulations which curbed the amount of 'corrupting', 'un-Aryan' jazz influences in music played in the Third Reich. Although Nazi prohibition is more prescribing and articulated than the CJA, McKay has pointed out similarities.[55] Unsurprisingly, the Resistance in Western Europe bonded their allegiance in defiance to the occupiers by dancing at secret parties to jazz, jungle[56] and swing records (full of loud repetitive musical statements) imported from the USA.[57] Note that during moments when a particular music is outlawed (or repressed), a gramophone and box of records are logistically much easier in terms of transport and set-up than a full-on band.

Still, to come back to Adorno's 'rhythmically obedient' type, which, he stated, 'is not restricted to any one political attitude', the CJA seems to show a fear not so much of a perceived alien ethnicity nor of unregimented music *per se*, but rather of a united 'agglutinized' mob which is indeed regimented into a festive frenzy. While this 'mob' has the potential to go in any political direction, including the void of rave, the real paranoia seems to be of a 'mob' which is obedient to notions which represent extra-parliamentary interests. This may seem plausible, since the sound systems who are small and who negotiate with the police are often left alone,[58] while those who take a confrontational stance are often addressed without mercy.

Politics of pleasure 3: collective disconnection

The notion of collectivity (that is, the forming of a tight group that is obedient to its own internal logic, rather than to the state) is relevant in the context of the adoption of techno sound systems by those who, willingly or not, find themselves outside of the realm of 'citizenship'.[59] Henderson has written that 'a "disconnection index", recently prepared by Socioconsult (part of MORI), showed that 54 per cent of 18 to 24 year olds are proud not to be part of the British system'.[60] Many young people are disappointed with party politics. Henderson observed in 1996 that:

> Club 18–34 (7 million men and 7 million women) now make up a
> third of the voting population but nearly half of 18 to 25 year olds
> didn't vote in the last election and 1 in 5 of them do not register to
> vote (four times more than the rest of the population).[61]

One could argue that in a time of breakdown of a sense of national belonging, rave-like events do provide a sense of community, even when it's only on a superficial level for the duration of the party.

On the basis of his daughter's involvement, musicologist Philip Tagg has mused about the earlier raves that:

> rave is something you immerse yourself into together with other
> people. . . . you just 'shake your bum off' from inside the music. You
> are just one of many individuals who constitute the music as a whole
> . . . [D]oes this prefigure a new form of collective consciousness or
> does it mean the end of oppositionality and individualism?[62]

Dave Hesmondhalgh, who studies the current music industry, has replied to Tagg's comments that since a lot of people dance with their eyes closed, they disconnect from each other and 'retreat into the individual's response to the music'.[63] Occasionally, this may be so; with eyes closed, one can trance into what looks like a spiralling kaleidoscopic never-ending tunnel, so familiar from computer graphics at, for example, Goa trance events. However, outsiders' observations such as Hesmondhalgh's are problematic since this gaze disregards feeling. A rave is foremost a tactile-acoustic event, rather than a visual one, so visibility is of little importance; with the eyes closed one can flow with the groove of both the music and the surrounding bodies. If a collective feeling and physical closeness were not important to raves, people would not make such an effort to congregate, despite the law. In other words, if a tactile-acoustic group experience was not important, a pair of headphones in the living room would do. In addition, people are not in one singular state of being throughout the night. There are a variety of very practical reasons for closing one's eyes, such as tiredness, sweat on the brow and impaired visibility due to visual effects. When people do 'clock' each other, they will reach out; even a complete outsider of the dance scene can observe this in the pictures of rave crowds spreading out arms and fingers to each other (or towards the other motivators, the MCs and/or the DJ).[64] At techno events and at times when the use of Ecstasy is less prevalent, this reaching out is more restrained, but a collective awareness has not disappeared.

For most people, rave events are consumed in terms of a break, a holiday, to regenerate for the next working week; a weekend lifestyle rather than a way of life, since one needs to work to be able to afford transport and to pay for the events. Free parties could make a difference to this economic perpetuation of political positioning. In that case, certain countercultural ideas could flourish once more. One such idea is that being off one's face on whatever mind-altering substance can be obtained, delirious with lack of sleep and put into a dream-state by a trance-inducing beat,[65] could present an alternative to society in itself, like a Surrealist strike, 'creating a new way of life based on play; in other words, a *ludic* revolution'.[66] Within the academic milieu of New Left thinking, such an idea would be rejected. A certain amount of masochistic self-denial, losing one's ego to relentless machine rhythms of a Spiral Tribe techno gig, disappearing with revolutionary ideas and all down the trance whirlpool into an empty hole of oblivion, does not seem to create a strong counter-political force. It certainly takes the ground from under one's feet, making it difficult to articulate a position. The argument of confrontation (entering into the dialectic) versus 'losing it' and living out dreams is not new. For example, before the Second World War French Surrealist artists were rejected by Marxists for fluffy anarcho ideas like that, while during the sixties LSD-soaked drop-outs were looked down upon

by self-respecting organised protesters. Roland Barthes's notion of
jouissance as opposed to *plaisir* is useful here. The latter is a
comfortable self-confirming sense of pleasure, while *jouissance* is
more a sense of abandon and (sometimes frightful) bliss which can
provide new ways of seeing.[67]

An overwhelming soundscape can become a spiritual re-ener-
giser which is part and parcel of what Ray Pratt, in the context of
gospel music, has called 'a larger strategy of survival'.[68] For those
who feel they have been dislocated in a political sense, made
homeless in more ways than one, intense dance parties can provide
a strong sense of community, comparable to Caribbean sound
systems, hip hop gatherings, gospel congregations or gay clubs. At
times, the cultural output of the DiY dance scene seems to take on
a cultural logic which in some way is comparable to migrant and
diasporic communities. As Peter Manuel has observed with both
hip hop and diasporic Punjabi communities:

> The syncretic popular musics cultivated by such communities often
> exhibit such contradictions with particular clarity, combining pre-
> modern folk elements with the latest mainstream pop styles in a self-
> conscious and often deliberately ironic sort of eclecticism.[69]

The cultural effect can be a non-judgemental use of new technologies combined with pre-modern mythologies and musical instrument use. At DiY dance gatherings one often finds some drummers
and didgeridoo players. In fact, drone-like techno and trance can
be reproduced on such portable acoustic instruments, and, vice
versa, the recorded tracks seem to imitate those instruments. Some
sound systems and their crowds seem to show a real need for a
deeper, pre-modern, meaning which is often invented and constructed to suit the present circumstances. For example, Pendragon, a south London collective on the boundary between free party
and club organisation, who mainly organise cheap and friendly
('fluffy') legal full moon gatherings for London inner-city dwellers,
always subtitle their events with: 'invokes the tribal celtic spirit'.[70]
This longing for pre-modern roots can partially explain the adoption of a version of shamanism, which is generally accepted as
being a pre-Christian tradition of celebrating a feeling of community and of reaching a form of enlightenment. Its concepts of

death–rebirth fit well with the notion of losing a sense of self by breaking the boundaries of ego through exhaustion, repetitive beats and the use of certain (not always fun) drugs.[71] As Spiral Tribe's Mark said in the quote above, 'It's a shamanic thing'.[72] Futurist pre-modernism is an important aspect of a tradition of countercultural thought[73] and so it is not surprising that Mark declared, 'You can call us techno-pagans, whatever . . .'[74]

Techno folk music

As an example of how dance music acquires some of its sensibilities, it is useful to explore the sensibilities of its user group. Techno was played on that sunny Liverpool dockers day in Trafalgar Square, so I'd like to focus mainly on that. As has been shown, not all free sound systems play European acid techno, but it is prevalent, together with psychedelic trance. Wordless, its aggressive industrial sounds grind the dancers into an empty place where only 'now' is relevant. The producers of techno will tell you enthusiastically how it is the ultimate DiY music, home-made on consumer-friendly composition tools and self-released in small batches of vinyl. This is music by the people, for the people, and they will be heard. As Spiral Tribe's Mark has put it: 'Techno is folk music. Never has folk music been so loud.'[75] Buying some second-hand (or even new) digital equipment is cheaper than owning a big recording studio and less of a 'sell-out' than having to sign a record deal with professional money lenders such as a record company.

However, even though many studio musicians argue that if you really want something you'll get it, this may not be as easy for some as it is for others. Alan Durant, for example, has argued that the democratisation of digital music technologies depends on specific presumptions which do not take into account notions of access.[76] For instance, how does one gain access to these technologies? A long-term unemployed person, and especially someone who is homeless, has little economic means to buy and secure even one synthesiser let alone a sequencing computer. For someone who lives a long way from a metropolitan centre, this problem can be intensified, since there will be less affordable equipment to get hold of. So, those with some regular form of income and a relatively

safe (urban) home are privileged in this context. Access to distribution (points) of the actual records is another important point,
since not every shop sells this type of music. The makers of dance
music usually love to expose the world to their music, but due to
the independent nature of many of the productions, distribution
can be pretty limited. In the case of the underground dance scene,
most of the time it is only the DJs who have access to the right
records and those DJs in turn need to have access to mailing lists
and record shops. How one starts out as a DJ depends on whether
one's social circle is involved in the production and/or acquisition
of such records. If not, the task of gaining access to records for
DJing can be tough for the aspiring DJ. This is also the case if there
is no-one around to lend some record decks for a try-out or to show
you how they work. Durant points out that without access to
technologies, new skills or distribution, the claims for democratisation wear a bit thin. A similar point can be made for aspiring music
makers. Working in collectives can alleviate some of these problems
of access, however: collectives can spread the cost of (the loss of) a
rig, and can create a pool of equipment; the music may only have
relevance to a particular musical posse, so a global distribution deal
may be unimportant; and new skills can be shared in an informal
manner.

Having said this, there seems to be a gender divide in the production of dance music, even on the more politically conscious DiY
scene. Although more women than ever have ventured into DJing
and into making dance music, access and the will to bridge the step
to new technological skills in this genre are still problematic. Henderson observed in the old E-driven rave scene that boys and girls
may have had a brief moment of bliss when E neutralised the
testosterone-driven ego complex, but that this didn't last for ever:

> It was liberating to roam in this girly world of physicality, sensuality
> and emotion, especially for the white, straight boys. . . . But the boy
> punters didn't stay all girly and united, didn't stay punters for long.
> . . . Many got uncomfortable and went their separate ways. Meanwhile
> there were those who didn't just want to be made to dance by
> someone else. They wanted to be the man up there in control of the
> crowd. Or the man selling the drugs, or organising the event. Leaving
> the girls . . . where exactly?[77]

Maybe pregnancy and bringing up children has kept some women occupied enough not to be bothered at all with late nights out; alternatively, even in the nineties, it is still difficult to negotiate with the father that mum should DJ and he should look after the kids. Another factor may be that learning to play with electronics and musical technologies has traditionally been a male bonding ritual which excludes women. Increasingly, however, women are breaking that mould. However, perhaps access to the running of the technologies aside, many girls are just not interested in crowd control.

Hardcore: rock encore?

On the DiY techno scene the gender divide seems to be articulated in terms of masculine hardcore and feminine fluffiness. For example, Jade, who spent a summer with techno outfit Spiral Tribe, remarked:

> They just seemed to be ego. There is no loving and caring, it's sheer anarchy. . . . Spirals are a bit chauvinistic. There aren't many women involved, they've got male ego. They seem to think that women are softcore and you got to be hardcore.[78]

Within the white boy-dominated hardcore techno scene, most other types of dance music are regarded as 'too soft'. For example, garage, with its melody lines, softer sounds, Latin rhythms and disco references, is often regarded as fluffy 'handbag' music.[79] 'Handbag' refers to women's and transvestites' disco accessories. The feminine has historically been vilified in rock ideology as 'pop', 'trivial', 'commercial' and 'mainstream'.[80] Even though techno owes some of its cultural history (especially the technique of the slow mix and the dancing to DJ-produced records) to African-American and Latino gay disco,[81] white techno fans seem more concerned with a type of rock ideology which elevates masculinity and, arguably, individualism.

In this context it is of interest to explore some of the old schisms between rock and disco. Richard Dyer observed in 1979:

Rock's eroticism is thrusting, grinding – it is not the whole body, but phallic. Hence it takes from black music the insistent beat and makes it even more driving; rock's repeated phrases trap you in their relentless push, rather than releasing you in an open-ended succession of repetition as disco does.[82]

Dyer concludes that rock is 'phallocentric', while disco provides an all-over body experience. In a similar way one could contrast garage to European techno.[83] Because European techno is often faster than 140 BPM, options for rhythmical variations in dance music have narrowed to a near 2/4 rather than 4/4 beat, leaving the dancer no other option than to wiggle to and fro, punch in the air or simply pogo. For a moment I can even picture the dancers as a type of phallus, or an extension of a phallic DJ. This adds to the effect of a macho mob, be it a crowd full of men or of women. It may give the impression of an armed presence, even though there is in effect only lots of loud industrial sound.

Whilst on this subject, the combat gear traditionally worn by crusties has added to this military spectacle. Sounds like Spiral Tribe especially are renowned for their uniform military anarcho look and the name Desert Storm refers to a military operation. Imagine mobile sound systems loaded on old trucks, sometimes acquired cheaply from ex-Eastern bloc army dumps, roaming across Europe like small combat units. The boys united, feeling omnipotent like they could conquer the world with a beat and seducing people with having a good time. It is one important motivation for travelling sound system people to withstand uncomfortable lives on the road. This is not new in terms of the armies of bands that have gigged along similar routes. The difference between bands and these types of sound systems is the self-contained aspect which makes the entire unit independent of venues in an ultimate quest for DiY sensibility. The rumbling, grating textures of techno go very well with this rough-and-ready attitude.

In support of the techno-has-a-rock-sensibility thesis, one could point to the presence of new individual leaders, who, like guitar heroes, whip up the crowd. A DJ who is able to keep the attention of the crowd with the sequencing of certain records becomes a star in their eyes. Such a DJ will pull the crowd again. To return to the shamanic reference, the traditional shaman is a person who, for whatever reason, has lived through severe moments of alienation and who is able to lead a community in and out of states of identity-loss. However, within our contemporary society, which puts emphasis on ego, the DJ-as-shaman could suffer from an overblown self-image. The DJ sometimes seems like a leader who can mould his flock, in a way that would make some think that the second coming of Hitler had arrived. To push the argument to a particular extreme, at such a moment the 'rhythmically obedient' have found their cult leader(s). The void has been alleviated, but at the price of a 'sheep mentality' of the alienated.

It has been necessary to take the rock–disco comparison to an extreme, since one hears these thoughts expressed in informal conversations. Now they can be addressed. First of all, star DJs can be found anywhere, from disco to techno. One could even point out that techno DJs are least concerned with stardom, even though a will-to-power does seem to be driving force. In the second place, many collectives provide a working relation that in effect prevents ego-mania. For example, Nottingham-based DiY's DJs have occasionally played as guests in dance clubs under the name of the collective, so you would never know exactly what the music would be like. In my own work on house music, I have even proposed that a truly effective DJ is more like a caring mother than an aspiring Führer, someone who guides rather than leads the crowd in a type of dialogue. The latter is the big difference between DJing and playing a tape or throwing people off course with a sonic wall of ego-pap. Any bedroom DJ who had his/her carefully prepared set confronted with a crowd in a different mood can bear witness to that: people vote with their feet.

In the case of the recording artists of contemporary dance, individualism is even more suppressed. This is due to the way that techno and related dance music is produced. The creator remains anonymous due to the process of recording – at another time and often in a different place than when/where it is 'performed' by the DJ. Records have been produced under the names of DJ collectives: Spiral Tribe, DiY, Desert Storm, The Lumpheads (of Sugar Lump), to name a few. Other records are produced under various pseudonyms, sometimes a different one for each project. Not always is anonymity intended for self-conscious ideological reasons; sometimes it may be necessary in order to evade copyright laws, which may confront the creative user of 'found sounds'.[84] Since techno is music for DJs, it is also often made by DJs and other record collectors. Inspired by the music they hear, play and own, new tracks are produced, sometimes with the help of a sampler. The latter enables and facilitates the recording and digital manipulation of fragments of sound, which can be sequenced in loops and as special effects. Culture, including sound, is commodified, so copyright applies to each 'borrowed' sound bite. However, not everyone is willing or has the financial means to play the game of seeking permission and paying licensing fees to copyright holders. So, as producers of 'dodgy' records which underline the notion that culture is a common good, they prefer anonymity over stardom. Sometimes even DJs don't really know who made a record or even what the title is; the tunes are recognised by the label design and a memory of textures and 'feel'.

Although a preference for masculinity can be identified on the hardcore techno scene, this is moderated in the more 'fluffy' hippie environments. A more colourful day-glo visual style is accompanied by trance music which carries some whirly-curly melody lines on top of a pushing rhythm section. At such events even garage and deep house can be heard, although these are given a marginal status of warm-up or backroom music. Techno, trance and garage cross each other's paths on the free festival scene, but their user groups have different allegiances.

Blinking into dawn

So, how can sound systems be seen as a threat to a mainstream establishment? And what are the politics of dancing? You could lose yourself to the beat, but this does not question the foundations of society. To take part in the act of dancing in our contemporary dance-drug culture, which roughly falls under the generic term 'rave', is not political in itself. It is even apolitical and amoral; no good or bad is recognised, only a collective surrender to the beat. More than anything, it is the celebration of a great void. What makes these parties seem so extreme, though, is the incredible effectiveness of current technologies of dance, in terms both of (re)producing music and of chemical nerve stimulation. Combined with a sense of disconnection from what is traditionally understood as citizenship, a gathering of chemically enhanced people moving to amplified beats can generate an intense response of ego-loss in a mass of dancing bodies. Losing one's self could provide a potential for change, but this depends on the context in which it takes place. Repetitive beats may induce a type of obedience to the groove, but do not impose a rational focus. Free parties allow more space for new insights than commercial dance events. In that context, dance-drug events can provide a real sense of community to those who feel politically dislocated and nationally disowned.

However, rather than generalising about sensibilities, attention must be directed towards the various user groups of dance-drug technologies. So, for example, even though both women and men happily (or aggressively) dance to European hardcore techno, the white rock ethos of some sound system collectives reinforces a particular gender division. However, within that same scene individualism of the performer seems to be less prevalent than on the rock scene, making way for cooperative social relations. This sense of cooperation helps to democratise the production of recorded music as well as of the dance events, by providing shared access, especially between the male participants, to equipment and skills in addition to independent product distribution. In general, free sound systems follow a DiY ethic which (in contrast to the Tory ethos of the eighties) is collective rather than competitive.

Most important in the politics of dance in Britain is that the restrained British body politic which keeps dance inside a rigidly regulated environment has criminalised those who believe in freedom of movement. In the wake of acid house parties and raves, this can be witnessed in various moral panics as well as in legislation attempting to regulate the dancing, musing body. In 1991, during my research into house music,[85] Dutch researcher Noot (a.k.a. Arno Adelaars) gave me a copy of his book on the history of Ecstasy,[86] which he signed with the joke: 'tien jaren cel for Gonnie' (ten years in jail for Gonnie [Hillegonda]). The Berlin Wall had come down, initiating the techno-driven Love Parade, while an invisible one was raised in the UK. Still, during the summer of 1997 countless small-scale free parties occurred all over the British countryside[87] and there are always city festivals like the Notting Hill Carnival, Pride and Manchester's Mardi Gras. 'Keep the faith', as Northern Soul fans say.

Notes

1 DiY Culture: notes towards an intro

1. Epigraphs are taken from the following sources, respectively. Ian Camp-
   bell, 'Music against the Bomb', in John Minnion and Philip Bolsover, eds,
   The CND Story, London: Allison & Busby 1983, pp. 116, 115; Nigel
   Fountain, *Underground: The Alternative Press, 1966–74*, London: Routledge
   1988, pp. 26–7; Jon Savage, *England's Dreaming: Sex Pistols and Punk Rock*,
   London: Faber 1991, pp. 230, 279; Cosmo, quoted in Nicholas Saunders,
   Ecstasy and the Dance Culture, London: self-published 1995, p. 173; Merrick,
   Battle for the Trees: Three Months of Responsible Ancestry, Leeds: Godhaven Ink
   1996, p. 9.
2. Stephen Booth, *Into the 1990s with Green Anarchist*, Oxford: Green Anarchist
   Books 1996, p. 83.
3. John Vidal, *McLibel: Burger Culture on Trial*, London: Macmillan 1997,
   p. 277.
4. It's often said that roads and animal rights are to the nineties what the
   Bomb and organised racism were to earlier decades: focuses of campaign
   and youth mobilisation. Yet strategies are different today. The time of the
   mass national CND or Rock Against Racism marches through London has
   passed, to be replaced by multiple, small-scale, 'in-yer-face' actions across
   the country, outside your sleepy port, your quiet market town.
5. Stephen Duncombe, *Notes from Underground: Zines and the Politics of
   Alternative Culture*, London: Verso 1997, p. 190.
6. Per Herngren, *Path of Resistance: The Practice of Civil Disobedience* (trans. by
   Margaret Rainey), Philadelphia: New Society Publishers 1993, pp. 9, 11,
   14.
7. Though when it works it is a spectacularly, even historically, successful
   strategy. The Ploughshares Movement in which Herngren is involved
   offers a recent example. In 1996 four women peace activists were tried for
   a number of charges, the main one being criminal damage to a Hawk
   fighter jet at an airbase in Lancashire, in an echo of Greenham women

invading airbases in the 1980s. Their defence in court, also echoing a strategy tried at Greenham, was based around the 1969 Genocide Act: their damage was justified because of the greater evil of the fact that the jets were due for export to the repressive regime of Indonesia to continue its brutal military domination of the people of East Timor. The jury accepted this and, in a historic verdict, the women were found not guilty. For Ploughshares activists, of course, non-violence is a fundamental feature of their direct action, since action is intended to protest against military weaponry, products designed for violence. Following the verdict, one activist against the arms trade said: 'It's all go for real direct action now. They'd better be increasing their security around all those bases and factories because there's a lot of people very keen on destroying the products of this sordid little industry bit by bit' (quoted in *SchNEWS*, no. 84, 2 August 1996). Indeed, energised by the success of the Hawks action, the Campaign Against the Arms Trade seriously disrupted the 1997 British arms fair at Farnborough in a mass protest.

8. Booth, *Into the 1990s with Green Anarchist*, p. 98.
9. Quoted in Duncombe, *Notes from Underground*, pp. 187–8.
10. Danny Burns, *Poll Tax Rebellion*, Stirling: AK Press 1992, pp. 31, 33. Welfare rights worker Steve Munby expresses reservations about such a direct challenge to implementation, however: 'I'm not convinced that the non-payment campaign got rid of the poll tax, but what I do know is that the "Can't pay, won't pay" campaign has had devastating consequences for tens of thousands of people on income support in poor communities who have been left with debts hanging over their heads.' Quoted in 'Directing the action', *New Times*, no. 131, 13 September 1997, p. 6.
11. Burns, *Poll Tax Rebellion*, p. 49.
12. For more on the road protest of Pollok Free State, see George McKay, *Senseless Acts of Beauty: Cultures of Resistance since the Sixties*, London: Verso 1996; Ben Seel, 'Frontline eco-wars! The Pollok Free State road protest community: counter-hegemonic intentions, pluralist effects', in Colin Barker and Mike Tyldesley, eds, *Alternative Futures and Popular Protest: Conference Papers*, vol. 1, Manchester: Manchester Metropolitan University 1996, no pagination; 'Pollock [*sic*] Free State lives on!', *Do or Die*, no. 5, 1995, pp. 7–10; Ali Begbie, 'Pollok Free statement', in Stacy Wakefield and Grrt, eds, *Not for Rent: Conversations with Creative Activists in the UK*, Amsterdam: Evil Twin Publications 1995, pp. 68–71.
13. Steve Platt, 'A decade of squatting', in Nick Wates and Christian Wolmar, eds, *Squatting: The Real Story*, London: Bay Leaf Books 1980, p. 15.
14. Brian Doherty, 'Paving the way: the rise of direct action against road-building and the changing character of British environmentalism', in Barker and Tyldesley, *Alternative Futures and Popular Protest*, vol. 1, no pagination.
15. Rik Scarce, *Eco-Warriors: Understanding the Radical Environmental Movement*, Chicago: Noble Press 1990, p. 49.

16. Alex Plows, 'The rise (& fall?) of the ego-warrior', *Do or Die*, no. 5, 1995, p. 89. The phrase 'womanly culture' about Greenham is taken from Barbara Harford and Sarah Hopkins, eds, *Greenham Common: Women at the Wire*, London: The Women's Press 1984, p. 5.

17. Personal correspondence, 1996.

18. Michel Maffesoli, *The Time of the Tribes: The Decline of Individualism in Mass Society* (trans. by Don Smith), London: Sage 1996, pp. 92, 93.

19. Scarce, *Eco-Warriors*, p. 48.

20. Robert Hunter, *The Greenpeace Chronicle*, London: Picador 1980, pp. 67, 17–18.

21. Thomas Harding, *The Video Activist Handbook*, London: Pluto 1997, pp. 90–91, 1. For other DiY groups such as *Green Anarchist* or (earlier) Class War, being mediagenic means aligning with the enemy, since if an action gains sympathetic press coverage it probably isn't spiky enough. For an underground magazine like *SQUALL*, as Jim Carey shows in his chapter here, there are also concerns about the cosy relationship between media and government.

22. Fountain, *Underground*, p. 24.

23. Or else a desperately sought hedonistic experience that sometimes led to death – on the dancefloor, outside the party. Is getting out of it *that* important?

24. Scarce, *Eco-Warriors*, pp. 260, 261.

25. *Do or Die*, no. 6, 1997, p. 63.

26. *The Book: Directory of Active Groups in the UK*, Brighton: Justice? 1995, p. 1.

27. A healthy disrespect of those suspected of discursive dilatoriness, like academics and experts, can be just that – healthy. I'm more concerned here to look at the possible weaknesses of direct action when it's offered, or ends up, as an end in itself.

28. Back cover blurb to *SchNEWSround: Issues 51–100*, Brighton: Justice? 1996. Depending on what number issue they have, the individual *SchNEWS* referred to elsewhere in these notes can be found collected in this book, or its earlier companion, *SchNEWSreader: Issues 0–50*, Brighton: Justice? 1995.

29. Scarce, *Eco-Warriors*, p. 31.

30. Daniel and Gabriel Cohn-Bendit, *Obsolete Communism: The Left-Wing Alternative* (trans. by Arnold Pomerans), Harmondsworth: Penguin 1969, p. 12; emphasis added.

31. Personal correspondence, 1997.

32. The best books to come out of DiY Culture to date exacerbate this lack of concern or curiosity for history. The *SchNEWS* collections bring together the weekly free newssheets from Justice? in Brighton in an annual publication – with a small amount of critical or reflective comment included. There are a small number of books in the form of transcribed interviews with DiY activists, but again with little analytical effort as part of the project. The DiY manuals, on topics from video activism to anti-roads

actions, valorise how-to knowledge over historical let alone theoretical material.

33. John Quail, *The Slow Burning Fuse: The Lost History of the British Anarchists*, London: Granada 1978, pp. 307–8.

34. Murray Bookchin, *Social Anarchism or Lifestyle Anarchism: An Unbridgeable Chasm*, Edinburgh: AK Press 1995, pp. 48, 49.

35. Road Alert!, *Road Raging: Top Tips for Wrecking Roadbuilding*, Newbury: Road Alert! 1997, p. 7. An article by Ian Welsh and Phil McLeish traces links between road protest and anarchism, particularly in the areas of direct action and decentralised, non-hierarchical organisation: 'The European road to nowhere: anarchism and direct action against the UK roads programme', *Anarchist Studies*, vol. 4, no. 1, 1996, pp. 27–44.

36. Maffesoli, *The Time of the Tribes*, p. 75.

37. Miss Pod, 'Where does it go from here?', *POD*, no. 6, no date, p. 11.

38. Pat Arrowsmith, 'The direct action debate', in Minnion and Bolsover, *The CND Story*, p. 140.

39. Road Alert!, *Road Raging*, p. 98.

40. Herngren, *Path of Resistance*, p. 18.

41. Scarce, *Eco-Warriors*, p. 12.

42. Doherty, 'Paving the way'.

43. David Henshaw, *Animal Warfare: The Story of the Animal Liberation Front*, London: Fontana 1989, p. 200.

44. Gaoled animal rights activist Keith Mann wrote to me from prison in October 1995 that 'it was the smashing of a windscreen at Shoreham one night in January that alerted the world to what was going on'.

45. *Poll Tax Riot: 10 Hours that Shook Trafalgar Square*, London: Acab Press 1990, pp. 18, 20.

46. Ronnie Lee, quoted in Henshaw, *Animal Warfare*, p. 100.

47. Seel, 'Frontline eco-wars!'

48. However, it's worth noting that the deployment of revolutionary violence by insurrectionary cells in the 1970s was partly justified by Ulrike Meinhof of the Red Army Faction as *a response to the violence directed towards the sixties counterculture*. Discussing the attempted assassination of German New Left activist Rudi Dutschke in West Berlin in April 1968, Meinhof said: 'The bullets fired at Rudi put an end to the dream of non-violence. . . . Those who do not arm themselves die, those who do not die are buried alive . . . in the prisons, the re-education centres, in the holes of suburban estates' (quoted in Vladimir Fišera, ed., *Writing on the Wall: France, May 1968: A Documentary Anthology*, London: Allison & Busby 1978, p. 18). Meinhof was found hanged in her prison cell in 1976, the first of a series of terrorist 'suicides' announced by the German state. In Britain meanwhile, from 1970, the Angry Brigade was releasing communiqués justifying its own actions: 'The question is not whether the revolution will be violent. Organised militant struggle and organised terrorism go side by side. These are the tactics of the revolutionary class movement. Where two or three

revolutionaries use organised violence to attack the class system . . . there
is the Angry Brigade. . . . No revolution was ever one without violence'
(Communiqué 6, in *The Angry Brigade*, Port Glasgow: Bratach Dubh
Publications 1978, p. 5). These extraordinary events across Europe in the
1970s do rather put contemporary fluffy/spiky tensions in some kind of
perspective.

49. Booth, *Into the 1990s with Green Anarchist*, p. 154; emphasis added.

50. The first quotation is from Road Alert!, *Road Raging*, pp. 1–2, emphasis
added; the second from Seel, 'Frontline eco-wars!'

51. For sure, privatisation also has a more authoritarian side in direct
connection to DiY Culture, as seen in the greater employment of private
security firms and private detective agencies by the state and related
concerns, which at the very least raises questions about the validity of the
rhetoric of freedom of speech and the right to protest. The advice and
support group Friends, Families and Travellers note that 'private security
firms . . . seem to be becoming increasingly involved in dealing with
unauthorised occupation of land. . . . [T]he Country Landowners' Association employed a security firm called SAS Security between 1984 and
1986. The man who ran the firm acted as an advisor to Wiltshire Police
during the Peace Convoy. He was reported by the Searchlight magazine
as being the national recruiting officer for the National Front, and had
been a recruiting officer for mercenaries for Rhodesia' (Friends, Families
and Travellers Support Group, *Confined, Constrained and Condemned: Civil
Rights and Travellers*, Glastonbury: FFT 1996, p. 33). And, as reported by
Road Alert!, 'The DoT has used private detectives to photograph, spy on,
serve legal papers on, film, and generally harass activists since the protests
at Twyford Down in 1992. One firm, Bray's of Southampton, has cornered
the market in this sad and shady speciality. . . . We suggest you make life
as difficult and unpleasant as possible for them at every opportunity' (*Road
Raging*, p. 48).

52. There is something of a new religious strand to DiY Culture, which may
be a sign of what *My First Little Book of Peaceful Direct Action* nicely calls 'the
leap of faith required to get people out of their car and in front of a
bulldozer'. In individual chapters here Alex Plows touches on neo-
paganism and Tim Malyon shows the appropriation of Rastafarian rhetoric
by the Exodus Collective, for instance. The resurgence of paganism is also
seen in an organisation like Dragon Environmental Network, which
connects pagan ideas of respect for and worship of the earth and natural
cycles with campaigns and actions to highlight environmental issues and
to resist development. It can be quite easy to map pagan beliefs on to road
protesters, even if it's done via a vaguely woolly redefinition of pagan as
'pagan with a small p' (Stephen McKay, 'A Pagan intifada? Eco-paganism
and the Land Rights Movement', in Barker and Tyldesley, *Alternative
Futures and Popular Protest*, vol. 1), which seems to me an instant effort to
reclaim a lost history, one which may be none too rigorous, may be

intuitive, may be lacking in the political framework necessary (possibly/ probably) to make wide sense of a challenge. Yet Graham Harvey insists on the radical greenness of paganism: 'At this point it offers its most radical challenge to the consumerism and individualism of contemporary culture. There are those who would like it to be part of the mainstream and resent the tree-dwelling Pagan eco-warriors, but the counter-cultural flow in Paganism is its lifeblood' (Graham Harvey, *Listening People, Speaking Earth: Contemporary Paganism*, London: Hurst 1997, p. 142). The phenomenon of rave Xtianity, as exemplified by the rise and fall of the Nine o'Clock Service in Sheffield in the early 1990s, shows if nothing else that rave culture can be an ideologically blank form, to be filled with anything from evangelism (happy clappy in white gloves) to anarchism (free party sound systems).

53. Peter Gartside, 'Bypassing politics? The contradictions of "DiY Culture"', *Soundings: A Journal of Politics and Culture*, no. 6, Summer 1997, p. 200. Talking of different languages, it's interesting that *SQUALL*, for example, deliberately eschews the use of terms like 'left-wing', 'right-wing', even 'anarchism', seeing these as media-loaded terms rooted in a past mentality it's trying to avoid.

54. Quoted in Duncombe, *Notes from Underground*, p. 40. More problematically for those believing in the *inherent* radicalism of DiY, Duncombe himself writes that 'in some ways the ideal of do-it-yourself is a far-from-radical proposition. The idea of not allowing your creativity to be stymied by any "authoritarian system" is the essence of American individualism. The far-from-dissident business section of the *New York Times* recently ran a piece entitled "The Do-It-Yourself Employer", with profiles on "DIY" accountants, real estate brokers, and public relations agents' (p. 179).

55. They have a pretty good track record of escaping capital too, of trying to bypass the economics of profit: through free festivals or parties, free newssheets, cheap independent production and distribution of goods (anything from records to wholefoods), squatting, LETS schemes, community bookshops, organic veggie boxes, low-impact communities, etc., etc.

56. Bookchin, *Social Anarchism or Lifestyle Anarchism*, p. 27. While Bookchin is here referring to the wider counterculture of the West Coast of America – 'the detritus of the 60s' is his surprisingly strong way of putting it (p. 51) – the comment is pertinent to the 1990s 'ecstasy industry' of rave and dance culture.

57. Colin Ward, *Talking Houses: Ten Lectures*, London: Freedom Press 1990, p. 9.

58. Quail, *The Slow Burning Fuse*, p. 225.

59. John Stewart, Jonathan Bray and Emma Must, *Road Block: How People Power is Wrecking the Roads Programme*, ALARM UK, undated, p. 4. The next quotation, from the Yorkshire road activist, is also taken from this book (p. 22).

60. Arrogant nonsense? It's always nice to hear an expert discussing their own speciality. The quotation is in Henshaw, *Animal Warfare*, p. 90.
61. These events are all looked at in detail in my book *Senseless Acts of Beauty.*
62. Merrick, *Battle for the Trees*, pp. 9, 21.
63. Both this and the following quotation on 'burnout' are from *My First Little Book of Peaceful Direct Action . . . A Quick Introduction to Protesting Against the Newbury 'Bypass'*, second edition 1996, p. 5.
64. 'Real women' feature, *Frontline*, no. 4, Spring 1997; 'PIERCED UP' feature, *Frontline*, no. 3, Summer 1996.
65. Campbell, 'Music against the Bomb', p. 115. Paul Oliver agrees that the trad jazz boom in the fifties was politicised; he just suggests that 'jazz symbolized what its proponents chose to find in it that supported their own aims and ideologies'. He maps things out: 'To the communists the ensemble improvisation of the traditional band symbolized the sharing of responsibility and skills of collective creativity without individualism; to the anarchists the traditional line-up meant freedom of expression and the loose, unshackled federalism of "head" arangements; to liberals the music spoke of responsibility and selflessness; to conservatives, the strength and continuity of traditions ensured the basis for the individual enterprise of front-line soloists' ('Introduction to Part Two', in Paul Oliver, ed., *Black Music in Britain: Essays on the Afro-Asian Contribution to Popular Music*, Buckingham: Open University Press 1990, p. 81). Maybe, then, jazz is no less of an ideologically blank form than rave (see note 52), or maybe instrumental music forms by their nature float free from fixed meaning.
66. Quoted in Paul Harris, *When Pirates Ruled the Waves*, third edition, Aberdeen: Impulse 1969, p. 2.
67. Maybe I'm overstating the oppositional thrust of pirate radio. At the launch of Radio Atlanta (soon to be renamed Caroline) in 1964, good luck messages were sent by Cliff Richard, Harry Secombe, Rolf Harris, Frank Ifield, Alma Cogan . . .
68. This and the cool Tory MP quotation following it are taken from Harris, *When Pirates Ruled the Waves*, pp. 6, 43.
69. The Desperate Bicycles, 'The Medium was Tedium'/'Don't Back the Front', Refill Records, 1977. The Poison Girls lyric is taken from 'Daughters and Sons', on *Total Exposure*, Xntrix Rcords, 1981.
70. Bookchin, *Social Anarchism or Lifestyle Anarchism*, pp. 20, 25.
71. In *Do or Die*, no. 6, 1997, p. 29.
72. In Wakefield and Grrt, *Not for Rent*, p. 79; emphasis added.
73. *SchNEWS*, no. 53, 15 December 1995.
74. To give a very brief sense of the CJA, the Criminal Justice and Public Order Act 1994, I'll quote from Part V, Section 63, which outlines 'Powers to remove persons attending or preparing for a rave': '(1) This section applies to a gathering on land in the open air of 100 or more persons (whether or not trespassers) at which amplified music is played during the night (with or without intermissions) and is such as, by reason of its

loudness and duration and the time at which it is played, is likely to cause serious distress to the inhabitants of the locality; and for this purpose – (a) such a gathering continues during intermissions in the music and, where the gathering extends over several days, throughout the period during which amplified music is played at night (with or without intermissions); and (b) 'music' includes sounds wholly or predominantly characterised by the emission of a succession of repetitive beats.' There's an entire chapter on the Criminal Justice Act and counterculture in *Senseless Acts of Beauty*; it's worth reading it alongside John Hutnyk's chapter in *Dis-Orienting Rhythms* to see the limitations (including my own in *Senseless Acts*) of opposition to it. Hutnyk argues that, 'While the inclusion of clauses to increase police powers in the inner urban areas was of special concern to Asian anti-racist organizations, these aspects were rarely addressed by white middle-class activists more concerned with the attacks on raves and parties. . . . The most political of responses from the white Left took up the attacks on demonstrations, the anti-terrorism clauses and the abolition of the right to silence . . ., but rarely the stop-and-search powers [predominantly used against urban black and Asian youth]'. (In Sanjay Sharma, John Hutnyk and Ashwani Sharma, eds, *Dis-Orienting Rhythms: The Politics of the New Asian Dance Music*, London: Zed Books 1996, p. 159).

75. *Ideal Home: Survival Edition*, Hooligan Press 1986, p. 56.

76. In Harford and Hopkins, *Greenham Common*, p. 71.

77. The quotation is from Lynne Jones, ed., *Keeping the Peace: A Women's Peace Handbook*, London: The Women's Press, 1983, p. 97. While Greenham Common Peace Camp is well documented, what of the other one hundred? Is there a single book which tells their story, the history of that extraordinary nationwide phenomenon of opposition? Aren't we in danger of being a bit careless with our own radical history here? It's not even *old* history.

78. Harford and Hopkins, *Greenham Common*, p. 5.

79. Seel, 'Frontline eco-wars!'

80. While government is busy trying to think up new laws to block such creativity and action, why doesn't it try instead to celebrate our diversity, and help out with some space? It has done this on at least one occasion: in 1975 the Labour government helped provide a site for that year's People's Free Festival, following the violent trashing of the 1974 event at Windsor by police.

81. I'm aware that these aren't mutually exclusive, but often mutually reinforcing: a DiY protest space *is* a temporary illustration of alternative living, a low impact community such as a bender village on communally-held land is also implicitly a protest, a rejection of the social values of the dominant society.

82. *Do or Die*, no. 6, 1997, pp. 63–4.

83. This and the following quotation are from Road Alert!, *Road Raging*, pp. 76, 82.

84. Merrick, *Battle for the Trees*, p. 53.
85. Quoted in Quail, *The Slow Burning Fuse*, p. 228.
86. This and the following quotation are from Simon Fairlie, *Low Impact Development: Planning and People in a Sustainable Countryside*, Charlbury, Oxfordshire: John Carpenter 1996, p. xi.
87. Though landowners and huntspeople – usually targets rather than practitioners – have recently threatened to take direct action themselves in protest against the 1997 Labour government's proposed legislation to ban fox-hunting.
88. This and the following quotation are from Fairlie, *Low Impact Development*, pp. 16, 127.
89. Booth, *Into the 1990s with Green Anarchist*, p. 17.
90. Personal correspondence, 1996.
91. Rupa Huq, 'Asian Kool? Bhangra and Beyond', in Sharma et. al, *Dis-Orienting Rhythms*, p. 79; emphasis added.
92. Gartside, 'Bypassing politics?', p. 204.
93. Colin Ward, 'The early squatters: six centuries of squatting', in Wates and Wolmar, *Squatting: The Real Story*, p. 107. Another surprising historical correspondence in the context of squatting, and another which sadly confirms the lack of knowledge of tradition of radical history, is the Squatters' Estate Agency set up by Justice? in Brighton in February 1996. This was 'a place where you can go for squatting advice and subversive literature. With pictures of empty properties in the window, complete with handy hints: '"Three bedrooms, nice garden, window open at rear"' (*SchNEWS*, no. 64, 8 March 1996). The 1990s Squatters' Estate Agency became a ten-day media event, in squatted premises closed down before bailiffs arrived. The significant point here is that the nineties activists had no knowledge of the seventies precedent, the Ruff Tuff Cream Puff agency set up by activists in 1974, which itself featured prominently in the media at the time. The similarities are remarkable, but went entirely unremarked as far as I am aware. This indicates a degree of ahistoricism on the part of nineties activists, but also is a symptom of the apparent lack of historical narrative or even knowledge available to countercultural groups. For the story of the Ruff Tuff Cream Puff agency, see Heathcote Williams, 'The squatters estate agency', in Wates and Wolmar, *Squatting*, pp. 192–7.
94. Platt, 'A decade of squatting', p. 39.
95. See *Senseless Acts of Beauty* for more on the 1990s Free States at road protest sites, including Wanstonia, Pollok Free State, Cuerdenia.
96. Platt, 'A decade of squatting', pp. 91, 93.
97. Quoted in Wakefield and Grrrt, *Not for Rent*, p. 33.
98. Danny Penman, *The Price of Meat*, London: Gollancz 1996, p. 12. The following quotation is also taken from ibid., p. 202.
99. Personal correspondence, 1995.
100. This could have been better phrased: I doubt very much whether the activists here wanted to say that they 'hate' animal rights, anti-roads protest

and wilderness. Maybe, *pace* the slogan by Justice? that 'a single action is worth a thousand words', some activists should stick to actions not words. Incidentally, such multiplicity of interest is commonplace as activists cross between one campaign group and another, as Alex Plows illustrates in her chapter on Earth First!.

101. Hunter, *The Greenpeace Chronicle*, p. 55.
102. Henshaw, *Animal Warfare*, p. 8. Following the outrageous infiltration of London Greenpeace by private detectives paid for by McDonald's to glean information on those who would become the McLibel anarchists, adding a couple of undercover spies to this list would bring it up to date. See *SQUALL*, no. 14, Autumn 1996. A wide-ranging special feature on the McLibel trial was published in *SQUALL*, no. 11, Autumn 1995, pp. 44–55.
103. Merrick, *Battle for the Trees*, pp. 13, 52.
104. I've written about Little Englander issues in relation to fears of Americanisation in the introduction to my collection *Yankee Go Home (& Take Me With U): Americanization and Popular Culture*, Sheffield: Sheffield Academic Press 1997. One thing that interests me is the extent to which we rely on America for our models of liberatory politics (from the hippie counterculture to Earth First!). It's interesting that, in the context of animal rights, a campaign organisation like the Animal Liberation Front was a British export to the United States, rather than the other way round.
105. *Green Anarchism Its Origins and Influences*, no publishing information, p. 5.
106. See Matthew Kalman and John Murray's 'New-Age Nazism', *New Statesman and Society*, 23 June 1995, pp. 18–20, for a more detailed account of extreme right-wing appropriation and activity in Britain and the United States.
107. *Lost in Concrete: Activist Guide to European Transport Policies*, Amsterdam: A SEED Europe 1996, p. 25.
108. Peter Staudenmaier, 'Fascist ecology: the "green wing" of the Nazi Party and its historical antecedents', in Janet Biehl and Peter Staudenmaier, *Ecofascism: Lessons from the German Experience*, Edinburgh: AK Press 1995, p. 8.
109. Daniel Gasman, quoted in ibid. p. 8.
110. Biehl and Staudenmaier, *Ecofascism*, p. 2.
111. Staudenmaier, 'Fascist ecology', pp. 15, 19.
112. The two Adorno quotations are from 'Theses against occultism', in Stephen Crook, ed., *Adorno: The Stars Down to Earth and Other Essays on the Irrational in Culture*, London: Routledge 1994, pp. 130, 128. It's worth considering the extent to which Adorno's connection of the irrational with the authoritarian overlooks the possibility of an *anti*-authoritarian irrationalism (as in the anarchic New Age-tinged Peace Convoy, or the Dongas Tribe in Britain, for instance).
113. This and the following quotation are from Kalman and Murray's 'New-Age Nazism', p. 20.
114. If you're really interested in anarchist in-fighting see Luther Blissett and Stewart Home on *Green Anarchist* in *Green Apocalypse*, London: Unpopular Books, no date.

115. Henshaw, *Animal Warfare*, p. 92.

116. Quoted in Duncombe, *Notes from Underground*, p. 183; emphasis added.

117. Staudenmaier, 'Fascist ecology', p. 26.

118. Tim Jordan, *Reinventing Revolution: Value and Difference in New Social Movements and the Left*, Aldershot: Avebury 1994, p. 50.

119. Quoted in Miss Pod, 'Where does it go from here?', p. 11.

120. I think that the subject range of the chapters in this book confirms these lacunae; I also think that their relative absence from the book is a reflection of the limits of DiY Culture as a self-invented movement rather than of the editorial position of the book. I'm basing the judgement both on what's presented in DiY media and on discussions with activists of different persuasions and generations. Of course I could have commissioned chapters on the direct action campaign of, for instance, Outrage or the Disabled Action Network, but my feeling is that I would then have been presenting DiY Culture as I thought it ought to be rather than (hopefully) roughly as it was. (As I said earlier, there's enough material around now that uncritically celebrates DiY.) And if there *is* the odd gap in my construction of DiY Culture as presented by the range of chapters here I should just delicately explain that, at least in part, that's down to the odd activist-writer I commissioned who ended up believing too much that 'a single action is worth a thousand words', let alone a chapter-length five thousand.

121. Mark Simpson, quoted in Andy Beckett, 'On the gay and narrow', *Guardian*, G2 section, 3 July 1997, p. 2.

122. Seel, 'Frontline eco-wars!'; emphasis added.

123. *Do or Die*, no. 5, 1995, p. 10.

124. Michele Wallace, 'Reading 1968: the great American whitewash', in *Invisibility Blues*, London: Verso 1990, p. 195. The second quotation from Wallace is also from ibid., p. 194.

125. *The Book*, p. 1.

126. Sharma et al., *Dis-Orienting Rhythms*, p. 11.

127. 'Re-sounding (anti)racism, or concordant politics? Revolutionary antecedents', in ibid., p. 139.

128. Koushik Banerjea and Jatinder Barn, 'Versioning terror: Jallianwala Bagh and the jungle', in ibid., p. 214.

129. Quoted in Wakefield and Grrrt, *Not for Rent*, p. 64.

130. Winfried Wolf, *Car Mania: A Critical History of Transport* (trans. by Gus Fagan), London: Pluto 1996, pp. 205-8.

131. Lorna Reith, quoted in 'Directing the action', p. 7. Interestingly Reith's justification of direct action – to provoke *greater* state intervention – distances it from the anarchist emphasis I've placed on DiY Culture through this introduction.

132. Personal correspondence, 1997.

133. Wolf, *Car Mania*, p. 210.

134. Colin Ward, *Anarchy in Action*, second edition, London: Freedom Press 1972, pp. 137-8.

135. John Vidal, *McLibel*, p. 287; emphasis added.
136. Bookchin, *Social Anarchism or Lifestyle Anarchism*, p. 18.
137. Ibid., p. 57.

3 *Viva camcordistas!* Video activism and the protest movement

1. Thomas Harding, *Video Activist Handbook*, London: Pluto Press 1997, p. 16.
2. Ibid., p. 135.
3. Merrick, *Battle for the Trees: Three Months of Responsible Ancestry*, Leeds: Godhaven Ink 1996, pp. 23–4.
4. Adapted from Harding, *Video Activist Handbook*.
5. Stephen Booth, *Into the 1990s with Green Anarchist*, Oxford: Green Anarchist Books 1996, pp. 110, 114. In 1998, I made a video with Stephen raising awareness of the GANDALF (Green Anarchist and Animal Liberation Front) trial, where he and two others were gaoled for reporting direct actions.

4 The politics of anti-road struggle and the struggles of anti-road politics: the case of the No M11 Link Road campaign

1. *Contributions to the Revolutionary Struggle Intended to be Discussed, Corrected and Principally Put into Practice without Delay*, London: Elephant Editions 1990, p. 12.
2. *New Musical Express*, 4 June 1994, p. 6.
3. Thanks to Mike Edwards and Paul Morozzo for comments on the earlier version of this chapter. For further material on the issues covered here, see 'Auto-struggles: the developing war against the road monster', *Aufheben*, no. 3, Summer 1994.
4. For more on our 'intellectual heritage', see the Editorial in *Aufheben*, no. 1, Autumn 1992.
5. The circulation of *commodities* has very different imperatives than the movement of goods would have in a world orientated to human needs instead of profit. For capital, commodities are essentially locked-up value, which must be realised as soon as possible. This need to free the value contained in commodities is not a neutral need for 'efficiency', but the need of capital to minimise circulation time – circulation time being that period when capital is not sucking the blood out of its human prey by putting them to work.
6. See, for example, Edward Balls, 'Growth and greenery can still be friends', *Guardian*, 1 August 1994, p. 11.
7. Estimates for the policing cost alone for the fifteen-month campaign were put at £200 million. However, the signal-workers' dispute cost the same amount to business in just nineteen strike days over five months!

8. Costs to capital and the creation of a climate of resistance are of course bound up; there will be no climate of confrontation with capital unless there is at least some threat to capital's reproduction of itself.
9. The contrast between such a form of life and the way we tend to conduct most other types of struggle is clear, for example, by comparison with the poll tax struggle. In our fight against the poll tax, we had meetings, riots, prison pickets, bailiff pickets, and so on, but (for most of us) large sections of our life, activity, time and living space were easily sectioned off from the poll tax struggle in time and space. That is not a criticism of the way we did things, but it is a fact of the nature of that particular struggle and indeed most struggles. Although most of the people living in Claremont Road had other places where they could go, when they were on Claremont Road, they were living the struggle: life was the campaign and the campaign was life.
10. See for example Raoul Vaneigem (1967), *The Revolution of Everyday Life* (trans. by Donald Nicholson-Smith), London: Rebel Press/Left Bank Books 1994.
11. One obvious difference between the concerns of the Situationists and those involved in the No M11 campaign is the concern with the future. 'And above all I would promote this one watchword: "Act as though there were no tomorrow,"' declares Vaneigem (ibid., p. 116). Despite the fact that many of us involved in the No M11 campaign saw spontaneity and immediate pleasure as essential components of the struggle itself, an important element of the campaign's rationale was the apparent *lack* of concern of the car/road empire for the future. Hence the common argument within the campaign, 'There'll be no future for our children (if the road is built etc.).' In fact, the car/road empire *does* have a concern for the future (that is, the future of its profits; hence its concern with planning), although the future it envisages is neither as global or as long term as that evoked by the No M11 participants.
12. 'The desire to live is a political decision' (ibid., p. 18). 'People who talk about revolution and class struggle without referring explicitly to everyday life, without understanding what is subversive about love and what is positive in the refusal of constraints – such people have a corpse in their mouth' (ibid., p. 26).
13. For more on the advances and limits of the Situationist International, see 'Decadence', *Aufheben*, no. 3, Summer 1994.
14. Michael Randle, *Civil Resistance*, London: Fontana 1994.
15. In contrast to these ideologues who actually believe in the project of modern democracy and all it entails, there were some involved in the No M11 campaign who wanted to be sneaky and position the campaign within the discourse of liberal democracy in order to legitimise our action and get wider participation. But the discourse is one of *recuperation* of struggles, and is more likely to moderate our radicalism, channelling it into the useless dead-end of alienated (representational) politics, rather than

functioning as some kind of 'transitional demand'. (See the point below about 'use' of the media operating as an appeal to the very ideas we want to subvert.)

16. Another argument which assumes the legitimacy of the democratic process is the suggestion that 'our argument is with the Department of Transport, not with the police or security guards'. Again, while this is true at one level, the problem of it is that it seems to accept that the police and security are just some kind of neutral layer. But of course, both groups protect the sovereignty of private property and state capital, so they can't be neutral. Moreover, to say that our argument is simply with the DoT not the people on the ground in a way flies in the face of the very *raison d'être* of direct action – which is to intervene *on the ground*. This is why so many people in the No M11 campaign spent so much time disputing with the construction workers and security. The argument seems to reduce direct action merely to publicity-seeking when it ought to be environment-changing and self-changing in its own right.

17. One example is the question of the physical appearance of No M11 campaigners. Although it was recognised that the good burghers of Wanstead would like campaign participants better if we all wore suits instead of scruffy clothes when we invaded work sites, people involved in the campaign felt that this was not a price worth paying!

18. There is an important distinction between the public silence within the campaign about theft and criminal damage (discussed earlier) and this issue of an acceptable public image. The first refers to our relations with the police, and was driven by practical (legal) considerations; the second refers to our relations with the mass media and was driven by ideological considerations. Hence the former was more a matter of tacit agreement and individual decision within the campaign (as 'common sense'); and the latter was agonised over and consciously decided upon by groups representing the collective as a whole.

19. Vaneigem, *Revolution of Everyday Life*, p. 139.

20. A version of this section appeared originally in 'Kill or chill? Analysis of the opposition to the Criminal Justice Bill', *Aufheben*, no. 4, Summer 1995.

21. The concept of 'proletarian subjectivity' has nothing to do with the miserable questions generated by sociology and cultural studies about the attributes, tastes and norms of those in manual occupations, and everything to do with Marx's distinction between a class *in* itself (its objective relation to capital) and a class *for* itself (the class's recognition of its objective relation to capital and hence itself as a class).

22. The complexities and contradictions of DiY-fluffy ideas and practices merits a lengthier analysis – for example, tracing the changing nature of DiY-fluffyism before and after the CJB became law. But this is beyond the scope of the present article. See 'Kill or chill?'

23. See the article 'Solidarity with the Liverpool dockers: why our movement should be involved', available from *Earth First! Action Update*, Dept 29,

1 Newton Street, Manchester M1 1HW. See also the Reclaim the Streets article in *Do or Die*, no. 6, 1997, c/o South Downs EF!, PO Box 2971, Brighton BN2 2TT, UK.

24. See the critical appraisal of this demo in the spoof newssheet *Schnooze*.

25. Of course, the new Labour government shows a slightly different ideological gloss, with its talk of 'inclusion' and 'stakeholding', reflecting perhaps an even greater emphasis than the Tories' on imposing alienated labour on everyone. The 'Welfare to Work' programme is a ruthless and well-resourced attempt to bring the young into 'society' and away from dole-based political activity and other forms of 'crime'.

26. The term 'DiY Culture' serves to restrict our historical antecedents to post-war Britain, privileging explicitly cultural phenomena, at the expense of connections to, say, the Russian, German and Spanish revolutions, or the history of 'workers' struggles' in the UK.

27. Recuperation is an attempt (not necessarily deliberate) to appropriate antagonistic expressions, transforming them into something harmless and integrating them ideologically into the aims and purposes of capitalist relations. See our critique of George McKay's *Senseless Acts of Beauty* (London: Verso 1996) in *Aufheben*, no. 5, Autumn 1996. Much of what we said about the recuperative function of that book could apply to the present one, although the difference is that this one at least allows those engaged in struggles to speak for themselves. It is to be hoped that our own contribution will make the recuperative functions of the present book more problematic.

5 The art of necessity: the subversive imagination of anti-road protest and Reclaim the Streets

1. There is not space in this chapter to elaborate on the history and theory of the agitational avant-garde. One could trace a history of subversive imaginations back from DIY Culture, through the Situationists, Surrealists and Dadaists. For a brief and somewhat partisan overview see: Stewart Home, *The Assault on Culture: Utopian Currents from Lettrisme to Class War*, London: Aporia Press/Unpopular Books 1988. For a view of art activism (as opposed to activist art) produced by the contemporary avant garde, see Nina Felshin, ed., *But is it Art? The Spirit of Art as Activism*, Seattle: Bay Press 1995.

2. I have just stumbled upon an article in *The Times*, 12 August 1997, which presents an ironic twist to the issues in this essay. Art and life became confused when a 'mock protest' stunt to advertise an anti-road play at the Edinburgh Festival turned into a 'real protest' when 200 Edinburgh Reclaim the Streets activists turned up and blocked the road for several hours. The photo caption reads 'Anti-road campaigners who took the mock protest a little too seriously yesterday. Several were arrested.'

3. Coined by American Earth Firster Jasper Carlton and quoted in Christopher Manes, *Green Rage: Radical Environmentalism and the Unmaking of Civilization*, Boston: Little Brown 1990, p. 26.

4. Ibid., p. 28.

5. When art remains a tool of representation, art *about* political issues, it fails. Applying art and creativity to real political situations is what I am talking about in this essay. German Artist Joseph Beuys used the term 'social sculpture' to describe the process of creatively moulding society rather than conventional artists' materials, such as clay, wood or paint. An interesting encroachment of representative art into the DiY protest movement was the Art Bypass event, where 'art objects' created by professional artists were placed beside the route of the much contested Newbury bypass in Berkshire, southern England. Art Bypass succeeded as a publicity stunt for the media and middle England's liberal intelligentsia. It was also unique in that it was curated by an artist working for Friends of the Earth as part of their campaign strategy. But it failed as socially engaged art practice. The tree houses and numerous direct actions against the bypass were where true art and radical creativity lay.

6. Guy Debord, *The Society of the Spectacle*, 1967, p. 115, quoted in Sadie Plant, *The Most Radical Gesture: The Situationist International in a Postmodern Age*, London: Routledge 1992, p. 16.

7. Jean Dubuffet, quoted in Andrea Juno and V. Vale, eds, *Pranks*, San Francisco: RE/Search 1987, p. 4.

8. Raoul Vaneigem (1967), *The Revolution of Everyday Life* (trans. by Donald Nicholson-Smith), London: Rebel Press/Left Bank Books 1994, p. 190.

9. The first wave of activists on the M11 had come from Twyford Down, where UK DiY protest was born in 1992.

10. A strategy which was to become invaluable to the movement and repeated at all the subsequent protest camps.

11. The Criminal Justice Act outlaws many of the direct action tactics used on the M11.

12. Richard Schechner, *The Future of Ritual: Writings on Culture and Performance*, London: Routledge 1993, p. 1.

13. A D-lock is a bike lock that fits perfectly around pieces of machinery and your neck. The machinery has to stop and contractors have to bring in bolt croppers to remove you. See Road Alert!, *Road Raging: Top Tips for Wrecking Roadbuilding*, 1997 (available from Road Alert! PO Box 5544, Newbury, Berkshire, RG14 5FB, UK, for £3) for a fantastic guide to direct action techniques.

14. Victor Turner, 'Body, brain, and culture', *Zygon*, vol. 18, no. 3, 1983, quoted in Schechner, *The Future of Ritual*, p. 25.

15. Hakim Bey, *TAZ: The Temporary Autonomous Zone, Ontological Anarchy, Poetic Terrorism*, Brooklyn, NY: Autonomedia 1991, p. 98.

16. The M11 saw several sites of resistance. First, there was the Chestnut Tree on George Green, Wanstead (evicted December 1993), which was to be

the inspirational spark that ignited the whole direct action campaign against the M11 link road. This was followed by the first houses to be squatted and turned into the 'Independent Free Area of Wanstonia' (evicted February 1994), and a whole series of evictions in the spring and summer of 1994, including Leytonstonia, an area of woodland, 'Euphoria', and then the final house left on the route (July 1995). Claremont Road was by far the largest and the most significant site for the final months of the campaign.

17. Dolly became ill after the first attack of the DoT on Claremont Road (2 August 1994) and was moved to a nearby residential home. Mrs Leighton (aged 78) was less lucky – the state provided 11 bailiffs, 40 security guards and 160 policemen to move her from her house around the corner from Claremont Road, and she died a few months later – homesick and heart-broken.

18. *Détournement*: a French term which literally means a diversion or a re-routing. It was developed as a Situationist concept and is defined by Greil Marcus, in *Lipstick Traces*, as 'theft of the aesthetic artifacts from their contexts and their diversion into contexts of one's own devise' (*Lipstick Traces: A Secret History of the Twentieth Century*, London: Secker & Warburg 1989, p. 168).

19. Claremont Road was a prime example of what Hakim Bey terms a Temporary Autonomous Zone. For more on this concept see Bey, *TAZ*.

20. Tyres proved to be both practically and symbolically a perfect barricading material. They fill space efficiently and are easy to move by hand, but difficult for bulldozer buckets to shift because they bounce!! At the end of the eviction the Department of Transport was left with the burden of disposing of some of the unsustainable waste product of its own car culture.

21. The conflict between art and political action was repeated here when some campaigners decided to close the art house down and turn it into a barricade for defensive reasons. The 'artists' argued that it should be left as it was so that when the bailiffs arrived they were confronted with the prospect of destroying something beautiful. Perhaps a naive belief: why should they see art as more beautiful and valuable than a 300-year-old yew tree, that they cut down without blinking a few months before?

22. The tower was inspired by a French children's book, *The House that Beebo Built* (London: Paul Hamlyn 1969), which tells the story of Beebo and his friend whose fantasy self-built house is to be demolished by developers. It ends with him escaping from bailiffs up an enormous wooden tower on the top of his house.

23. This was a direct act of defiance, as the Criminal Justice Act had been passed weeks before, and it had made a point of singling out rave music.

24. Many activists left London and went on to become key participants at other road protest camps that were starting up, including Pollok Free State in Glasgow, Fairmile in Devon and Newbury in Berkshire.

25. 'Reclaim the Streets was originally formed in London in autumn 1991,

around the dawn of the anti-roads movement. . . . Their work was small-scale but effective and even back then it had elements of the cheeky, surprise tactics which have moulded RTS's more recent activities. . . . However the onset of the No M11 Link Road Campaign presented the group with a specific local focus, and RTS was absorbed temporarily into the No M11 campaign in East London' (Del Bailie, 'Reclaim the Streets', *Do or Die*, no. 6, 1997, p. 1). This issue has several articles about Reclaim the Streets, as has no. 5, all written by activists.

26. Del Bailie, in *RTS Agitprop*, no. 1, July 1996.
27. From ibid. Reclaim the Streets agit-props present a multifaceted collage of texts that attempt to describe the group. Some of the texts are written by individual activists, others stolen or paraphrased from outside sources. The DiY direct action movement defines itself more by deed and strategy than by theory – not what are we *about* but what do we *do*.
28. These alliances were conscious strategies of Reclaim the Streets, intended to highlight the common social forces against which radical ecologists and social justice campaigners are fighting. 'We're saying that the power that attacks those who work, through union legislation and casualisation, is the same power that is attacking the planet with over-production and -consumption of resources; the power that produces cars by 4 million a year is the same power that decides to attack workers through the disempower-ment of the unions, reducing work to slavery' (Ian Fillingham, 'Why Reclaim the Streets and the Liverpool dockers?', *Do or Die*, no. 6, 1997, p. 9).
29. *RTS Agitprop*, no. 1, July 1996.
30. Jean-Jaques Lebel, 'Notes on political street theatre 1968–69', *Drunken Boat*, no. 1, 1994.
31. Phil McLeish, activist on M11 and RTS, *Agitprop*, no. 1, July 1996.
32. Quoted in Bailie, 'Reclaim the Streets', p. 5.
33. Paraphrased from Del Bailie, *Agitprop*, no. 1, July 1996.
34. Lautréamont (Isidore Ducasse), *Poésies*, London and New York: Allison & Busby 1980, p. 75.
35. Reclaim the Streets does not just put on street parties. Two road blockades using tripods have taken place, at Greenwich and Streatham in South London – and various small-scale actions, including hanging an enormous 'MURDERERS' banner outside the Shell AGM, locking on to the entrance of the Nigerian High Commission, numerous acts of subvertising (creatively changing car billboards) and a procession and banner hang during the Earls Court Motor Show. For the sake of this essay I am concentrating on the street party form.
36. Wooden tripods had been used before by antilogging campaigners in Australia. Reclaim the Streets were the first to substitute metal scaffolding poles. The idea of a tripod is that it can block a road and the police cannot pull it down without risking serious injury to whomever is suspended from the top of the tripod 20 feet above ground. See Road Alert!, *Road Raging*, for details of making and erecting tripods.

37. A reference to the Paris '68 graffito 'Beneath the cobblestones – the beach'.
38. Exactly a year after the Reclaim the Street party, Islington Council held an *official* street party in Upper Street as part of the Islington festival. Recuperation or inspiration?
39. Schechner, *The Future of Ritual*, p. 84.
40. Author's conversation with Del Bailie, July 1997.
41. An ecological *détournement* of 'Beneath the cobblestones – the beach' – 'Beneath the tarmac – the forest'.
42. Schechner, *The Future of Ritual*, p. 83.
43. 'The dispute was provoked when a docker, who had already worked a 12 hour shift was told to do overtime. He refused and was sacked on the spot. The strike then ensued, with 500 men staying solid behind the principle of resisting the erosion of working rights' (*SchNEWs*, no. 93, 4 October 1996).
44. Ian Fillingham, *RTS Agitprop*, no. 2, July 1997.
45. Title of the Labour Party's horrendous pop 1997 general election campaign anthem.
46. A direct reference to the Sex Pistols' 1977 LP, *Never Mind the Bollocks, Here's the Sex Pistols*.
47. Tree FM first broadcast from up a tree at the Newbury bypass protest.
48. These charges were later dropped and we are now pursuing a civil action against the police for wrongful arrest, imprisonment and trespass of goods.
49. *Express on Sunday* and *Mail on Sunday*, respectively. Both Sunday, 13 April 1997.
50. *Mixmag*, no. 73, June 1997, cover story, p. 101.
51. *Muzik*, no. 25, June 1997, no page numbers.
52. Ernst Fischer, *The Necessity of Art* (trans. by Anna Bostock), London: Peregrine Books 1978, p. 7.
53. Michael Fuerst, Earth First! activist, quoted in Manes, *Green Rage*, p. 225.
54. Quoted in Fischer, *The Necessity of Art*, p. 7.

6 Earth First! Defending Mother Earth, direct-style

1. Either I've got the best of both worlds – an academic overview with privileged insider knowledge – or I've sold out my protester principles and still haven't achieved academic cred/viability. I know which one I hope it is!
2. At least, this is how things are supposed to work.
3. Rik Scarce, *Eco-Warriors: Understanding the Radical Environmental Movement*, Chicago: Noble Press 1990, p. 62.
4. Again, I am not attempting to speak for everyone in the movement, but to identify what I believe to be the most commonly held position. I personally know people in the British EF! movement who think that the sooner humanity dies out as a species the better for the planet – but most campaign

with the hope of 'leaving the planet in better condition for the next generation'.

5. See, for instance, Murray Bookchin, 'Defending the Earth', in Lori Gruen and Dale Jamieson, eds, *Reflecting on Nature: Reading in Environmental Philosophy*, New York: Oxford University Press 1994.

6. Consider the direct action campaign against a second runway for Manchester Airport in 1997: this site of protest touched local, national *and* global concerns all in one.

7. http://www.hrc.wmin.ac.uk/campaigns/earthfirst.html.

8. *Do or Die*, no. 4, 1994.

9. See Road Alert!'s book *Road Raging: Top Tips for Wrecking Roadbuilding* (Newbury: Road Alert! 1997) for comprehensive advice on networking direct action campaigns.

10. 'An open letter to the Minister for Transport', *Do or Die*, no. 5, 1995, p. 5.

11. Dave Foreman, quoted in Scarce, *Eco-Warriors*, pp. 25–6.

12. Though, for instance, these features didn't stop the anarchist campaign group London Greenpeace being infiltrated by fast food organisation McDonald's spies in 1989–91. As John Vidal reports in *McLibel: Burger Culture on Trial* (London: Macmillan 1997), the two private-eye agencies hired to do the dirt on activists 'led to inevitable farce at London Greenpeace meetings with spies spying on spies and being observed in turn by suspicious anarchists. Sometimes there would have been as many – or more – spies at a meeting as anarchists' (pp. 193–4).

13. Though note this more critical realist voice from *Do or Die*: 'Is "everybody welcome"? We hand out thousands of leaflets saying so, but it is not true. If we are to continue to protest and to win, we have to accept different levels of commitment and ability. Those we have welcomed have not always been the best activists and we are too nice to turn some away. Whole sections of road campaigns have been abandoned to "Brew Crew" and "acid casualties", as the rest of us find their behaviour offensive'. *Do or Die*, no. 6, 1997, pp. 19–20.

14. Zygmunt Bauman, *Life in Fragments*, 1995, p. 31.

15. Stephen Sterling, 'Towards an ecological world view', in J.R. Engel and J.G. Engel, eds, *Ethics of Environment and Development*, London: Belhaven Press 1990.

16. 'An open letter to the Minister for Transport'.

17. Bauman, *Life in Fragments*.

18. *Confined, Constrained and Condemned: Civil Rights and Travellers*, Glastonbury Friends, Families and Travellers Support Group 1996, p. 10.

19. Letter in *Do or Die*, no. 5, 1995, p. 92.

20. Zygmunt Bauman, *Postmodern Ethics*, Oxford: Blackwell 1993, pp. 198–9.

21. Others *are* that ambitious. One slogan on the magazine *Green Anarchist*'s masthead reads: 'For the Destruction of Civilization'.

22. 'Tree spirit and earth repair', *Do or Die*, no. 5, 1995, pp. 72–3.

23. John Barry, 'Sustainability, political judgement and citizenship', in Brian

Doherty and Marius DeGeus, eds, *Democracy and Green Political Thought*, London: Routledge 1996, p. 123.

24. For copies of the written-up minutes of the NVDA workshops (*Ego Warriors and Energy Vamps*) send SAEs to 'Alternatives', PO Box 7, Llangefri, Anglesey, North Wales.

25. Sterling, 'Towards an ecological world view'.

26. Denis Goulet, 'Development Ethics', in Engel and Engel, *Ethics of Environment and Development.*

27. Alex Plows, 'The Donga Tribe: practical paganism comes full circle', *Creative Mind: Magazine of Living Philosophy*, no. 27, Summer 1995, pp. 25–9.

28. Rolston Holmes, 'Science-based versus traditional ethics', in Engel and Engel, *Ethics of Environment and Development.*

29. Goulet, 'Development ethics'.

30. See David Pepper, *Communes and the Green Vision*, London: Green Print 1991.

31. Quoted in ibid.

32. OK, sympathetic magic example. Sympathetic magic owes more than a little to group psychology but there's more to it than that, something indefinable. It's working on an instinctive level (. . . by any means necessary . . .). There were some OK security guards at Twyford Down, but most (or at least the ones I encountered!) were of the heavyweight ex-army sadist variety. Violent men. And the machines – impossibly huge, driven by lunatics. And we were running at these guards to get through and past them and up the still-moving machines day in, day out. But we believed in our own protection, spiritually and physically. We were fighting for Mother Earth and she would take care of us. This belief, this energy, was consciously evoked: we'd get drums and chants going before we went on site, raise the energy levels, get the group as a unified whole. We'd face-paint each other up, dance about a bit, get a rhythm going, then we'd go for it . . . shrilling and ululating. I hope we scared the fuck out of them. We sure as hell vibed them out. Of course, they still caught us and pressure-pointed us and threw us off the machines (on yer average day, anyway) but that was relatively nothing, considering what they could have got away with, in those early days when the world's media were nowhere to be seen. I used to carry around a handmade wooden pentacle (a five-pointed star) – for me, a sign of protection. Many guards saw it as 'black magic' and stayed clear – the protection worked.

A group with the kind of energy we'd consciously danced and drummed up, with a belief in its own protection, can do practically anything, can get away with leaping under machines, climbing the arm of a digger while the driver swings it about and security guards pull at your ankles . . . and not get hurt. Well, not badly, considering what we got away with. Of course, as I said, all this has a lot to do with group psychology . . . as the Celts knew . . . scare your enemy and boost your own mental/physical strength. But more than this, we were tuning in to the earth's heartbeat, to a frequency you find only through faith and instinct. (And I don't need science to give this natural law a name to 'prove' its existence, although one of these days it will. . . .)

33. In *Communes* and especially in *Eco-Socialism: From Deep Ecology to Social Justice*, London: Routledge 1993.

34. See for instance Lynn White's 'Images of nature', in Gruen and Jamieson, *Reflecting on Nature*. These are complex concepts which I am touching on here extremely briefly – primarily because I am running out of energy . . . my newborn baby is getting highly fed up with mum spending so much time scribbling! . . . I'd recommend Karen J. Warren's collection *Ecological Feminism* (London: Routledge 1994) to anyone interested in following this line of thought further.

35. John Purkis, ' "If not you, who? If not now, when?" Rhetoric and reality in the vision of Earth First!', *Alternative Futures and Popular Protest*, conference papers, vol. 2, Manchester: Manchester Metropolitan University 1995, no pagination.

36. 'Earth First! But what next?', *Do or Die*, no. 6, 1997, pp. 18–20.

7 Reclaim the fields and country lanes! The Land is Ours campaign

1. This chapter is based on my 1996 Schumacher Lecture, first published in *Resurgence Magazine* (no. 181, March/April 1997) under the title 'Land reform in Britain'.

8 Tossed in the fire and they never got burned: the Exodus Collective

All unattributed quotations are taken from unpublished interviews by the author.

1. From BBC Radio 4 *Kaleidoscope Feature*, 'Raving in revolt', October 1996.

2. From the Twinkle Brothers, 'Never Get Burn', on *Free Africa* (Virgin Records, 1990).

3. *New Statesman & Society*, 24 June 1994, Criminal Justice and Public Order Bill Supplement, 'United you're nicked', pp. x–xi.

4. This and the following extract from DJ Hazad taken from *Kaleidoscope Feature*, 'Raving in revolt'.

5. The role of women in Exodus has been an interesting, if perhaps problematic one. On the one hand, women are closely involved in the organisation and management of Exodus and unanimously point to the liberation from sexual harassment at the dances, as compared to attitudes in pubs or some clubs to women, especially single women. On the other hand, some women within Exodus play what seems to be a traditional role, especially when they

have had children. They hotly deny any suggestion of oppression, however, saying that they have chosen this role for the period when the children are young. And, to further complicate the issue, fathers tend to play a strong role in parenting, as does the whole community, analogous in some ways to tribal communities, where everyone considers themselves responsible for the children.

6. *New Statesman & Society*, 'United you're nicked', pp. x–xi.
7. Ibid.
8. Ibid.
9. Ibid.
10. Ibid.
11. Ibid.
12. From *Kaleidoscope Feature*, 'Raving in revolt'.
13. *SQUALL*, no. 12, Spring 1996, p. 62.
14. *SQUALL*, no. 13, Summer 1996, p. 64.
15. Vox pop and Inspector Kimble's quotes from *Kaleidoscope Feature*, 'Raving in revolt'.
16. *SQUALL*, no. 15, Summer 1997, p. 42.
17. *New Statesman & Society*, 'United you're nicked', pp. x–xi.

9 Dangerous dancing and disco riots: the northern warehouse parties

1. Hakim Bey, *TAZ: The Temporary Autonomous Zone, Ontological Anarchy, Poetic Terrorism*, Brooklyn, NY: Autonomedia 1991, p. 128.
2. R. Winstanley and D. Nowell, *Soul Survivors: The Wigan Casino Story*, London: Robson Books 1996, p. 20. For another excellent insider account, see Pete McKenna, *Nightshift*, Dunoon, Argyll: ST Publishing 1995.
3. It is a sad fact that many of the original warehouse DJs now make a living playing 'classics' retrospective nights.
4. Even then the illegality of the parties was often far from cut and dry. The police had to search out obscure laws and apply them in a different context from that intended, as I discovered several years later when I interviewed the officer in charge of policing the parties in the Blackburn region: 'We started having some difficulty [in identifying it as a crime], and needed quite close scrutiny of the law by our legal people to actually find what offences were being committed.' But by refusing dialogue – 'The rationale in Lancashire was: We're not actually going to negotiate with these people' – the police locked both sides into an escalating series of confrontations in a process of contestation from which neither could escape. (From an interview with Chief Inspector Jeff Beaty, at Lancashire Police Force Head-quarters, Preston, 15 July 1995. Chief Inspector Beaty was not involved in the public disorder incidents discussed below, and I do not wish any comments made here to reflect negatively on him personally.)

5. In the words of the police's own analyst, Malcolm Young, police work is cast 'into the required framework of combative warfare directed against a common (male) enemy.' (Malcolm Young, 'The police, gender and the culture of drug abuse and addiction', in Maryon McDonald, ed., *Gender, Drink and Drugs*, Oxford: Berg 1994, p. 55).

6. Respect is due to everyone involved in the Hardcore Uproar collective.

7. 'Safety was paramount, because people would panic, and they'd run around in a dark environment and you'd have people crushed and trodden to death' (Chief Inspector Beaty – who had no involvement in this incident).

8. No Damn Cat is the company name of two photojournalists who were involved with the LAB.

9. The ART LAB was first raided on 27 May 1995, and then again on 17 March 1996 and 17 August 1996.

10. The subsequent ventures of the LAB carry a poignant warning against complacency, as on the first occasion that they attempted to take the ART LAB concept into a licensed venue they were ripped off by an unscrupulous club manager and left disillusioned and in debt. Further excursions in the underground have proved more successful, however.

10   The Great British Ecstasy revolution

1. Metanoia means a radical change, a spiritual conversion, a change of life. A revolution in your head.

2. It is impossible to give accurate figures, but this estimate, from drug agency Lifeline, is commonly quoted.

3. This history of MDMA relies heavily on the work of Nicholas Saunders. For more information, read his latest book *Ecstasy Reconsidered*, London: self-published 1997.

4. Quoted from Nicholas Saunders, *Ecstasy and the Dance Culture*, London: self-published 1995, p. 16.

5. Derogatory term from Scotland used to describe people living on housing schemes. Irvine Welsh's contemporary classic *Trainspotting* (London: Secker & Warburg 1993) is based on the proliferation of heroin use on housing schemes in 1980s Edinburgh.

6. Alexander Shulgin, and Ann Shulgin, *PIHKAL*, Berkeley: Transform Press 1993. The title of this book stands for Phenethylamines I Have Known And Loved.

7. Ibid., p. 736.

8. Ibid., p. 72.

9. Ibid., p. 70.

10. See Saunders, *Ecstasy and the Dance Culture*, p. 51.

11. Richard Smith, and Tim Maughan, *Youth Culture and the Making of a Post-Fordist Economy: Dance Music in Contemporary Britain*, Discussion Paper,

DP97/2, Department of Social Policy and Social Science, Royal Holloway College, University of London, 1997.

12. M.A. Wright, 'Freedom to party: an investigation into the British dance/ rave scene and the implications of the Criminal Justice and Public Order Act', *Yearbook for Ethnomedicine and the Study of Consciousness*, no. 3 pp. 343–51.

13. Alberto Melucci, 'The symbolic challenge of contemporary movements', *Social Research*, vol. 52, no. 4, p. 797.

11 Repetitive beats: free parties and the politics of contemporary DiY dance culture in Britain

1. As seen on a banner in Trafalgar Square, 12 April 1997.

2. See their website: http://www.network23.org/.

3. Beats per minute.

4. See, for example, Steve Redhead, ed., *Rave Off: Politics and Deviance in Contemporary Youth Culture*, Aldershot: Avebury 1993; Sarah Thornton, *Clubcultures*, Cambridge: Polity 1995; Jonathan Fleming, *What Kind of a House Party is This? History of a Music Revolution*, Slough: MIY Publishing 1995; Matthew Collin with John Godfrey, *Altered State*, London: Serpent's Tail 1997; Steve Redhead with Derel Wynne and Justin O'Connor, eds, *The Clubcultures Reader*, Oxford: Blackwell 1997; Hillegonda Rietveld, *This is Our House: House Music, Cultural Spaces and Technologies*, Aldershot: Ashgate 1998.

5. *Evading Standards*, 25 April 1997, and *SQUALL*, no. 15, Summer 1997.

6. *Mail on Sunday*, 13 April 1997.

7. *Sunday Express*, 13 April 1997.

8. *Guardian*, 14 April 1997.

9. *Independent*, 23 July 1990.

10. Criminal Justice and Public Order Act 1994, c. 33, Part V, Section 63, p. 44.

11. Collin with Godfrey, *Altered State*.

12. Julian Kossoff, 'Pills, thrills and bellyaches', *Time Out*, no. 1403, 13–20 August 1997.

13. An exact quantitative history will be hard to trace due to the underground nature of these sound systems and their reliance on mostly word of mouth (and some micromedia) publicity.

14. Brighton-based underground newssheet published by Justice? 'in defiance of the Criminal Justice Act'. See *SchNEWSreader: Issues 0–50*, Brighton: Justice? 1995.

15. George McKay, *Senseless Acts of Beauty: Cultures of Resistance since the Sixties*, London: Verso 1996. See also Adam Brown, 'Let's all have a disco? Football, popular music and democratisation', in Redhead et al., *The Clubcultures Reader*.

16. 'Shamanarchy': shamanistic-inspired anarchy. 'Zippies', derived from 'zen-

inspired person'. According to Fraser Clark, 'A Zippy is a combination of the '60s hippy and the late '80s technoperson – a person who is using new knowledge and technology for the good of the individual' (*Bres Magazine*, 1989, cited in *Encyclopedia Psychedelica International*, vol. 11, Spring 1989, p. 445).

17. Quoted in Richard Lowe and William Shaw, *Travellers: Voices of the New Age Nomads*, London: Fourth Estate 1993.

18. Collin with Godfrey, *Altered State*.

19. Hillegonda Rietveld, 'Marshall Jefferson and the Lumpheads: Chicago legend vs South London sound-system', in Sarah Champion, ed., *Trance Europe Express 5*, London: Volume 1996.

20. Jez Tucker, 'All systems are go', *SQUALL*, no. 13, Summer 1996 (anonymously reprinted in *Dream Creation Inc.*, Global Trance and Acid Techno Issue, July/August 1997).

21. McKay, *Senseless Acts of Beauty*; Collin with Godfrey, *Altered State*.

22. Amy Garner, 'Czech', Frontline website: http://www.c–ccomm.demon.co.uk/frontline/frontline.html. Also known as 'technivals', see Tina Jackson, 'Technivals: Britain's vibe tribes in Europe', *The Big Issue*, no. 181, 13–19 May 1996.

23. Rachel Newsome, 'Tribe on a quest', *Muzik*, no. 28, September 1997.

24. Based on various conversations with Drew Hemment, Joe Marshall and Danny Baxter during 1995. See also Ally Fogg and Joe Marshall, ' "Storm"in' the desert', *SQUALL*, no. 13, Summer 1996.

25. *Mixmag*, vol. 2, no. 75, August 1997, p. 21.

26. For arguments to this effect, see Hillegonda Rietveld, 'The house of Chicago', in Redhead et al., *The Clubcultures Reader*; Will Straw, 'Systems of articulation, logics of change: communities and scenes in popular music', *Cultural Studies*, vol. 5, no. 3, 1991; Peter Manuel, 'Music as symbol, music as simulacrum: postmodern, pre-modern, and modern aesthetics in subcultural popular musics', *Popular Music*, vol. 14, no. 2, 1995.

27. Jon Savage, 'Introduction' to *Industrial Culture Handbook*, San Francisco: RE/Search no. 6–7, 1983.

28. Ibid.

29. Rietveld, *This is Our House*.

30. 'Entactogenic': a technical term invented specifically in relation to MDMA and its effect of increasing the tactile senses.

31. Simon Reynolds, 'Rave culture: living dream or living death?', in Reynolds et al., *The Clubcultures Reader*, p. 106.

32. Ibid., p. 104.

33. Hillegonda Rietveld, 'Living the dream', in Redhead, *Rave Off*.

34. Sheila Henderson, *Ecstasy: Case Unresolved*, London: Pandora 1997, pp. 118–26.

35. A main drawback of E, it seems, was that not long after its peak in British popularity and the first round of moral panic, E was found to be increas-

ingly diluted with unknown substances, mostly due to its illegal status and subsequent lack of quality control.

36. See, for example, McKay, *Senseless Acts of Beauty*.
37. See Les Back, 'Coughing up fire', *New Formations*, no. 5, 1988, for a description of the South-East London sound system Saxon.
38. Collin with Godfrey, *Altered State*.
39. Cynthia Rose, *Design After Dark*, London: Thames & Hudson 1991, p. 20.
40. Lu, conversation with the author, London, October 1993. For more information on Crass, see McKay, *Senseless Acts of Beauty*, chap. 3.
41. Rietveld, 'The house of Chicago'.
42. Rietveld, 'Living the dream'.
43. Ibid.; Steve Redhead, *Unpopular Culture: The Birth of Law and Popular Culture*, Manchester and New York: Manchester University Press 1995.
44. Allon White, 'Hysteria and the end of carnival', in Nancy Armstrong and Leonard Terrenhouse, eds, *The Violence of Representation*, London and New York: Routledge.
45. British children are therefore not educated in a self-regulating drinking protocol, while having a family is indirectly penalised.
46. Rietveld, 'Living the dream'; Collin with Godfrey, *Altered State*; Rietveld, *This is Our House*.
47. Wayne Anthony, 'Class of 88: Genesis & Biology presents future power people News [*sic*] Years Eve 1989–90', *DJ*, no. 187, 12–25 April 1997.
48. Thornton, *Clubcultures*, pp. 116–62.
49. Louise Veares and Richard Woods, 'Entertainment', in *Leisure Futures*, vol. 3, London: Henley Centre for Forecasting 1993.
50. *UK Club Guide 5*, 1996.
51. Both clubs are very different, not only due to their geographical locations but also due to the difference in music policy. But that's another story. Check out the Ministry of Sound's website for an example of marketing approach: http://www.ministryofsound.co.uk/home.html.
52. Collin with Godfrey, *Altered State*.
53. Theodor W. Adorno (1941), 'On popular music', in Simon Frith and Andrew Goodwin, eds, *On Record: Rock, Pop and the Written Word*, London: Routledge 1990, p. 312.
54. Ibid.
55. McKay, *Senseless Acts of Beauty*, p. 164.
56. 'Jungle' here (as distinct from its contemporary usage as a synonym for 'drum'n'bass') is used to indicate a type of jazz which became popular in Harlem during the war years. It was characterised by a relatively fast tempo and a heavy drum beat and was played by African-American musicians with a line-up of drums, double bass and brass.
57. Radcliffe A. Joe, *This Business of Disco*, Lakewood, NJ: Billboard Books/Watson-Guptill Publications 1980, p. 13. Also my father, who had been involved in the Dutch Resistance, was a jazz record collector and there were

mutterings in my family about some good secret parties in Rotterdam during the German occupation in the Second World War.

58. Tucker, 'All systems go'.

59. Without full rights of existence within a lifestyle of choice and without one's interests being represented in parliament.

60. Henderson, *Ecstasy*, p. 123.

61. Ibid., p. 119.

62. Philip Tagg, 'From refrain to rave: the decline of figure and the rise of ground', *Popular Music*, vol. 13, no. 2, 1994, p. 219.

63. Dave Hesmondhalgh, 'Technoprophecy: a response to Tagg', *Popular Music*, vol. 14, no. 2, 1995.

64. Fleming, *What Kind of House Party is This?*

65. Hillegonda Rietveld: 'Pure bliss', *Difference Engine*, http://www.gold.ac.uk/difference.rietveld.html (an earlier version is available in print: *Popular Musicology*, no. 2, June 1995); *This is Our House*.

66. Bob Black, 'The abolition of work', *Semiotext(e) USA*, no. 13, 1987, p. 15.

67. Roland Barthes, *The Pleasure of the Text* (trans. by Richard Miller), London: Cape 1976.

68. Ray Pratt, *Rhythm and Resistance: Explorations in the Political Uses of Popular Music*, London: Praeger 1990, p. 49.

69. Manuel, 'Music as symbol, music as simulacrum', p. 235.

70. Flyer for a one-off Saturday-night party.

71. See, for example, Rogan Taylor, *The Death and Resurrection Show*, London: Antony Blond 1985; Gilbert Rouget, *Music and Trance: A Theory of the Relations between Music and Possession*, Chicago and London: University of Chicago Press 1985; and Ioan M. Lewis, *Ecstatic Religion: A Study of Shamanism and Spirit Possession*, London: Routledge 1989. In relationship to the current dance scene, see Collin with Godfrey, *Altered State*; Rietveld, *This is Our House*.

72. Quoted in Lowe and Shaw, *Travellers*, p. 169.

73. Collin with Godfrey, *Altered State*, pp. 207–8.

74. Quoted in Lowe and Shaw, *Travellers*, p. 168.

75. Quoted in ibid.

76. Alan Durant, 'A new day for music? Digital technologies in contemporary music-making', in Philip Hayward, ed., *Culture, Technology and Creativity*, London: John Libbey 1990.

77. Henderson, *Ecstasy*, p. 116.

78. Quoted in Lowe and Shaw, *Travellers*, pp. 179–80.

79. For an insider's account by a female club-goer of handbag girls vs techno boys, see Geraldine Geraghty, *Raise Your Hands*, London: Boxtree 1996.

80. For a comparative piece, see Simon Frith and Angela McRobbie, 'Rock and sexuality', in Frith and Goodwin, *On Record*.

81. Rietveld, *This is Our House*.

82. Richard Dyer (1979), 'In defence of disco', in Corey K. Creekmur and

Alexander Doty, eds, *Out in Culture: Gay, Lesbian and Queer Essays on Popular Culture*, London: Cassell 1995, p. 411.

83. There is a difference between European techno and Detroit techno. Simply put, European techno is faster and pushes like rock, while Detroit techno is funky and uses fewer digital textures.

84. Thomas G. Schumacher, '"This is a sampling sport": digital sampling, rap music and the law in cultural production', *Media, Culture and Society*, vol. 17, 1995; Rietveld, *This is Our House*.

85. Rietveld, *This is Our House*.

86. Arno Adelaars, *Ecstasy: de opkomst van een bewustzijnsveranderend middel*, Amsterdam: In de Knipscheer 1991.

87. Dan Lambert, 'Free people, free parties', *DJ*, no. 196, 16–29 August 1997.

Notes on contributors

Aufheben is a magazine which has appeared approximately annually since 1992. Most of the people involved in it came together during the anti-poll tax movement of 1990. Our project in *Aufheben* draws inspiration from, but ultimately seeks to go beyond the limits of, the most recent high points in proletarian theory and practice, such as the Situationist International and the Italian *autonomia* movement. Current and back issues are available from *Aufheben*, PO Box 2971, Brighton BN2 2TT, UK. Most of the articles from past issues can be viewed on our website at: http://jefferson.village. Virginia.EDU~spoons/aut—html/aufledit.html.

Jim Carey is a co-editor of *SQUALL* magazine, a freelancer writer and a media tart/grafter for just causes. He also DJs under the name Seed & the Bridge and helps organise free parties. He has been a squatter since 1983. The *SQUALL* website is to be found at http://www/squall.co.uk. *SQUALL* magazine is available from *SQUALL* PO Box 8959, London N19 5HW, UK (£10 for four issues; Europe £15; rest of world £20 [includes p & p]). Cheques payable to *SQUALL*. E-mail: squall@dircon.co.uk; website: http://www. users.dircon.co. uk/~squall; fax: 0171 561 0800.

Thomas Harding is director and co-founder of Undercurrents. He has been a video activist since 1992 and has trained hundreds of people how to use camcorders to support their campaign work. He has written the *Video Activist Handbook* (London: Pluto Press 1997) as well as articles for the *Guardian, Independent* and *New Internationalist.* He was associate producer for the *Rainbow Reports* series for BBC in 1992 and producer/co-editor for *Major Resistance: The Underground Tapes*, a two-part series for Channel Four in 1997. To order a subscription to *Undercurrents* (three issues for £32.95 including p & p [UK – add £3 per tape for overseas subscriptions], credit cards accepted) or for more information contact 16b Cherwell Street, Oxford OX4 1BG; tel.: 01865 203662; fax: 01865 243562; or check out our website (http://www.undercurrents.org).

Drew Hemment was resident DJ at the 'acid blues' Twilight Zone in Leeds before becoming involved in the Blackburn parties. After a time promoting clubs around Leeds he hung up his decks and returned to university, which led to participation in events such as Digital Chaos, Virtual Futures, Thinking Alien and *FUTUREsonic*. He has written for the academic journal *New Formations*, as well as various magazines, including *On*, *Mixmag*, *Herb Garden* and *Mute*, and Internet sites such as Luxus and Out-of-Order. He is currently studying for a PhD and, until its premature demise, was editor of the ART LAB fanzine the *Daily Rumour*.

John Jordan spends his life trying to juggle social art practice, direct action, university teaching and looking after his three-year-old son Jack. His most recent art project, 'Consuming Desire', explored men's relationship with pornography, using invisible art strategies (a spoof sex shop and a spoof porn CD-ROM), media interventions (TV/radio and press exposure), and therapeutic work with men addicted to pornography. From 1988 to 1997 he was a co-director with the London-based interdisciplinary art and social science group PLATFORM. To earn his bread and butter he teaches Live Art at Sheffield Hallam University. For more information on Reclaim the Streets contact: Reclaim the Streets, PO Box 9656, London N4 4JY, UK; tel.: 0171 281 4621; e-mail: rts@gn.apc.org; website: http://www.hrc.wmin.ac.uk./campaigns/rts.html.

George McKay is a writer on radical culture. He was born in Glasgow and brought up in Norfolk. He's been a punk, anarchist, squatter, double bassist. He teaches in the Department of Cultural Studies at the University of Central Lancashire in Preston (e-mail address is g.mckay@uclan.ac.uk). His other books are *Senseless Acts of Beauty:*

Cultures of Resistance since the Sixties (London: Verso 1996) and, as editor, *Yankee Go Home (& Take Me with U): Americanization & Popular Culture* (Sheffield: Sheffield Academic Press 1997). He has two daughters.

Tim Malyon is a freelance writer, photographer, radio journalist and windsurfer who co-compiled *New Statesman*'s Criminal Justice and Public Order Bill supplements 'United you're nicked' and 'DIY politics'. A contributor to *SQUALL* magazine, he was voted British Telecom 1996 Radio Journalist of the Year. His world view changed when he witnessed massed police violence during the eviction of the last Windsor Free Festival. A decade later he photographed similar incidents in a beanfield on Salisbury Plain. The experience fired up widespread reporting of travellers, festivals, squatting, road protests and rave culture. Tim Malyon also reports extensively on drug policy, appropriate development and Himalayan culture.

George Monbiot is the author of the investigative travel books *Poisoned Arrows* (London: Abacus, 1989); *Amazon Watershed* (London: Abacus, 1991) and *No Man's Land* (London: Picador, 1994). He is *persona non grata* in seven countries and has a life sentence *in absentia* in Indonesia. In Britain he started the campaign against mahogany imports, became involved in the direct action movement against road-building and helped found The Land is Ours campaign. He writes a column for the *Guardian*. From 1993 to 1995 he was a Visiting Fellow of Green College, Oxford. In 1997, he was appointed Visiting Professor at the University of East London.

Alex Plows has been involved in roads protest since 1992, as one of the Dongas Tribe who took direct action at Twyford Down, Hampshire. She has continued to actively protest both nationally (Solsbury Hill, Newbury, and so on) and locally, in North Wales. As part of North Wales Earth First!, Alex campaigns on a number of grassroots issues, in particular the proposed Anglesey Euroroute, and gave evidence at the recent public inquiry (by any means necessary!). Alex is currently finishing an MA and intends to undertake a PhD on the values/ethics of direct activists, her primary aim being to highlight/communicate the philosophies and perspectives of those within the NVDA movement. She has published several papers on this subject.

Hillegonda (Gonnie) Rietveld is a senior lecturer in media and society at South Bank University, London, and is a former post-graduate student and researcher at the Unit for Law and Popular Culture and Manchester Institute for Popular Culture at Manchester Metropolitan University. She actively takes part in contemporary dance culture and is author of *This is Our House: House Music, Cultural Spaces and Technologies* (Aldershot: Ashgate 1998).

Mary Anna Wright has a deep passion for dance music, which flourished during her clubbing experiences in Liverpool at the end of the 1980s. She changed career from marine biology by using an MSc dissertation to record events at Castlemorton festival in 1992. The Centre for Human Ecology has since been thrown out of Edinburgh University for encouraging such radical work. She is now completing a PhD at City University looking at dance culture's oppositional potential. This research is rooted in DiY philosophy, being self-funded through writing for magazines, books and as a researcher for Nicholas Saunders's *Ecstasy and the Dance Culture*.

Artists/photographers: contact details

Iain Cartwright Sarphati Park 103¹, 1073 CV, Amsterdam; e-mail: inxmas@hotmail.com

Nick Cobbing 19 Burghley Road, London N8 0QG

Kate Evans Orange Dog Productions, 7 The Green, Biddestone, nr Chippenham, Wiltshire SN14 7DG

Julia Guest c/o Platform, 7 Horselydown Lane, London SE1 2LN

Gideon Mendell c/o Platform (see above)

No Damn Cat c/o Morgan on 01929 864150

Paul O'Connor c/o Undercurrents, 16b Cherwell Street, Oxford OX4 1BG; e-mail: underc@gn.apc.org; tel: 01865 203661

The editor and publishers would like to thank all of the artists and photographers for permission to use their work in this book.

Index

304   INDEX

Temporary Autonomous Zone 7, 139
  see also protest camp; street party
Thatcher, Margaret 6, 17, 21, 53, 65,
  71, 254
Thatcherism 19, 20, 22, 27
Third Way fanzine 43
Thornton, Sarah 255
Tilbury Docks (1991) 81
TIMBMET, Oxford 154
Tinker's Bubble (Somerset) 31, 184
Torrance, Jason 80–81
Trafalgar Square Liverpool dockers
  free party (April 1997) 149–50,
  243–5, 251, 261
Trans-European Networks 41–2, 103
Transport 2000 157, 161
travellers 65, 184, 193
  see also gypsies; New Age
tree-dwelling 30, 154
Tropical Timber Federation 91
tube workers 147
Tunnel club (New York) 221
tunnelling 30, 125, 154
Turner, Victor 133
Twyford Down M3 motorway protest
  (1991–92) 22, 81–2, 102, 104,
  125, 140, 155
  Land is Ours campaign 179, 180,
  181, 185
  see also Dongas Tribe
Tzara, Tristan 129

Undercurrents 84–8, 95–9
Undercurrents magazine 2, 85, 90,
  91, 95, 96–7, 99
United States 4, 11, 42, 43, 80, 230
United Systems 250
Uys, Peter-Dirk 75

Vaneigem, Raoul 117, 131, 140
Vidal, John 2, 53
video activism 10, 79–99
  beginnings 82–4
  beginnings of DiY movement
    80–82
  funding 88–93
  inventiveness 94–5
  other groups, emergence of 93–4
  see also Undercurrents
Video Activist Handbook 91
Vietnam Solidarity Campaign 8
Vietnam War protests 40, 83
violence 15–16, 116, 217–18

Wallace, Michele 47
Wandsworth (London) 174, 175,
  176–80
Wanstonia period (January–February
  1994) 106, 117
Wanstead 124
Ward, Colin 20, 34, 51–2
warehouse parties/raves 2, 26, 123,
  212, 246, 252–5, 267
  see also Blackburn
Westminster, Duke of 176
Whatley Quarry, Somerset 154
Whiteread, Rachel 136
Whiteways Anarchia
  (Gloucestershire) 31
Wigan Casino 211–12
Wilson, Tony 68
Wolf, Winfried 49–50
'womanly culture' 9
Women's Environmental Network
  157
Woods, Rev. Roger 205
Wright, Mary Anna 23, 50, 228–42

Zelter, Angie 80
zero tolerance 218–19